Imperial Ru

Why did colonial subjects mobilize for national independence from the French empire? This question has rarely been
posed because the answer appears obvious: in the modern era,
nationalism was bound to confront colonialism. This book
argues against taking nationalist mobilization for granted.
Contrary to conventional accounts, it shows that nationalism
was not the only or even the primary form of anti-colonialism.
Drawing on archival sources, comparative historical analysis,
and case studies, Adria K. Lawrence examines the movements
for political equality that emerged in the French empire during the first half of the twentieth century. Within twenty years,
they had been replaced by movements for national independence in the majority of French colonies, protectorates, and
mandates. Lawrence shows that elites in the colonies shifted
from demands for egalitarian reforms to calls for independent
statehood only where the French refused to grant political
rights to colonial subjects. Where rights were granted, colonial
subjects opted for further integration and reform. Nationalist
discourses became dominant as a consequence of the failure to
reform. Mass protests then erupted in full force when French
rule was disrupted by war or decolonization.

Adria K. Lawrence is Assistant Professor at Yale University
and a Research Fellow at Yale's Whitney and Betty MacMillan
Center for International and Area Studies. Her publications
include *Rethinking Violence: States and Non-State Actors
in Conflict* (coedited with Erica Chenoweth) and articles in
International Security, American Politics Research, and the
Journal of North African Studies. Her research interests lie
in comparative politics and international relations; she studies
conflict, collective action, nationalism, and the Middle East
and North Africa. She holds a Ph.D. from the University of
Chicago.

Problems of International Politics

Series Editors:
Keith Darden, American University
Ian Shapiro, Yale University

The series seeks manuscripts central to the understanding of international politics that will be empirically rich and conceptually innovative. It is interested in works that illuminate the evolving character of nation-states within the international system. It sets out three broad areas for investigation: 1. Identity, security and conflict; 2. Democracy; and 3. Justice and distribution.

Titles in the Series:

Imperial Rule and the Politics of Nationalism

Anti-Colonial Protest in the French Empire

ADRIA K. LAWRENCE

Yale University

CAMBRIDGE
UNIVERSITY PRESS

32 Avenue of the Americas, New York, NY 10013-2473, USA

Cambridge University Press is part of the University of Cambridge.

It furthers the University's mission by disseminating knowledge in the pursuit of education, learning, and research at the highest international levels of excellence.

www.cambridge.org
Information on this title: www.cambridge.org/9781107640757

© Adria K. Lawrence 2013

First published 2013

Printed in the United States of America

A catalog record for this publication is available from the British Library.

Library of Congress Cataloging in Publication data
Lawrence, Adria, 1973–
Imperial rule and the politics of nationalism : anti-colonial protest in the French empire / Adria K. Lawrence.
    pages   cm
Includes bibliographical references and index.
ISBN 978-1-107-03709-0 (hardback) – ISBN 978-1-107-64075-7 (paperback)
1. Anti-imperialist movements – France – History. 2. Postcolonialism – France. 3. France – Colonies. 4. Nationalism – France. 5. France – Politics and government. I. Title.
JV1811.L38   2013
325'.344–dc23   2013014270

ISBN 978-1-107-03709-0 Hardback
ISBN 978-1-107-64075-7 Paperback

Contents

vii

Figure and Tables

Figure

Tables

Preface

When the first carton of French colonial reports that I was to sift through arrived on my desk at the Château de Vincennes, home of the French army's historical archives, I thought the task before me was clear. I wanted to understand how colonial subjects came to form the nationalist movements that would confront the imperial state in the mid-twentieth century. I intended to extract information about nationalist protests in colonial Morocco from administrative and police reports and compile this information in a dataset that I would use to test hypotheses about the triggers of nationalist protest. It was a plan that I expected to be time consuming, particularly given the copious and meticulous documentation by French officials, but it was also, I thought, conceptually straightforward.

And yet, as I began delving into monthly reports on early protest activity in Morocco, I found myself unable to answer the most basic question: what counts as a "nationalist" protest? A June 1936 report described a demonstration in Casablanca; thirty "nationalists" protested against a local *moussem*, or religious festival, on the grounds that such celebrations of local saints are not sanctioned by Islam. What made these protestors nationalist, I wondered? The following month saw a series of protests in the towns of Casablanca, Khourgiba, and Fes when French and Moroccan workers went on strike for better working conditions.

Should this event count as nationalist, or does the participation of French workers make it distinctly non-nationalist? In Meknes, more than 400 demonstrators took to the streets in September 1937 to protest changes to the existing water-sharing arrangement; infuriated that the waters of the Oued Boufekrane were to be redirected for use by French settlers, protestors shouted, "Not one glass of water for the settlers!" Should this be coded as nationalist? In November 1937, protests spread; protestors in multiple towns demanded reform, including the right to free speech and the right to unionize, but no one spoke of independence. Were these protests nevertheless nationalist? In January 1944, protestors took to the streets across the country to demand an end to French rule and independence for the Moroccan nation. Were these the first protests that should be called nationalist or were the earlier ones nationalist, too?

I could hardly begin building a dataset of nationalist protests without knowing which protests belonged and which did not, and yet I did not have a ready answer. From one standpoint, it makes sense to group all of these protests under the umbrella of nationalism. Regardless of what any individual protest was about – wages, water, civil rights, or independence – protests during the colonial period tended to pit Moroccans on one side against the French on the other. Looking at the *identities* of the actors involved, nationality appears paramount, the primary cleavage of the conflict. These protests thus appear to be instances of one nation asserting itself against exploitation by another and may all be called nationalist.

Yet the idea of ignoring differences among these protests in order to fit them into the single category of nationalist action troubled me. Although the sides were defined by nationality (for the most part, although not completely) the protests were not all about nationality or nationhood. That is to say, protestors did not always describe their struggle in nationalist terms or assert national differences. Instead, protestors expressed a wide variety of substantive concerns. At times they explicitly de-emphasized differences between the French and Moroccans, pointing to values and aspirations shared across national boundaries, such as the desire for decent employment, the right to have a say in one's own governance, or the right to free expression. It seemed inaccurate and unjust to act as if these protests were all instances of the same thing, to disregard how the protestors themselves spoke about their objectives. Focusing on the stated *goals* of the actors, rather than their identities, produced a much more complex picture of protest during the colonial era.

I had not anticipated this conceptual difficulty, largely because I had expected that all protest activity by Moroccans living under French colonial rule could be easily and unproblematically called nationalist. I assumed protests would reflect one abiding concern: an end to rule by a foreign power, by the "other." Morocco was, after all, among the most contentious territories of the French empire, acquired late in the colonial period and fully conquered only in 1934. A sense of national identity predated the conquest; indeed, the French established a protectorate, rather than a colony, in part because Morocco already had an internationally recognized national character. Further, according to most accounts, nationalist resistance occurred from at least the 1930s onward. My prior reading of Moroccan history had not prepared me to encounter so much diversity in the kinds of concerns that protestors expressed when they confronted the colonial administration.

Attention to the diversity of demands made by activists in Morocco and across the wider twentieth-century French empire forced me to question my preconceptions about the nature of anti-colonial movements and ultimately shaped the arguments in this book. I noticed that colonial subjects criticized the colonial power not only by using the discourse of nationalism, but also by appealing to another powerful idea: political equality for all, regardless of race, religion, or ethnicity. Opponents of colonialism spoke of the ideals of *egalité*, *fraternité*, and *liberté* in their efforts to reform colonial rule and rid it of its inequalities. They rejected the inferior status of colonial subject and insisted that France live up to its inclusionary rhetoric. One of the main arguments this book seeks to demonstrate is that nationalist demands began when and where the French refused calls for political equality. Exclusion led to nationalist movements seeking to end colonial rule.

Had I focused solely on the *identities* of the actors in conflict in the French empire rather than their *goals*, and taken anti-colonial protest to be tantamount to nationalist protest, I might have failed to pay attention to how colonial subjects reacted to French decisions to offer or withhold political equality. I would have overlooked the shift from discourses about individual equality to claims about national self-determination, and I would have missed the opportunity to consider how and why social movement objectives change over time. I also would have done a profound disservice to those who expressed alternative visions of how empire's inequalities could be addressed and whose voices have already been neglected in nationalist histories.

Reading through French administrative and police reports on Morocco drove home another point about anti-colonial protest: it was very difficult to organize. As events like those of the Arab Spring, Color Revolutions, or collapse of the Soviet Union make manifest, the most hated regimes can prove durable for decades; there is no easy formula for getting people to disregard their safety and take to the streets. Protest requires opportunities that lead people to estimate that taking to the streets can produce change. The French monitored their Moroccan critics closely, drawing up reports on suspected troublemakers, limiting access to the press, and shutting down meetings deemed threatening to French interests. Seventy-one out of the 263 monthly reports I read document the use of repression against Moroccan activists: they were jailed, exiled, or attacked with force for more than a quarter of the period from "pacification" through independence. Under these circumstances, leaders had difficulty organizing opposition. Political exclusion was not enough to prompt nationalist protest. The second argument this book makes concerns the importance of disruptions in the political order for triggering nationalist protest. In the French empire, mass protests erupted when French rule was disrupted by outside forces. When French authority was compromised in a territory, protestors poured into the streets to demand independence for the nation.

These arguments reflect two broader conclusions I reached over the course of this project. The first is that nationalist mobilization is far more contingent than might be expected. The resonance of nationalism in the context of imperial rule is often taken for granted, but as this book seeks to show, the eruption of nationalist movements was neither easy nor inevitable, not even for those living under foreign rule in the mid-twentieth century.

The second is that it matters how rulers treat those they intend to govern. Nationalist conflict is not solely a consequence of the presence of a foreign ruler; the ruler's behavior is also important. Foreign rulers in a variety of contexts have retrospectively explained outbursts of nationalist resistance by claiming that people were bound to oppose foreigners, regardless of the way they behaved. These claims are often, at least in part, self-serving fictions: by claiming that inter-group antagonism is natural, foreign rulers avoid taking responsibility for their own failed policies and actions. More generally, the assumption that nations have a tendency to be in conflict with one another leads to a failure to investigate the factors that fuel antagonism. In the French empire, it mattered whether the French treated people as inferior subjects or political equals. Nationalist conflict was not a given because of the existence of different nationalities but was the result of an interactive, iterative process between the colonizer and the colonized. That process was a political one, in which demands were issued, responses given, and platforms recast.

The desire for equality, I learned, lay beneath much of the political activity of the colonial era. Persistent inequality heightened the boundaries between the French and their colonies and paved the way for nationalist demands. Activists looked to independence to bring the equality that imperial rule had failed to provide. In the postcolonial world, where authoritarian rule and elite privilege persist, many are still waiting.

Acknowledgments

The idea for this book first took shape when I had the privilege of attending a class on Francophone Africa with William Foltz at Yale University. At the time, I was reading Douglas Porch's marvelous popular history, *The Conquest of Morocco,* and I began to wonder just why it was that reactions to colonial rule in the twentieth century varied so significantly across the African continent, from Casablanca to Dakar, Tunis to Tananarive. Professor Foltz was the first to encourage me to take a fresh look at the era of anti-colonialism, applying the insights from decades of work on nationalist conflict to a set of cases that political scientists have tended to overlook.

Since then, I have incurred many personal and intellectual debts; it is a pleasure to be able to acknowledge the kindness and generosity of the many people and organizations that have lent their support to this project. As a graduate student at the University of Chicago, I was the fortunate recipient of helpful advice and support from my advisers. Lisa Wedeen, the chair of my committee, provided valuable guidance and incisive comments throughout my years in graduate school. Stathis Kalyvas taught me the importance of wedding important questions to a rigorous research design. Following long-standing Chicago tradition, Carles Boix and John J. Mearsheimer pushed for sharp, strong argumentation. I am also grateful to other mentors at Chicago:

Cathy Cohen, Charles Lipson, Robert Pape, and Ronald Grigor Suny. For their friendship and intellectual companionship, I thank my graduate school classmates at Chicago, particularly Bethany Albertson, H. Zeynep Bulutgil, Anne Holthoefer, Jenna Jordan, Michelle Murray, Harris Mylonas, Emily Nacol, Sebastian Rosato, Keven Ruby, John Schuessler, and Frank Smith.

I had the very good fortune to engage in research and writing for this project among a terrific group of colleagues and mentors at the Olin Institute for Strategic Studies at Harvard University and the Belfer Center for Science and International Affairs at the Harvard Kennedy School. For their feedback, I thank Erica Chenoweth, Lindsay Cohn, David Cunningham, Kathleen Gallagher Cunningham, Michal Ben-Josef Hirsch, Terence Lee, Sean Lynn-Jones, Jeffrey Mankoff, Steven E. Miller, Stephen Peter Rosen, and Jessica Stanton.

I benefited from critical feedback from many others who read portions of the manuscript at workshops and conferences. I thank Rogers Brubaker, Keith Darden, Philip Gorski, Francesca Grandi, Paul Kenny, Dominika Koter, Matthew Longo, Sarah Parkinson, Leonid Peisakhin, Emmanuelle Saada, Jillian Schwedler, Josh Simon, Dan Slater, Peter Stamatov, and Jonathan Wyrtzen. Mark Beissinger read a substantial portion of the manuscript; I am especially grateful for his comments. The Northeast Middle East Working Group has provided a supportive critical forum for my research; I thank Melani Cammett, Amaney Jamal, and David Patel in particular for their comments and advice.

I am especially grateful to Frederick Cooper, who read the manuscript and hosted me at his home for a challenging and enlightening feedback session; his work on the colonial period profoundly influenced my own ideas as the project developed. I thank him for his insightful comments, encouragement, and willingness to traverse disciplinary boundaries.

At Yale University, I am grateful to Thad Dunning, Ellen Lust, Nuno Monteiro, Ian Shapiro, Susan Stokes, Steven Wilkinson, and Elisabeth Wood, who offered advice and support at crucial moments. Thanks also to Sigrun Kahl, for both her comments on the manuscript and her friendship. I could not have asked for a better intellectual environment than the Department of Political Science at Yale University during the final stages of this project.

In my years of traveling to and living in Morocco, I have not ceased to be astounded by the hospitality many Moroccans have shown to me. I thank Driss Maghraoui at Al Akhawayn University, Mustapha Qadery at the National Library, Mohammed Zade at Le Haut commissariat aux anciens résistants et anciens membres de l'armée de libération, and Abdelhay Moudden and Farah Cherif d'Ouezzan at the Center for Cross Cultural Learning. Younes Amehraye provided research assistance and good conversation during my fieldwork in Morocco. I extend a heartfelt thanks to the former anti-colonial activists who sat down with me to discuss the struggle for national liberation over mint tea. Finally, without the friendship and good humor of Nicole Bennett during the years we spent in Morocco, I would never have come to know and admire the country so well.

I was fortunate to have considerable institutional support for my archival and field research. In France, I consulted archives at the Ministry of Defense in the Château de Vincennes, the Ministry of Foreign Affairs in Nantes, and the Centre des Archives d'Outre-Mer in Aix-en-Provence. I thank the staff at these institutions for their assistance. Awards from the Fulbright-Hays Doctoral Dissertation Research Abroad Program, the American Institute for Maghrib Studies, and the Harry Frank Guggenheim Foundation provided funding for this project.

Finally, I extend my love and gratitude to my family. My parents, Gerald Lawrence and Elaine Lawrence, were my first and most important teachers. Together with Elizabeth Ching, Michael Lawrence, Joanna Ialuna, and Neil Lawrence, they have encouraged my personal and intellectual development in countless ways with their love and support. My daughter Audrey Elena arrived halfway through my work on this book; with her happy, spirited, fun nature, she has made these years my very best. Louisa Ava, my youngest daughter, made her appearance as the book went off to press and provided yet another reason for joy and gratitude. Last, but certainly not least, I thank my husband, Matthew Kocher, whose brilliance and intellectual enthusiasm have inspired me since the day we met. He not only had faith in me and this project from the beginning, he also generously read and criticized several drafts of both the book and the dissertation on which it was based. His contributions to this book are immeasurable. This book is dedicated to him, with my love, admiration, and gratitude.

1

Introduction

The Politics of Nationalism in the French Empire

In late 1945, elected representatives to France's First Constituent Assembly began the task of constructing a new postwar constitution for the Fourth French Republic. In the Overseas Committee, the issue at hand was the place of France's colonial possessions in the new constitution. Delegates wrestled with questions about how the empire would be governed in the postwar era, what status colonized subjects would have, and how to manage cultural differences within a wider polity.[1] To answer these questions, the delegates needed not only to reconcile their own views, but also to think about the great diversity of opinions and aspirations of colonized populations throughout the French empire. For as the debates took place in Paris, various political movements were underway in the colonies and territories. Ho Chi Minh had just declared Vietnam independent to cheering crowds in Hanoi. Political leaders from Martinique, Guadeloupe, Guiana, and Réunion were seeking to turn their territories into French departments. In Morocco, the Independence Party had formed in 1944 and was organizing demonstrations in favor of national independence. Tunisia's nationalist movement had demanded autonomy. In Madagascar, the leaders of the Malagasy National Socialist

[1] For more on the French Constituent assemblies, including the failure of the first, see Benoist (1982); Chafer (2002, 60–67); F. Cooper (2009); Marshall (1973).

Party had asked for autonomy in April 1945. In other parts of French Africa, African leaders favored reforming colonial rule in an egalitarian direction, asking that Africans be accorded the political rights of French citizens while maintaining their distinct cultural identities. The Senegalese deputy Léopold Sédar Senghor had just urged his fellow Africans to "assimilate, do not be assimilated."[2] Algeria was still reeling from the May 1945 events in Sétif, where after a nationalist demonstration had turned violent and resulted in European casualties, a period of brutal retaliation and repression had ensued.[3] Despite the viciousness of the French reaction, there was not, as yet, a consensus among Algerian leaders in favor of independence; some organizations advocated independence but others sought reform within the existing colonial system.[4] In Paris and across the empire, political leaders and colonial subjects expressed diverse wishes for the postwar order.

In hindsight, it is easy to believe that the delegates to the constitutional assemblies had been handed a Sisyphean task: no matter how sincerely they tried to address the inequalities of colonial rule or what proposals they put forth to redefine the relationship between France and her colonies, their efforts were bound to come crashing down eventually, in part because of the allure of nationalism. Nationalism is frequently described as a wave that swept the colonized world in the wake of World War

[2] Quoted in F. Cooper (2009, 98).
[3] Accounts of the initiation of violence in Sétif are contradictory and unclear. The police decided to stop a demonstration, and reports suggest that either the police fired first, or that they responded with gunfire when some of the demonstrators fired or threw stones. The small police force was overwhelmed, and over the next few days, 103 Europeans were killed and another 110 injured. The number of Algerians killed in the reprisals carried out by the French army and area settlers is unknown, although even the lowest numbers suggest that it was a vastly disproportionate response. Horne (1977, 27) gives figures that range from 1,020 to 45,000 killed, and says that most French historians accept a figure of 6,000. On the uprising in Sétif, see also Stora (2001) and Jauffret (1990).
[4] The question of Algeria's postwar status would be tabled until 1947, when seven different proposals for the *Statut d'Algerie* were considered (Ageron 1991a, 104).

II, a ubiquitous force that characterized politics and identity in places ruled by empires.[5] The nationalist movements demanding independence or autonomy that were already underway in 1945 offered clues as to what the future would bring to the rest of the empire; the mystery is why the French did not see it coming.

Indeed, after the colonial period ended, the French and other observers saw nationalism in the colonies as predictable. In his memoirs, Charles de Gaulle (1970, 38) suggested that the very act of bringing French civilization and notions of nationhood to the colonies produced the desire for self-rule.[6] Others thought nationalism was inevitable for reasons less flattering to imperial powers, arguing that the inequalities and injustices of colonial rule made nationalism the obvious response.[7] Global changes also made nationalist responses throughout the colonial world seem natural; Woodrow Wilson's Fourteen Points, the founding of the League of Nations, and the creation of the United Nations are among the events that rendered imperial rule illegitimate and self-determination an internationally recognized right. As Lamine Guèye, once the great Senegalese spokesman for assimilation, said when francophone African states became independent in 1960, "One cannot hold back the ocean with one's hands."[8]

In the academy, understanding colonial history through the lens of nationalism has become, as Gary Wilder (2005, 127) put it, "intellectual common sense."[9] To take a few examples, Roger Owen (2000, 20) writes in his history of Middle Eastern states that the colonial state gave birth "to the familiar dialectic by

[5] For examples of this type of language, see Emerson (1969, 4); Grimal (1985, 6); Landau (1956, 141); Smith (1975, vii), among others.

[6] See Young (1994, 208), who suggests that colonial powers preferred to describe the outcome as inevitable because they sought to portray the outcome as a part of their plans, not a failure. Shepard (2006, 4) argues that "French bureaucrats, politicians, and journalists rewrote the history of imperialism and antiimperialism so that decolonization was the predetermined end point."

[7] Examples include Abun-Nasr (1975, 313); Emerson (1960); Owen (2000, 20); Pratt (2007, 29); Rivlin (1955).

[8] Quoted in Morgenthau (1964, 165).

[9] Wilder is not endorsing the reliance on nationalist norms to understand colonial history, but calling attention to its dominance in U.S. scholarship on the colonial period.

which imperial rule cannot help but generate the nationalist forces that will eventually drive it out." In a similar vein, Edmund Burke III (2000, 21) states that "the violence and cultural hubris of European colonialism called forth its violent negation in the national liberation movements of the 1950s." Likewise, Clement Henry Moore (1970, 34) and Nicola Pratt (2007, 29) suggest that European rule planted "the seeds of its own destruction." To put it another way, empire was an "unstable equilibrium." (Abernethy 2000). Other depictions of the colonial era do not directly state that nationalist responses were bound to occur, but still tend to assume that they are natural and do not require scrutiny. Colonialism and nationalism appear to go hand in hand, the former eventually prompting the latter. In a world organized into nation-states, the eruption of movements using the discourse of nationalism in places where empires still ruled seems unremarkable. Although scholars typically avoid explicitly claiming that any political development is inevitable, it is tempting to look back at the close of the colonial period and see nationalism as, if not foreordained, at least hardly very surprising.

Yet such a view is mistaken for three reasons. First, by taking the resonance of nationalism in the colonial world for granted, scholars and observers overlook the other ways that people responded to empire. Nationalist claims were not the only claims colonized populations articulated; indeed, in many places and time periods, they were not the dominant way to oppose colonialism. Activists living under French rule had multiple reactions that are not easy to classify in the binary terms of collaboration or resistance. Submitting to imperialism or demanding independence were not the only choices. Activists aspired to a better life, they asked to be treated as equals, they defended religion, and they proposed a variety of solutions to the injustices of colonial rule, including federal arrangements and incorporation. Their proposals were creative, audacious, and diverse; they cannot be reduced to assertions about the primacy of nations and nation-states. Yet in the postcolonial era, these alternatives have too often been subsumed into the dominant nationalist history or considered weak precursors to nationalism. Some scholars, however, have called attention to these neglected forms of opposition.[10] And with good reason, as not only are other types of opposition important for their own sakes, but they can also help us understand why nationalist movements took place. This book argues that we cannot understand how nationalism came to be so widespread in much of the colonial world without first considering what happened to the political movements that preceded demands for national autonomy and independence. Put otherwise, we cannot grasp why nationalist movements took place without examining the full range of variation in political organizing.

Second, nationalist opposition to colonial rule is puzzling because it required collective action against a powerful authoritarian state. Theorists have long stressed the difficulties involved in mobilizing people to obtain public goods.[11] In the colonial world, the obstacles to collective organizing were immense.[12] In their empire, the French repressed nascent movements, jailed activists, and confronted mass protests with displays of force and sometimes violence. They fought two major wars in Algeria and Indochina to defeat nationalists, resulting in one of the century's bloodiest decolonization processes.[13] Under these circumstances, the eruption of nationalist demonstrations requires explanation, unless one assumes that the ideology of nationalism is so appealing that collective action is somehow no longer a challenge. Yet there are good reasons to suppose that it was indeed difficult; nationalist

---

[10] For examples, see McDougall (2006); Thompson (2000b). F. Cooper (2002; 2005) has led the way in pointing out the diversity of claims in French Africa. Their work can be considered part of the larger scholarly effort to demonstrate the ways in which studies of the colonial period are beholden to nationalist interpretations of history. Although considerable work has gone into demythologizing the nationalist period in sociology, anthropology, and history, in political science and policy circles the appeal of nationalism is often considered self-evident.

[11] This argument originates with Hume (1978 bk. 3, part 2, sect. 8, p. 538), and was formalized by Mancur Olson (1971).

[12] See Wallerstein (1961, 58).

[13] See Spruyt (2005); see also Lawrence (2010a; 2010b) on nationalists' turn to violent resistance in the French empire.

mobilization in the colonial world was not omnipresent, and long periods passed with little activity. Studies that depict nationalist opposition as the clear consequence of colonial rule overpredict its occurrence and cannot account for temporal and spatial variation in nationalist mobilization. This book points to specific circumstances that provided openings for opponents of colonial rule and facilitated nationalist activity.

A final reason to question the obviousness of nationalist responses to colonial rule is that they were not, as it turns out, foreseeable at the time. Writing just over a year before the Independence Party in Morocco was formed and mass demonstrations erupted, French administrators wrote: "The attachment Moroccans have to France is deeper and more sincere than ever."[14] The delegates drafting France's postwar constitution likewise failed to anticipate that African colonies, too, would experience nationalism or that Algerians would unify under a nationalist platform.[15] During the immediate postwar period, it was not clear just how popular, important, or irreversible nationalist trends would be.

The insight that nationalist movements were to be expected in the mid-twentieth-century colonial world is a retrospective one that depends on knowledge of the outcome. Only in hindsight do nationalist movements and the transformation of colonies into independent nation-states appear to be part of a "tide of history."[16] This point has been made more starkly in the context of the collapse of the Soviet Union, where the suddenness of nationalist revolutions stunned both observers in the West

[14] *Bulletin de Renseignements Politiques*, November 1942. Biweekly report of the Political Affairs Bureau, French Residency in Morocco, SHAT 1414.

[15] Young (1994, 182–183) writes that no one foresaw the collapse of empire immediately after the war. Maalem (1946), like other Algerian activists, did not anticipate widespread mobilization for independence in Algeria during the postwar period. Writing in 1953, Keris (1953, 13) still did not predict significant nationalist mobilization in the Empire, seeing nationalism in Madagascar, Vietnam, Morocco, and Tunisia as the result of causes specific to those places and not part of a wider trend.

[16] See Shepard (2006, 3–10), whose discussion of decolonization as an invented tradition that has been depicted as part of a "Tide of History" could likewise be applied to nationalism.

and dissidents in the East. Although initially surprising, those nationalist uprisings later came to be seen as the inevitable consequence of multiple factors.[17] As in the Soviet Union, nationalist movements in the French empire became predictable only after the fact.

Starting from an outcome and looking back into history to identify patterns that produced it is not necessarily misguided; sometimes patterns are only discernible after time has passed. But, as Frederick Cooper (2005, 18) points out,

[O]ne risks anachronism: confusing the analytic categories of the present with the native categories of the past, as if people acted in search of identity or to build a nation when such ways of thinking might not have been available to them. Even more important is what one does not see: the paths not taken, the dead ends of historical processes, the alternatives that appeared to people in their own time.[18]

Hindsight can thus produce biased explanations. Knowledge of the outcome can lead one to erroneously believe that preferences for the outcome caused it to happen, even when the existence of such preferences has to be assumed.[19] Analyzing past events

---

[17] Beissinger (2002) examines just how the "seemingly impossible" disintegration of the Soviet Union became the "seemingly inevitable" by 1991. Derluguian's (2005, 166) analysis describes "the contentious processes behind what was perceived in the contemporary political imagination as the inevitable consequence of the existence of nationalities." Kuran (1991, 12) argues that hidden preferences make such contentious processes difficult to predict. Hale (2008) provides an explanation for the timing of movements seeking independence. For more on nationalism and the collapse of the former Soviet Union, see also the seminal works by Brubaker (1996); Bunce (1999) and Suny (1993).

[18] See also the discussion in Rivet's (2002) introduction.

[19] Kuran's (1991) explanation for nationalist mobilization in the East European revolutions of 1989 rests on the private preferences of ordinary citizens, who reach a "revolutionary threshold" when hiding their dislike for the regime becomes more costly then acting against it. This theory helps explain why revolution is so surprising, but because it depends upon preferences that are by definition unobservable, it is essentially unverifiable. One has to take the outcome as evidence for the explanation of that outcome. Anticipating this objection, Kuran (1991, 48) states that the theory predicts unpredictability and thus can be falsified if predictable revolutions are observed, but unpredictability is also consistent with other explanations for nationalist uprisings, including accounts that focus on contingency and political opportunities.

with the end result in mind can make an outcome that was not predicted paradoxically appear easily predictable. Looking back after the fact, it is easy to focus on the "winners" who succeeded at collective action or gather only the evidence that appears most relevant to producing nationalism. But by ignoring (or simply failing to see) the alternatives to nationalism, we miss the opportunity to investigate why one mobilization platform succeeds while others fail.

Moreover, we risk being overly influenced by the winners' perspectives. Part of the reason that nationalism seems so inevitable comes from nationalist ideology itself, which, like Marxist metanarratives or ideologies of inexorable Western expansion, explicitly puts forth a teleological view of history. Nationalists vigorously maintained that the imperial status quo was untenable and nationalism was bound to triumph. Some scholars and observers looking back at the period have accepted those claims as fact. There are normative reasons for doing so; emphasizing the contingent nature of nationalist responses might be interpreted as diminishing the accomplishments of national liberation movements, or even implying that colonial rule was viable or inoffensive. Yet, as this book seeks to demonstrate, an investigation into how colonized populations came to articulate nationalist objectives can help illuminate just what made colonial rule in the mid-twentieth century so objectionable.

Nationalist responses to empire do require interrogation. The tendency to see nationalism as the obvious organizing idiom for people living under colonial rule in the mid-twentieth century has obscured important puzzles about the causes of nationalist mobilization. Most importantly, taking nationalism for granted serves to conceal the contingent nature of the eruption of movements seeking autonomy or independence from colonial empires. Yet this outcome did not have to unfold as it did. Specific circumstances gave rise to movements in particular times and places. This book looks at some of the ways that mobilization varied in the French empire, addressing several questions. Why did mobilization in favor of independent statehood supplant movements to reform and reshape colonial rule, where it did so?

What prompted those living under imperial rule to begin making nationalist demands? Why did nationalist demonstrations erupt in particular places and times?

Concepts: Nationalism, Nationalist Mobilization, and Decolonization

Nationalist mobilization in the French empire is the subject of interest here, not decolonization or nationalism, two related but distinct phenomena. My investigation benefits from a significant body of scholarly work on the colonial period, but nationalist mobilization is typically not the central outcome these studies seek to explain. To begin with, nationalist mobilization in the colonial world is usually analyzed for its effects rather than its causes. Thus, there is an ongoing debate about how much credit nationalist movements can take for achieving independence: did they win liberation or did independence result from a European-initiated process of decolonization?[20] These questions focus on decolonization or the achievement of independence, depending on the stance of the author. Nationalism is one factor, among others, that potentially produces independence.[21] The major puzzle of interest is the European loss of territory. Studies of the postcolonial period have likewise looked at the effects of mobilization, examining what nationalist movements achieved and failed to achieve in the years following independence.[22] Fewer studies have focused directly on nationalist movements

---

[20] For a recent discussion of this debate, as well as a discussion of the existing consensus on the factors that led to decolonization, see Shipway (2008).

[21] For studies that take decolonization or the end of empire as the outcome of interest, see Ageron (1986a; 1991b); Betts (1991); Chafer (2002); Chamberlain (1999); Clayton (1994); Duara (2004); Easton (1964); Gifford and Louis (1982); Grimal (1985); Le Sueur (2003); Low (1991); Lustick (1993); Pervillé (1991); Smith (1975); Spruyt (2005); von Albertini (1975); Yacono (1971). See also Roeder (2007) on the formation of nation-states.

[22] For instance, on North Africa, see the seminal works that focus on postindependence politics by Entelis (1980); Moore (1970); Waterbury (1970); and Zartman (1964). L. Anderson (1986) theorizes the impact of colonial rule on post-independent Tunisia and Libya. On postcolonial politics in Southeast Asia, see Slater (2010); for Africa, see MacLean (2010).

themselves, placing their fate and not the fate of the colonies at the center of the analysis.[23] An investigation of the causes of nationalist mobilization has implications for understanding the transition to independence, but explaining empire's end is not the objective here. This analysis examines why people came to mobilize for national liberation, not why colonialism collapsed, a question others have carefully and convincingly considered.

Whereas studies of the colonial period typically emphasize independence as the outcome of interest, there is a considerable body of work with wide geographic and temporal scope that is directly concerned with the development of nationalism. This study draws on insights from the nationalism literature, but it is important to highlight the distinction between taking nationalist *mobilization*, rather than nationalism, as the outcome of interest. It is more common for scholarly work to focus on nationalism, understood primarily as ideology or identity, than nationalist mobilization, which is explicitly concerned with human action. My objective is to investigate when and why people come to take action in the name of the nation, not when they start identifying with a nation or how nationalist ideologies are constructed.

This is not unfamiliar terrain; Beissinger (2002) likewise focuses on mobilization in his study of the breakup of the Soviet Union.[24] He points out that most studies see nationalist behavior "as merely an externalization of nationalist ways of thinking brought into being well before the onset of nationalist action" (Beissinger 2002, 9). These studies imply that the origins of national identity deserve the bulk of scholarly attention because identity explains action or, if it does not fully explain it, at least predisposes people to take certain actions.[25] It is noteworthy that this view does not imply that studying action is unimportant. Rather, because

---

[23] A number of important works do focus on nationalism in the colonial context, particularly those that examine the case of India. See Chatterjee (1993a; 1993b); Goswami (2004). See also Duara (1997), on China.

[24] See also Hechter (2000), who defines nationalism as collective action. See Beissinger (2002, 21–27) on the importance of systematically studying events. For a discussion of events as a theoretical category, see Sewell (1996).

[25] For this view, see the classic work by Hroch (1985); as well as the discussion of Hroch in Beissinger (2002). For more recent examples that privilege an

mobilization is the consequence of identity, it need not be theorized as a distinctive outcome.

The purported causal link between identity and action has prompted a number of criticisms suggesting that the causal relationship is far less straightforward than might be expected.[26] Identity change does not prompt immediate action, and few would propose that it is either a proximate trigger of or a sufficient condition for mobilization.[27] The more common formulation is that identity is an important background condition: identities are not expressed through action in all times and places, but they become politically salient under specific conditions.[28]

The circumstances under which identities are expressed in behavior remain opaque; some identities become the basis for mobilization whereas others do not, even some that appear to resonate very strongly with people. A group identity may not be salient for political action for years on end, remaining essentially "latent." Identifying the roots of particular identities may therefore explain political behavior only indirectly; the effects of identity on action may be delayed by years or may not manifest themselves at all.[29]

Given the difficulty of connecting identities to instances of mobilization, it is fruitful to focus on the conditions that give rise to mobilization at particular moments in time, not the identities that underlie it. If people take action to defend or promote an identity only under particular circumstances, surely it is in understanding those circumstances, and not in focusing on the origins of the identity, that we are likely to gain the most explanatory power,

account of the origins of national identity, see Greenfeld (1993) and Darden (Forthcoming).

[26] This debate mirrors an older one in the literature on revolutions over the role that ideology played in causing revolution. See Skocpol (1979, 14–18).

[27] Yashar (2005, 18) provides a critique of work that focuses on identity and neglects questions about the timing of action.

[28] Roger Gould (1995, 19), for instance, has suggested that critical events can heighten preexisting identities; circumstances can both encourage action and render identities politically salient. See Varshney (2003) for further discussion of the relationship between national identity and nationalist action.

[29] On the rarity of conflict among ethnic groups, a related issue, see Fearon and Laitin (1996).

even if identity formation is an important long-run antecedent of action.[30] Put another way, to understand mobilization that is episodic – that varies over time and place – the best potential explanations should also be episodic, and therefore capable of accounting for the observed variation.

This approach is particularly useful if it is the case that pre-existing identity is not, in fact, necessary for action. Existing scholarship reflects serious disagreements about whether a prior sense of national identity is required for mobilization. Instead, identities may gain salience as a consequence of mobilization. Gould (1995, 14–15) exemplifies an approach to studying collective action that seeks:

> To avoid the reductionist tactic of assigning causal priority either to existing identities or to the social interactions they inform in determining the shape of social conflict. Instead, I hope to demonstrate the merits of a theoretical perspective according to which collective identities undergird normative commitments to social protest, but are at the same time the product of the very social relations that are both affirmed and forged in the course of protest.

Identifying as a member of a nation, like identifying as a worker in Gould's study, may precede or result from experiences of nationalist protest. Indeed, the very words and actions enacted during a protest may serve to call nationalist actors into being. As Beissinger (2002, 11) puts it, "Collective action itself may be constitutive of nationhood."[31] Brubaker (1996, 19–20) maintains that nationalism can erupt as an event that "suddenly crystallizes rather than gradually develops, as a contingent, conjuncturally fluctuating, and precarious frame of vision and basis for individual and collective action."[32] If

---

[30] To take a few examples of this approach, scholars have shown that institutional rules and contexts can make some identities politically salient and alter behavior (Chandra 2007; Posner 2005) or states and elites may manipulate existing national identities to provoke action (Gagnon 1994; Wilkinson 2004a).

[31] Nationalist actions can be understood as performative, in Bourdieu's (1991) terms. See the discussion of Bourdieu and Arendt applied to nationalism in Wedeen (2009, 88–89).

[32] See Darden (Forthcoming) and Haas (1997) for opposing views; they see nationalist frames as enduring once constructed, not precarious.

national identity is malleable and constructed, as recent scholarly work suggests, it may get constructed before, during, or after episodes of mobilization.[33] National identity may thus at times be a consequence of action, changing rapidly during periods of mobilization that serve to heighten boundaries between social actors – an insight that renders problematic the assumption that identities must be causally prior to action.

A study that seeks to explain nationalist mobilization need not resolve the causal relationship between identity and action. Given the unsettled nature of existing debates, it would be imprudent to pursue a research strategy that assumes a particular causal link. The arguments I make in this book allow for national identity to be an important precondition for those who engage in nationalist mobilization, or it may be a precondition for some but not everyone, or identity may change as a consequence of mobilization. In other words, my account is consistent both with the view that mobilization is shaped by preexisting loyalties and commitments and that nationalist expressions may be fleeting and context dependent.[34] By positing an account of mobilization that allows multiple roles for identity, I seek to avoid assuming either that action is a consequence of identity or that identity is irrelevant to action.

An understanding of identity formation is not a prerequisite for investigating political action. The question of how national identities are forged is distinct from an investigation into nationalist action.[35] Studying nationalist mobilization rather

---

[33] For examples of work on the construction of nationalism and nations, and the provisional nature of nationalist expressions, see B. Anderson (1983); Brubaker(1996); Sahlins (1989); Suny (2001b).

[34] Lomnitz (2001, xiv) argues that nationalist consciousness was uneven at the time of Mexican independence, both in terms of its content and the extent to which it had disseminated. This unevenness likely existed in many places in the French empire, although it is difficult to say given the paucity of measures. The lack of data is part of the reason I make no attempt to posit a causal relationship between national identity and action.

[35] The question of why, how, and whether people in the French empire came to see themselves as part of a national community is a worthy one, but not one I address here. Such an analysis would require a different research design; for many places it would necessitate going beyond the colonial period into the era of independence. The pieces in McDougall (2003), for instance, focus on identity formation before and after independence.

than national identity is analytically useful in three respects. First, one of the key objectives of this analysis is to understand the timing of nationalist events – why people take action in the name of the nation when they do. This focus on timing is a way to put Brubaker's (1996) call for an "eventful" approach to nationalism into practice; it focuses on what people do and say, not who they are. Studying action is particularly appropriate in the context of the colonial world, where nationalist mobilization often appeared to erupt suddenly, taking the authorities and outside observers by surprise.

A second reason to focus on mobilization is to facilitate comparisons with other kinds of political opposition. In the French colonial empire, nationalist mobilization was not the only kind of political dissidence. By comparing nationalist movements to mobilization around alternative frames, we can identify how different contexts promote particular discourses of action.

A third reason to avoid taking sentiment or identity as the outcome of interest stems from problems of measurement. Focusing on mobilization eliminates the need to demonstrate either the existence of stable, long-standing "nations" or the presence or absence of nationalist commitments among a specified population. Providing evidence of identity is a difficult problem; in many contexts, it is insurmountable.[36] Scholars of nationalism often have two available routes to observing it – they can either rely on the statements of elites (via press, poetry, or other writings), or they can take behavior as evidence of identity. The first approach illustrates nationalist sentiments, but potentially only among a small, unrepresentative group. For this reason, studies that focus on elite statements often claim to be looking for the origins of the nation, rather than demonstrating its wider appeal,

---

[36] Darden's (Forthcoming) measurement of national identity is the clearest: he codes a place as having a national identity once literacy reaches 50 percent. By this measurement, however, no French colony has national identity by independence, making the occurrence of mass mobilization in favor of national independence puzzling if one assumes that a widespread sense of identity is required for mobilization. Laitin (1998) uses language as an indicator of identity.

and the mechanisms by which it spreads to the rest of the population are left unspecified. The second approach is more inclusive, but it requires assuming that behavior is a straightforward reflection of identity, and thus ignores the criticisms previously outlined. Taking nationalist behavior as evidence of nationalist identity is particularly problematic if the latter is posited to cause the former, as it entails assuming the cause from its consequent.

My approach is to explicitly embrace nationalist mobilization as the outcome to be explained. The discussion does have implications for understanding why national identities became salient, but identity is not the primary focus. I consider mobilization to include the kinds of contentious activities described in the social movement literature[37] – such as boycotts, demonstrations, strikes, and other protest activity – but I also include non-contentious collective action such as voting for or joining nationalist parties.[38]

This discussion has thus far defended an emphasis on mobilization rather than identity, but what does it mean to say that mobilization is nationalist? Deciding which events ought to be counted as nationalist is tricky, as in the colonial context there is a tendency to consider all opposition as nationalist in nature. My view is that nationalist acts are discursively constructed as such.[39] When mobilized actors articulated demands for independence or autonomy on behalf of a separate nation, I consider the event nationalist. This understanding is simple: it relies on what people were saying about what they were doing. It does not claim to read their minds; nationalist action does not have to imply the mobilization of those with a

---

[37] See McAdam et al. (1996); McAdam et al. (2001); Tarrow (1994); Tilly (1978); Tilly and Tarrow (2007).

[38] Throughout the text, I also use synonyms of mobilization, such as "activity" or "action." When invoking nationalism as a form or identity or identification or as an ideology, I am careful to use those terms.

[39] A discursive approach comes out of the view that nations and nationalism are primarily constructed via the various discourses that call them into being. On the merits of a discursive approach to nationalism, particularly given "the diversity and heterogeneity of nationalist discourses and practices," see Gorski (2000, 1460–1461); see also Burton and Wilder (2003, 5). McDougall (2003, 3) likewise advocates paying attention to people's articulation of their identities.

deep sense of national identity.[40] Rather, mobilization is nationalist if actors framed their actions using the discourse of nationalism.

My focus on demands for independence on behalf of a nation invokes a standard, widely shared understanding. Ernest Gellner (1983, 1) defined nationalism as a political principle that holds that the political and national unit should be congruent, or as Wedeen (2008, 8) put it, "Nationalist ideology presumes a congruency between 'the people' and state institutions." Expressions of nationalism reflect the view that the world is divided into nations, these nations are sovereign, and that sovereignty implies statehood.[41] Nationalist discourses wed nation to state; they invoke the nation as the basis of the right to statehood.[42]

It is true that nationalist utterances are not limited to expressions of a desire for unrealized political independence or autonomy; states in many places have promoted national identity and encouraged nationalist displays even when independence has already been achieved. Some have thus made distinctions between state-seeking and state-led expressions of nationalism.[43] The cases in this book are instances of state-seeking mobilization. The reason all these types are classified as nationalist is that they share the core claim that nations are independent units with the

[40] One might object that to call mobilization nationalist in the first place, it must be carried out by those with national identity, but this requires assuming the causal impact of identity on action. The approach here is to take seriously how actors described their goals, without making assumptions about the strength or depth of their identification to the nation.

[41] See Hechter (2000, 7); see also Gorski (2000, 1432–1433).

[42] Not all demands for independence may be classified nationalist; I define demands for independence as nationalist if they are made on behalf of a nation. Demands for independence could be issued on behalf of other entities. For instance, a monarch could insist on the right of the monarchy to rule the state, demanding independence without invoking a nation. I thank Josh Simon for this point.

[43] Tilly (1995). Wimmer (2008, 13) also notes that nation building may be pursued by the state or against the state. Brubaker (1996, 4–5) offers a different typology, describing three "distinct and mutually antagonistic nationalisms," the nationalizing efforts of newly independent states, transborder nationalisms, and nationalism by minorities within a state. See also Hechter (2000, chapter 1), who discusses four types of nationalism and does seek to decouple nationalism from demands for statehood.

right to self-governance in a given territory.[44] Both those seeking states and states engaged in promoting nationalism assert this claim. Thus, the discourse used by those in the French empire resembles nationalist claims in other settings.

It may be tempting to widen the definition of what counts as nationalist by including discourses that fall short of claiming the right to self-rule in a specified territory, but such a move risks "conceptual stretching" (Sartori 1970). Broadening the concept of nationalism beyond a commitment to distinct, self-governing entities sacrifices conceptual clarity and risks conflating national commitments with identifications to other kinds of groups.[45]

The Arguments

This book makes two arguments to explain nationalist mobilization in the French empire. First, it investigates the goals of mobilization, positing an argument to explain why nationalist movements demanding independent statehood supplanted calls for political equality in many parts of the empire. Second, it addresses the problem of mobilization, explaining how it became possible to organize nationalist movements in a setting that restricted political opposition. Together, these arguments account for variation in the timing and location of public demonstrations in favor of independence.

Political Equality and Inequality
Local elites in French colonies initially asked the French to treat them as political equals. These elites espoused French republican principles and advocated the extension of French political institutions

[44] Additional characteristics have sometimes been taken as fundamental aspects of nationalism, for instance the sense that nationalism is a necessarily modern, secular ideology that implies certain understandings of time. Gorski (2000) argues against the view that nationalism is a solely modern phenomenon. Wedeen (2008) calls into question the relationship between secularism and nationalism and points out that other ideologies imply similar understandings of time.

[45] Other groups do indeed make references to nationhood as a way to emphasize their distinctiveness and legitimacy without any pretension to sovereignty or peoplehood; the 1990s radical gay group Queer Nation comes to mind as an example.

to the colonies. In many places, calls for political equality took the form of demands for full French citizenship; elites asked the French to live up to their promises to assimilate colonized populations. In other places, elites sought political equality via the establishment of local representative institutions that would permit colonized subjects to share political power, eliminating a system that privileged French citizens. These demands were shaped by French promises; activists used the imperial power's stated justifications for colonialism to point out the disparity between colonial principles and practices.[46] Proponents of political equality challenged the *authoritarian* nature of colonial rule, not its *foreignness*.

Demands for political equality are often portrayed as epiphenomenal, an initial response to colonialism that primarily served to set the stage for nationalist claims. Conventional accounts imply that pleas for political equality constituted a preliminary stage in the progression toward nationalism; nationalist demands were the logical next step. Still, the question of what would have happened if political equality had succeeded has been a subject of speculation. Some scholars have suggested that if the French had been able to meet demands for political equality, nationalism might have been forestalled, whereas others have maintained that political equality would never have been an acceptable alternative to national independence. I evaluate these claims and provide evidence that elites successfully mobilized for nationalist goals only when and where demands for equality failed to produce results. Exclusion from the democratic institutions of France led to nationalist mobilization; inclusion did not.[47]

This argument speaks to the question of how nationalist goals replaced alternative demands made on the colonial state. It addresses the kinds of claims that opponents of colonial rule articulated, explaining why the organizing idiom of mobilization switched to nationalism. It operates primarily at the elite level; the experience

[46] On attempts to put colonial principles into practice in the French empire, see Conklin (1997). See also Strang (1992), on colonial contradictions.
[47] This formulation of the argument goes further in establishing the causality between political exclusion and nationalist mobilization than others have advocated, but in doing so generates clear observable implications.

of persistent political inequality despite calls for change affected elite views about the desirability of remaining in the French empire and led to an emphasis on national differences and statehood.

The consequences of political equality and exclusion have been obscured by the tendency to dismiss early calls for equitable reform and focus on the first stirrings of nationalist mobilization. This tendency is not unreasonable given the historical record. After all, calls to reform imperial rule and transform colonial subjects into equals were unsuccessful in many places. Exclusion was the dominant response to assertions of political equality in the French empire; subsequently, most colonies were ultimately caught up in the nationalist wave of the twentieth century and became independent. But proponents of equality also achieved successes. In a number of places activists made significant headway; a few cases achieved full incorporation as French departments. The fate of these movements varied, and this book takes advantage of this variation, examining successful cases, exploiting subnational variation, and engaging in counterfactual analysis to demonstrate the effects of political equality and exclusion. The argument accounts for the negative cases, those that saw little to no nationalist mobilization, as well as the positive. In an era of widespread nationalist opposition to empire, the absence of nationalist mobilization is puzzling.

Given that the cases of exclusion outnumber the cases where political equality was granted, however, why should we pay close attention to the latter? What is at stake, if political equality was not ultimately an option for many colonies? The argument that nationalist mobilization was a consequence of denying political equality is an important one, regardless of whether political equality was extended in many cases or few, because an understanding of the consequences of equality and exclusion reveals serious flaws in the way we think about nationalism and decolonization more broadly.

First, it forces us to ask why political equality was not extended in many cases. The literature implies that political equality was impossible or doomed because it was unacceptable to the colonized population, whose aspirations were bound to turn nationalist. In contrast, I show that the reason was not a lack of willingness on the part of colonized peoples to entertain incorporation on fair and equal terms. It was the French who could not live up to their promises of political equality. Chapter 3 explores some of the reasons why the French ultimately denied political equality to many parts of the empire, but the point to be emphasized is that the obstacle was not the colonized population or the existence of national differences. Attention to differences between the French and the people of the colonies has, I shall argue, led analysts to underestimate how much people care about being treated as equals and overestimate how much they care about national divides.

This point has implications beyond the French empire for how we understand conflict between members of different groups. Although states and empires have, throughout history, extended forms of political equality to minority populations,[48] the potential for equitable policies to reduce or diffuse intergroup antagonism has been masked by the conviction that such antagonism is in some way natural in the modern age of nationalism, and not a function of policy. But the substantive grievances in nationalist conflicts may have less to do with given attributes of populations and more to do with how they treat one another.[49] In cases of foreign conquest and occupation, the ruling power may not even consider that a higher degree of equality between the occupier and occupied could work to diffuse conflict. Perhaps political equality would have been on the policy agenda more often if rulers did not assume it would be unacceptable to those they ruled. Alternatively, as in the French empire, it may be that the rulers and not the ruled are the obstacle to equitable policies. This analysis therefore invites a reconsideration of the factors that can make political equality unfeasible.

---

[48] See the conclusion for a discussion of cases outside the French empire where political equality was extended to conquered populations. See also Mylonas (2013), on state decisions to assimilate, accommodate, or exclude ethnic groups.

[49] See also Hechter (2009), who argues that the evidence for the pervasiveness of antagonism toward alien rule has been overstated; he argues that alien rule can be acceptable when it is fair and efficient.

Second, this argument challenges our understanding of decolonization. There is a widely held belief that nationalism, and more generally racial, ethnic, and religious difference, made imperialism unsustainable. This book shows the limit of this claim. If political equality was another remedy to imperialism and nationalism was not inevitable, then our beliefs about the relationship between nationalism and decolonization are mistaken. Social scientists seek to identify the right causal mechanisms; we need to know about the link between political inequality and nationalism, or we will misunderstand the pathway to the collapse of the empire.

Disruptions in Order

The denial of political equality was not enough to trigger nationalist action. Mobilization did not automatically happen when demands for equality went unmet. Mobilization requires openings, particularly in an authoritarian setting that limits free speech and association. In the second half of the book, I argue that disruptions in imperial authority at the level of the colonial territory prompted participation in nationalist activities. The imperial power's control over a territory could be disrupted by invasion and occupation, as occurred in some but not all French colonies during World War II, or by the very decision to decolonize. These events produced a situation in which the colonial power's local authority was either partial or nonexistent. It provided opportunities for political opponents to take to the streets and stage nationalist demonstrations.

This argument draws on insights about the consequences of state crises from the literature on revolutions and connects them to the study of nationalism.[50] It explains why the timing of nationalist activity varied, helping make sense of the sudden onset of contentious, nationalist politics. Nationalist mobilization did not begin all at once in the empire; in some places it began early in the twentieth century, while others did not experience it until 1960 or later. Nor did it spread from one colony to its neighbors; geography cannot account for the variation in timing. I explore this variation

[50] See Skocpol (1979), on the role of state crises in revolution.

and argue that it was the state of authority at the local level that mattered. Through attention to the local context within individual colonies, I identify the proximate causes of action, rather than the background conditions that serve to facilitate it.[51] Explaining the timing of mobilization is a notoriously difficult problem for social movement theorists; focusing on periods of disruption helps account for when mobilization occurred in the French empire.

This argument counters studies that see disorder or imperial collapse as a consequence of nationalist mobilization. Instead, I suggest that disorder and ineffective state control preceded widespread participation in nationalist movements. Mobilization then served to exacerbate already-existing problems of order. Counterintuitively, in some instances, nationalist mobilization was endogenous to decolonization.

Discussion and Implications

This book thus argues that nationalist mobilization happened where equitable reforms no longer appeared achievable and when changes in imperial control created opportunities for public demonstrations against colonial rule. These two arguments provide an account of the motive and opportunity for nationalist action against the empire.[52] They point to the ways that context shapes political action. Opponents of French colonialism were both empowered and limited by what appeared possible, by the menu of options they saw before them. Their options were wider than we often think when we look back at the period; their choices and actions were determined only in part by their national identity. By pointing to the capacity for colonized

---

[51] See Collins (2008, 20–21) on this distinction.

[52] There is a long-standing debate in the literature on ethnicity and nationalism regarding the fruitfulness of focusing on motives and grievances (see, for instance, Gurr 1971; Horowitz 1985; Petersen 2002) or on opportunities and structures (see the discussion in Skocpol 1979; see also Fearon and Laitin 2003a). The difficulty in measuring motives and grievances has led to increased attention to more observable structural and institutional factors. My account stresses the importance of both motivational microfoundations and structural factors, pointing to specific grievances with observable implications that can be assessed.

populations to engage in both assimilating and differentiating practices (as well as combinations of the two), I show that they had significant agency. But their choices were not limitless; they were bounded by the particular circumstances of living in the twentieth century French empire.

The French were similarly limited by what appeared possible for a colonial ruler at that time, and the factors that I argue prompted nationalism were often largely out of their control. Vying political factions and fragile political coalitions in France affected decisions on colonial policy and shaped colonial administrators' interactions with political activists in the colonies.[53] The changing fortunes of war also constrained the colonizer's actions.

Further, actors' options were shaped by a wider global context in which particular political frames were gaining currency while others were in decline.[54] These arguments are thus historically situated; they cannot be transferred wholesale to explain other nationalist conflicts because the menu of options differs across time periods and settings.[55]

Yet these arguments suggest the importance of thinking about how the local context affects the possibilities for mobilization and considering the ways the state, colonial or otherwise, can create the conditions that produce nationalist opposition against itself.[56] States can shape the very language of opposition by promoting particular ideologies and worldviews that opponents may appropriate. Just as opponents of French colonialism drew on republican ideology to criticize colonial policy,

---

[53] See Spruyt (2005) for more on how domestic politics in European states affected their actions in the colonies.

[54] See Ageron (1986a).

[55] Moreover, it may well be the case that explanations capable of accounting for timing are less well suited to generalizing across many different cases, a trade-off that may be worth making. For more on the importance of developing dynamic theories, see Lawrence (2010b).

[56] Yashar (2005) provides a model for considering how the state affects social movement action. The puzzle here is similar to the one she investigates: the uneven emergence, timing, and location of indigenous protest in Latin America.

pointing to the ways in which colonial rule was inconsistent with republican principles, critics in other parts of the world have pointed out discrepancies between states' principles and their practices. In times of crisis, these criticisms can form the basis for mass action.

My arguments also challenge the conventional wisdom on nationalism in the colonial world. They call into question accounts that see nationalist responses as obvious or easy in the context of empire, pointing to the precariousness of nationalist action in an authoritarian, colonial setting. Before vibrant nationalist movements developed, efforts to redress the inequalities between subjects and citizens had to be abandoned, and imperial authority itself had to be radically disrupted. These conditions were not easy to meet, and they did not happen everywhere. These arguments thus help explain why imperial rulers were able to maintain control for long stretches of time despite deep dissatisfaction with colonial rule.

My arguments privilege local processes over the international trends that are thought to be so crucial for the onset of nationalist opposition in the twentieth century. Below, I discuss existing explanations for nationalist mobilization in the colonial world. Factors other than the two I focus on here undoubtedly helped inspire and produce nationalist opposition. My claim is not that nothing else mattered, but my aim in putting forth a parsimonious theory is to pinpoint the variables that are best able to account for variation in the timing and location of nationalist organizing across the twentieth-century French empire. Before I turn to other explanations, however, I put my arguments in context, describing the cases and methodology.

Case Selection and Research Design

The colonial cases are often studied by historians and anthropologists who have described the dynamics of nationalist resistance in case studies and comparative histories. This rich literature points to a number of explanations for the rise of nationalist movements that have rarely been subjected to rigorous empirical tests aimed at isolating key causal variables. An approach that is informed by political methodology can thus contribute by constructing tests to systematically assess the relative strength of competing explanations.

Such an approach faces challenges of data availability, however. Although there are excellent sources on the colonial period, the data are not organized in a way that facilitates systematic hypothesis testing. Colonial reports that can be accessed in the archives are typically descriptive. When the French did amass quantitative records, their data-collection methods differed across territories and even over time in the same place, making comparisons difficult. Secondary sources provide a wealth of information, but they are likewise not designed to assist the kind of sophisticated quantitative testing common in political science. The cross-national datasets often used by political scientists contain many missing values for colonial territories prior to independence; indeed, political scientists continue to lack reliable current statistics on many areas of the world that experienced colonial rule in the past. The absence of easily accessible data means that politics during the colonial era have largely escaped the attention of political scientists.[57]

The state of the data requires an approach that takes advantage of the existence of good historical sources to construct ways to consider explanations for nationalist mobilization systematically. I take a multi-methodological approach, combining archival research, field work, and comparative historical analysis. In the chapters that follow, I draw out the implications of competing explanations and construct tests that utilize the information obtained using these methodologies. Following the recommendations of Brady and Collier (2010), I rely not only on dataset observations but also on causal-process observations that can suggest the relative merits of competing explanations. I thus draw on historical qualitative evidence to consider whether the

---

[57] Mitchell (1991) provides an exception. There is also a growing literature in economics and political science that looks at the effects of colonial legacies for current development. See, for instance, Acemoglu and Robinson (2001). Wilkinson (2004b) outlines plans for a new dataset that includes a diverse set of variables from the colonial era.

observable implications of rival theories are borne out. I also conduct counterfactual analyses, constructing alternative scenarios and considering how nationalist mobilization might have differed.[58] Additionally, I carry out simple quantitative tests using the data that are available.[59] Fortunately, it is not necessary to employ sophisticated econometric models, or even to count very high, to observe that some of the most common explanations for nationalist mobilization in the colonial world do not hold up to empirical scrutiny.

Throughout the book, explanations are evaluated at two levels of analysis. The first is a medium-N cross-colony analysis of the territories of the French empire. Investigating variation in nationalist mobilization within one empire provides several advantages. Studies of the decolonization era often compare broadly across empires, but by doing so they lower the size of their sample and lose cross-colony variation. Studies that compare the British, French, Belgian, and Portuguese empires, for example, tend to privilege metropole-based explanations because the research design itself prompts investigation into the differences between imperial powers. By comparing cases within one empire, I hold the colonial power constant and investigate why nationalist mobilization varied even within one empire. The French empire in particular provides a useful set of cases because it was the second-largest twentieth-century empire, with thirty-five colonies and territories (see Table 1.1) that varied in important ways that facilitate the consideration of rival explanations.

A medium-N approach permits hypothesis testing without excessively sacrificing data quality. A large-N study that drew on multiple empires would not only introduce considerable unit heterogeneity, but would also suffer from serious measurement error and missing values on many variables of interest. A medium-N

---

[58] On the use of counterfactuals for causal analysis in political science, see Fearon (1991); Lebow (2010); Tetlock and Belkin (1996). Tetlock and Lebow (2001) point to both benefits and pitfalls that stem from openness to historical contingency.

[59] On the virtues of simple tools, see Collier, Brady, and Seawright in Brady and Collier (2010, 199).

TABLE 1.1. *French Colonies and Overseas Territories*

Vietnam	Ubanghi-Shari (CAR)	French Polynesia
Cambodia	French India	New Caladonia
Laos	Reunion	French Guiana
St Pierre and Miquelon	Mayotte	Mauretania
Martinique	Madagascar	Senegal
Guadeloupe	Comoros	Guinea
Cameroon	Wallis and Futuna	Ivory Coast
Djibouti	Syria	Dahomey (Benin)
Togo	Lebanon	French Sudan (Mali)
Chad	Morocco	Upper Volta (Burkina Faso)
Gabon	Tunisia	Niger
Middle Congo (PRC)	Algeria	

approach, although still susceptible to error, makes data collection easier, and the number of cases is not so small that there is no leverage to evaluate competing explanations.

The purpose of the cross-colony analysis is not to bring new data sources to light, but to use existing sources to mediate between competing explanations. Historical accounts of the French empire and case studies of individual territories tend to be inclusive and nuanced, listing many plausible factors that could account for the onset of nationalist opposition. This book seeks to narrow the field, identifying those that best account for the observed variation in nationalist mobilization across the empire.

The second empirical strategy is subnational analysis.[60] The chief case considered is colonial Morocco.[61] The Moroccan case is particularly useful because it provides a "hard test" of

---

[60] See Kalyvas (2006) on the use of subnational microcomparative evidence; his book promotes and explicates systematic hypothesis testing through making comparisons across similar units within states.

[61] For this case, I collected archival and other primary source material in France and Morocco from September 2005 to May 2006, and I carried out participant and expert interviews in Morocco in the spring of 2006. I also relied on descriptions of nationalist mobilization in secondary sources, such as the excellent work by Hoisington (1984).

the arguments proposed here. It is not easy to make the case that nationalist mobilization in Morocco was contingent in the ways that I suggest. Although scholars have described other forms of opposition besides nationalism in Algeria and French Africa, Morocco is typically taken to be a place where nationalist mobilization was the dominant response to colonialism. This view is shaped by the knowledge that Moroccans already had a sense of national identity when colonialism began, unlike many other places in the empire. The concept of a Moroccan nation predates the establishment of French rule in 1912.[62] Morocco was a state with a sovereign leader, the sultan, before the arrival of the French. In the protectorate treaty, France acknowledged Morocco's sovereign status and promised to uphold the sultan as the legitimate leader of Morocco.[63] The French therefore did not propose a policy of assimilation for Moroccans, as it did when it acquired other colonies.

Morocco's history of statehood and recognized nationality might be expected to facilitate nationalist organizing, and make it the obvious idiom with which to oppose colonial rule. Indeed, the French anticipated that they would encounter nationalism in Morocco early in the colonial period.[64] We thus might expect my arguments to have little explanatory power, and nationalist mobilization to have occurred relatively easily in Morocco.

[62] The dominant conception of Moroccan nationalism sees it as centuries old (Stora 2003, 15), but it is impossible to know how many Moroccans felt themselves to be part of a Moroccan nation prior to the colonial period. Some scholars have argued that the origins of nationalism lie in the precolonial period. See particularly Burke (1976) and Laroui (1977). Others have dated its appearance to 1930, when protests broke out in response to French attempts to divide the Berbers and Arabs; political activists argued at this time that Berbers and Arabs were part of one nation. See Halstead (1969a), among others. The history of nationalism in Morocco is discussed in Chapters 2 and 5.

[63] See Lewis (2008) on what protectorate status meant for Tunisia; she argues that the protectorate treaty affirmed Tunisia's sovereignty under the Ottoman bey; the same could be said for Moroccan sovereignty under the sultan in the protectorate treaty with Morocco. In addition, France promised to uphold all prior international agreements between the bey's government and other states, thus seeking to placate rival powers.

[64] Report to the military cabinet of the Residency, Rabat, January 1932. SHAT 3H247.

Nationalist mobilization did develop in Morocco, as we might expect, but it varied considerably over time and location. Despite a prior history of nationhood, nationalist responses were neither automatic nor ubiquitous during the colonial period.[65] The language used to oppose the colonial regime varied over time, from demands for reform within the context of French rule to demands for separation from France. Mobilization also varied: strikes, protests, and riots took place at some times and not others, and participation fluctuated. These sources of variation provide opportunities to consider why nationalist mobilization occurs at some times and not others. Further, nationalist action occurred not only in French Morocco, but also in the northern zone controlled by Spain; the division of Morocco into two protectorates provides another basis for comparison.

The subnational analysis employs an original dataset on nationalist mobilization in Morocco from 1934 to 1956, which I constructed from biweekly and monthly French reports on the political situation in Morocco collected in French archives. I rely on these data, as well as participant interviews, primary documents, and the historical literature to evaluate my arguments at the subnational level. Focusing on one case permits a richer discussion of the mechanisms of mobilization and interaction between French administrators and their opponents. It also allows consideration of other factors that mattered for nationalist mobilization, but which cannot be easily evaluated at the cross-colony level given the paucity of data.

In addition to Morocco, I examine subnational dynamics in other cases, including Senegal and Algeria. Both of these cases were among France's oldest and most valued colonial possessions. Algeria is often taken to be a paradigmatic example of the connection between colonial rule and nationalist opposition, but the historiography of the period suggests a wide range

---

[65] Morocco is a good case for isolating the causes of nationalist mobilization from the causes of national identity, as they do not appear at the same time. National identity appears to predate the outbreak of demands for independence, making it an unlikely proximate cause of mobilization.

of responses to French rule.[66] Senegal was selected because its unique history provides subnational variation on one of the key independent variables: some Senegalese townships were granted French citizenship, while the rest of the colony was denied. This variation offers an opportunity to observe the effects of political equality and exclusion within one setting.

The combination of medium-N analysis across the empire and subnational studies facilitates the evaluation of explanations in a context in which systematic hypothesis testing is challenging. It is an approach that is fruitful for studying historical events, for it allows observation of the dynamics of those events both across and within cases.

"Developing" Nationalism: The International Climate and the Colonial Context

The rise of nationalist mobilization across the French empire in the mid-twentieth century has been attributed both to the international climate and to conditions in the colonies themselves. In the international arena, norms about the legitimacy of empire changed over the course of the twentieth century. Further, the early occurrence of nationalist movements in places such as Syria and India provided models for others living under European domination. Within colonies, changes in the economic and social conditions wrought by colonial rule, along with experiences of injustice, have been advanced as factors that facilitated nationalism. In this section, I discuss these international and domestic explanations.

These are not, I will suggest, proper alternatives to the arguments I propose. Rather than reject them, I show the limits of their explanatory power as well as the positive contributions they can make to understanding patterns of nationalist protest.

---

[66] Opposition to French rule in Algeria shares characteristics with opposition in other parts of the empire, but is far from being a typical case because of the heavy presence of settlers and the long war of independence that ensued. See Chapter 3 on the role of settlers in the empire. For more on settlers and nationalist violence, see Lawrence (2010a).

These factors were important background conditions that facilitated nationalist action. Some may have been necessary conditions for nationalist mobilization to occur. But they are, at best, partial explanations because they cannot account for variation in the timing and location of movement activity. Accounting for this variation is the aim of this book, but it has not been the objective of most other scholars writing on the colonial period. Most have been more concerned with describing the origins of national identity or the context in which nationalist movements operated than with specifying the triggers of nationalist mobilization. It is important to note these divergent objectives because they are likely to require different explanations. Although our purposes are not the same, it is useful to begin thinking about the triggers of nationalist protest by discussing the contextual factors that shaped the environment in which nationalist actors began to organize.

The International Climate: Norms and Diffusion

Scholars of empire have suggested that changes in international norms were important both for decolonization (typically the focus of these studies) and for the development of nationalist opposition in the colonies. Specifically, empire undeniably came to be seen as an outdated form of state as the twentieth century progressed. Lord Hailey (1943, 13) described the shift in international norms in a speech at Princeton University in 1943: "There was a period in the world's history when it seemed to be almost in the natural order of things that the more highly organized peoples should make use of their strength to acquire territory at the expense of the less-developed communities. That is not a view which would be implicitly accepted today."

As empire became increasingly illegitimate, imperial powers were forced to rethink their relationships with dependent territories and make decisions about whether and how to administer them. Changes in international norms also affected political leaders in the colonies and influenced their decisions about using the language of nationalism rather than requesting reform. The hypothesis that can be drawn for the purposes of this analysis is that nationalist mobilization should begin as empire becomes less acceptable internationally.[67]

One problem with this hypothesis concerns measurement: how exactly can we tell when international norms shifted? Lord Hailey suggests that empire was outdated by 1943, but others maintain that the shift occurred later. International events that contested the legitimacy of empire began with the American Revolution and the wars of Spanish decolonization and continued through Portuguese decolonization in the 1970s and the dissolution of the Soviet Union in 1991.[68] Which of these events delegitimated empire, and by how much?

For the French empire, a number of scholars have pointed to one crucial event: the defeat of France by Germany in 1940, which ostensibly damaged French prestige in the colonies, made France appear vulnerable, and prompted nationalist mobilization.[69] After 1940, the French simply no longer seemed invincible. Clayton (1994, 15), for example, states that France's collapse produced a "grave" loss of prestige throughout its empire, although the French managed to limit the damage in some places. Japan's subsequent takeover of French Indochina compounded perceptions of French weakness by showing their vulnerability to a non-European power.[70] The implication is that

[67] This hypothesis has been advanced in the form of a "stage" theory of history, in which nationalism supersedes colonial ideologies. See the discussion in Burke (2000).

[68] Burbank and F. Cooper (2010, 7–8) examine imperial history in a variety of settings, and note that empire has been an enduring state form. They suggest that the nation-state's triumph has been declared prematurely; in comparison with empires, "the nation-state appears as a blip on the historical horizon, a state form that emerged recently from under imperial skies and whose hold on the world's political imagination may well prove partial or transitory" (ibid., p. 3). This logic implies that the legitimacy of empire as a form of rule may still not be assumed to have ended.

[69] See Ageron (1991b, 59); Chafer (2002, 48); Chamberlain (1999); Clayton (1994, 15, 22, & 34); Damis (1970, 83); Hoisington (1984, 203); Owen (2000, 20); Pervillé (1991, 91); Smith (1975, 115); Springhall (2001, 30); Thomas (1998, 38–39); Tucker (1999, 42); Young (1994, 184); Zisenwine (2010, 17).

[70] See Chapter 4 for more on wartime Indochina.

the 1940 defeat marked a turning point for nationalist resistance, which increased during the war.

Given that France's experience in World War II appears crucial for nationalist organizing in the empire, Chapter 4 looks closely at the war's effects. But the claim that nationalists responded to a loss of French prestige faces several problems on its face. First, nationalist mobilization did develop in a number of French territories during the war, but in many others there was no activity at that time. An argument about prestige cannot account for these negative cases; it does not explain intra-empire variation. Second, it is difficult to see why potential nationalists would have interpreted France's defeat as a sign that they, too, could beat France. Colonized populations did not have armies comparable to German or Japanese forces and could not have expected to fare as well as these powerful states. Finally, the argument implies that prior to defeat, France was considered prestigious by colonized populations. There is little direct evidence to support this view, aside from the absence of nationalist mobilization itself in many territories of the empire. Although people in the colonies expressed loyalty to France when the war began and many fought for France, there is little to suggest that they were motivated by a sense of prestige or invincibility.[71] People in the colonial world had already seen the French fight and die in World War I and the wars of colonial conquest. This argument may thus exaggerate the extent to which colonized people perceived France as invulnerable before 1940.

It is quite difficult to reconcile the timing of any one international event with the pattern of onset of nationalist mobilization. No single event can explain variation across the empire, as nationalist movements began at different times in different colonies. A more reasonable, although imprecise, characterization may be that empire's legitimacy decreased over time as the century wore on. If so, we might expect to observe a general intensification in nationalist mobilization over time as nationalism became an

---

[71] On expressions of loyalty to France at the outset of war, see Smith (1975, 103); von Albertini (1975, 11); Yacono (1971, 43–44).

increasingly legitimate response to imperialism. Strang (1990) shows that the rate of decolonization accelerated rapidly after World War II, a finding that is compatible with this hypothesis.

But relying on the growing legitimacy of nationalist movements in the colonial world does not help explain the early cases of nationalist mobilization. Early cases may have helped produce the norm, rather than resulting from it. Likewise, nationalist movements that got underway late in the twentieth century remain perplexing if international norms produced mobilization in other places earlier on. Colonies where widespread nationalist mobilization never occurred are even more puzzling. Furthermore, mobilization in favor of independence even varied over time within colonies. Algeria, for instance, saw its first large nationalist protest in 1945, after which there were few nationalist public events until the war for independence began in 1954. A focus on changes in norms cannot explain why mobilization would fluctuate over time rather than growing in a linear fashion. The central problem is that international norms, by definition, hold for every place at a given moment in time: they take the same value for all cases and thus cannot explain cross-sectional variation without the interaction of case-specific variables.

An additional problem with relying heavily on international norms to explain twentieth-century nationalist movements stems from the existence of competing norms. International criticism of imperialism does not point solely toward nationalist responses. The belief that states ought to be democratic was likewise a norm that gained legitimacy throughout the century, and democratization was an alternative way to dismantle empire. International norms could also have encouraged those who wished to push empires in a more inclusive direction. Because support for democracy and national self-determination could both be found at the international level, it is difficult to see how international norms can explain a shift away from demands for reform and toward nationalist mobilization. The same international climate could promote both kinds of political organizing, which may explain why nationalist mobilization broke out in Morocco and Vietnam even as elites in Africa continued to insist on democratic participation in French institutions.

Yet international norms should not be deemed irrelevant. Changes in norms about the appropriateness of empire expanded the scope of the possible, making nationalism available as an option for activists in the colonies. Norm change likely increased the probability of nationalist mobilization throughout the twentieth century, but other factors are needed to explain why nationalist mobilization happened where and when it did. Norm change is best thought of as a facilitating condition, not a full explanation.

An alternative way that the international environment may have encouraged nationalist mobilization is via diffusion. Descriptively, nationalist mobilization appears to come in waves.[72] The eruption of nationalist mobilization in multiple locations in quick succession hints at their interdependence; nationalism can seem "contagious."[73] In the colonies, nationalists monitored movements in other places closely and drew inspiration from them.[74]

The difficulty lies in specifying a diffusion model that adequately captures the pattern of mobilization.[75] There are a few ways diffusion might have worked. Nationalist action may have diffused across empires, with cases in the British empire affecting those in the French and other empires. Many nationalists in the French empire were inspired by the organization and success of the Indian National Congress and explicitly adopted Gandhi's nonviolent tactics, for instance. Although there is evidence of the diffusion of ideas and practices, it is unclear how to make sense of the temporal or spatial configuration of movements. Mobilization does not appear to have spread to

---

[72] See Beissinger (2002, 27–34), who conceptualizes nationalist "tides" and "waves." He points out that tides are unusual; not all waves become the tides he describes in the context of the Soviet collapse.

[73] For an example of this language, see Wintrobe (2002).

[74] The idea that nationalists modeled themselves after earlier instances of nationalism is found in B. Anderson (1983, 67), who wrote that "the 'nation' proved an invention on which it was impossible to secure a patent. It became available for pirating by widely different, and sometimes unexpected hands." For a critique of Anderson's modular argument applied to the colonial world, see Chatterjee (1993a). See also Duara (1996) and Kelly and Kaplan (2001).

[75] For more on the difficulty of positing diffusion models, particularly for violent protest in the empire, see Lawrence (2010b).

geographically proximate neighbors, and nationalist action did not follow immediately in response to notable British cases. Diffusion may instead have been intra-empire, but once again, a pattern is not apparent. Nationalist mobilization in the French empire spanned many years, with the earliest instances arising in Syria and Lebanon in the 1920s; later movements did not mobilize until the 1950s and after.[76] Singer and Langdon (2004, 266) argue that the loss of Vietnam in 1954 triggered nationalist mobilization elsewhere in the empire, but many parts of the French empire already had movements prior to that date.[77] Alternatively, diffusion may have occurred within regions, across North Africa or sub-Saharan Africa, for instance.

Chapter 5 considers the impact of other nationalist events on political activity in colonial Morocco, and shows that external events did affect nationalist organizing. But as a primary explanation for the eruption of nationalist mobilization, diffusion is not a good candidate. The absence of a clear pattern of spread is a key problem; neither geographic proximity nor known networks appear to explain the order of their appearance.[78] The idea that nationalism diffuses does not produce straightforward predictions for where and when nationalist activity should arise. Ideas and news of events certainly did propagate, particularly among

[76] Strang (1990) shows that prior decolonization within the empire predicts further decolonization in the empire, but his dependent variable is decolonization, not nationalist mobilization. The result may be because of an imperial decision to withdraw from multiple territories rather than waves of nationalist resistance that lead to further decolonization.

[77] Gershovich (2003, 52) notes that Moroccans captured in Vietnam were invited to renounce their allegiance to France, and some did so. Returning soldiers is thus one potential way that nationalist mobilization could spread. There is evidence that former soldiers participated in nationalist mobilization, but not that mobilization coincides with their return. Some colonial soldiers remained intensely loyal to France, even after decolonization.

[78] In thinking through how a diffusion model might work, I drew on the example of the epidemiologist John Snow, who demonstrated that cholera is a waterborne disease. I considered various mechanisms of nationalist diffusion, and considered their implications for what should be observed. Unlike Snow, I did not find networks that transmitted nationalism across cases. See the discussion of Snow in Collier et al. (2010). On diffusion of social movements in other contexts, see McAdam and Rucht (1993) and Weyland (2010), among others.

students and political leaders from the colonies who congregated in France, but there is no immediate correspondence between the cross-fertilization of ideas and mobilization.

Further, although nationalist mobilization in the empire did sometimes appear wave-like, it is hard to know whether diffusion is the right mechanism. Diffusion arguments encounter particular trouble when it comes to explaining the negative cases, those that were not caught up in a wave. Chapter 4 offers an explanation for the wave of nationalist activity that occurred as World War II ended, one that focuses on local conditions rather than diffusion. This explanation is able to account for both the negative and positive cases.

Like explanations that rely on changing international norms, global nationalist activity may have mattered not because it denoted a cascade of interdependent cases, each triggered by another in a particular pattern, but because existing nationalist movements served to exemplify what could be achieved.[79] Nationalist movements and ideas provided a model for others to take up, but it is likely that these examples mattered most when the conditions in the colony were right. It is thus to internal conditions that we turn next.

The Domestic Climate: Modernization and Injustice

Conditions within colonized territories changed over the course of the colonial period in a number of ways. Two developments in particular have been linked to the growth of nationalist opposition: modernization and experiences of colonial exploitation. Both have the potential to explain patterns of nationalist mobilization. The chapters that follow consider further specific instances of modernization and colonial injustice, but here the aim is to highlight some general strengths and limitations of focusing on these factors as potential causes of nationalist organizing.

The idea that modernization may have led to nationalism in the colonial world draws from scholarly work on nationalism in other

---

[79] See Beissinger (2002, 31) on how successful challenges by one group can lead to emulation by others.

regions. A number of important studies have documented the ways in which modernizing European states encouraged the growth of nationalist sentiment, turning "peasants into Frenchmen" through state projects designed to give people living under a shared political system a common sense of identity.[80] Improvements in education and transportation, the introduction of conscription, economic development, and increased urbanization helped produce a sense of nationalism. There are limits to the relevance of the European experience in the colonial context, however.[81] In the colonies, nationalist mobilization had to grow without the help of the state. The colonial state ardently opposed nationalist organizations, policed and repressed nationalist movements, and tried to foster alternative forms of identification. Nationalism in the colonial world was anti-state, not a state project.

Although the state in the colonies opposed nationalist movements, it is still possible that the colonial state unintentionally helped produce nationalist mobilization via attempts to modernize colonial territories. Starting with Deutsch (1953), theorists have often wedded the growth of nationalism to modernization. European rulers may have created the conditions that encouraged nationalist responses to empire by increasing the productive capacity of the colonies and disrupting traditional economic practices. Further, urbanization, improvements in education, and the growth of newspapers, radios, and transportation systems may have facilitated the ability of colonial subjects to organize against colonial rule.[82]

---

[80] On nationalism in Europe, see Gellner (1983); Hobsbawm (1990); Tilly (1995); Weber (1976). Sahlins (1989, 9) offers a critique of state-centered approaches to nationalism in Europe; he examines nation making on the boundaries of Spain and France, and demonstrates that nationalism "appeared on the periphery before it was built there by the center. It appeared less as a result of state intentions than from the local process of adopting and appropriating the nation without abandoning local interests, a local sense of place, or a local identity."

[81] See Duara (2004, 5) for a discussion of the differences between nationalism in Europe and the colonial world.

[82] On these causes of nationalism, see B. Anderson (1983); Darden (Forthcoming); Sharkey (2003); Smith (1975), in addition to the works on Europe listed in footnote 80. On modernization as a cause of nationalism in the colonies, see Ansprenger (1989, 127); Cherif (1971); Coleman (1954, 411–412); Moore (1970, 34); Springhall (2001, 8–9).

If modernization leads to nationalist resistance to colonial rule, we might expect to observe that more modern French territories would experience nationalist resistance ahead of less modern territories. Chapter 3 analyzes this hypothesis, using data on urbanization as a measure of modernization. The analysis shows that there is no straightforward relationship between urbanization and nationalist mobilization. The more urbanized colonies did not necessarily undergo nationalist mobilization earlier, and places where nationalist mobilization erupted at the same time had widely ranging levels of urbanization. Some colonies with low levels of urbanization, such as Madagascar and Vietnam, saw nationalist mobilization much earlier than places with higher levels of urbanization, such as Senegal and Middle Congo.[83] Urbanization is, in general, a poor predictor of the eruption of nationalist movements.

This result makes sense for several reasons. First, modernization theories do not suggest clear hypotheses about timing, and it may thus be a mistake to rely on them to explain temporal variation in nationalist mobilization. Modernization is a gradual process that unfolds over time; it does not happen all at once. There is no sharp threshold for urbanization, education, or economic development at which we may say that a place is modern and expect nationalist mobilization to follow.[84]

In part, the absence of predictions about timing stems from the fact that those who focus on modernization do not necessarily intend to explain nationalist mobilization. Studies such as Benedict Anderson's (1983) *Imagined Communities* explore the mechanisms that lead people to identify themselves as members of a national community. The central concern is the spread of nationalist consciousness or identity, which may be a gradual evolutionary process that covaries with modernization. In

---

[83] The urbanization data is presented in Chapter 3, but in the mid-1940s, the percentage of the population living in towns greater than 20,000 for these 4 cases was: Madagascar, 6 percent; Vietnam, 7 percent; Middle Congo, 15 percent; Senegal, 17 percent (*Annuaire Statistique de l'Union Française 1939–1949*, Centre des Archives d'outre-mer, Aix-en-Provence).

[84] Indeed, many places in the French empire might not qualify as modern for the entire colonial period, depending on how it is defined. Most French territories lacked mass education, for instance, until after independence was attained.

contrast, nationalist mobilization is dynamic; it erupts at particular moments. Understanding why requires attention to factors that likewise vary rapidly over time, not just to macro factors that change rather slowly.

One further theoretical point can help make sense of the absence of a relationship between modernization and nationalist mobilization in the French empire. Modernization ought to facilitate all kinds of political opposition to colonial rule; there is no reason to expect it to prompt opposition that is specifically nationalist in nature. A better educated, more urban population should be easier to mobilize in general. To take a few examples, Senegal, Martinique, and Guadeloupe were more urbanized in the mid-twentieth century than most other places in the French empire. They had little to no nationalist mobilization, but they were not free of politics. Political activists in all three places opposed colonial polices and mobilized constituencies in favor of political equality. Political opposition existed, but it was not nationalist. These demands, however, were modern like nationalism. A degree of modernization may thus be important for facilitating any kind of opposition to the state, not just nationalism.

A large literature has suggested that it was not the colonial power's efforts to modernize that prompted nationalist opposition, but the exploitation and subjugation that accompanied colonial rule and made it unbearable.[85] The abuses of colonial

[85] Examples include Abun-Nasr (1975); Dirks (2004); Entelis (1980); Fanon (1963); Gelvin (1998); Hechter (2000); Keris (1953); Mamdani (1996); Pervillé (1991); Rivlin (1955); Sharkey (2003). Cole (2001, 17–20) provides a cogent discussion of the schools of thought on the effects of colonial rule. She describes three dominant trends in anthropological and historical studies of colonialism. The first emphasizes the power of indigenous groups to mediate outside intrusion. The second is a tendency to see the impact of colonial rule as pervasive and negative. Such studies at times seem to suggest that colonial rule entirely forecloses possibilities for opposition (see, for example, Mitchell 1991). The third trend "acknowledges the profound difference in power relations between colonizer and colonized while emphasizing the contingent and nonmonolithic nature of the colonial enterprise." Duara (2004, 2) has suggested that the historiography of the decolonization era has been shaped by the writings of nationalist statesmen and historians who were sympathetic to nationalist movements. Their influence may explain the tendency to focus on

rulers have been well documented. Colonized populations were subject to laws that were far harsher than those governing French citizens. Those who worked for the colonial power had limited opportunities for advancement and unequal pay. Land policies privileged French owners over indigenous populations. Economic policies favoring the French produced relations of dependency. Colonial subjects were forcibly recruited for work brigades and conscripted into the French army. The differences in the way France governed at home and in the colonies were clear to those who traveled to France or interacted with French administrators and settlers. De Gaulle (1970, 11) attributed nationalist opposition in part to "the wave of envious longing aroused among these deprived masses by the spectacle of the modern economy." His "deprived masses" were not only at an economic disadvantage, but also a political one. These experiences of injustice created grievances that may have made participation in a nationalist struggle appealing.

How might experiences of injustice contribute to an explanation for why nationalist mobilization erupted when and where it did? To some extent, the answer is obvious: it is necessary to have people with grievances to generate any kind of political movement. The more crucial question is whether an argument centered on these grievances can account for variation in nationalist mobilization. Many of these conditions were enduring facts of life across the French empire; it is thus hard to say when and where to expect nationalist resistance. It is intuitively plausible that injustices may pile up until they become intolerable, but it is hard to know when that point is reached. We may posit that nationalist mobilization occurred first in places where colonial policies were most unjust, a hypothesis I consider in subsequent chapters, although the data that can be used to compare relative experiences of injustice across cases is thin. Where grievances

injustice and exploitation as the root causes of nationalist resistance. In the nationalists' view, European domination proved intolerable to colonized peoples, and nationalism presented an ideology of resistance. This view is widely reflected in scholarly work on the colonial world, and explains why nationalist responses to colonial rule are often assumed rather than interrogated.

were relatively invariant, however, they are – like modernization – poorly suited to explaining why nationalist mobilization
would erupt at one moment but not another.[86] For a grievance
argument to answer this question, specific types of injustice must
be connected with subsequent mobilization.[87]

Further, like modernization arguments, experiences of injustice
need not produce solely nationalist reactions, but can instead
prompt demands for more just policies within existing political
structures. For example, a group of African soldiers who had
endured up to four years in German prisoner of war camps were
treated poorly upon their release: they received worse food and
housing than French prisoners of war, and their pay was withheld.
The soldiers responded by organizing a protest; they did not issue
nationalist demands (Chafer 2002, 46–47). Instances of injustice
may thus provoke diverse reactions, not only nationalism.

Studies that link modernization and experiences of injustice
to nationalism in the colonial world often reflect what Brubaker
(1996, 19) has called a "developmental" approach to understanding nationalism. Implicit in these understandings is the
sense that nationalism is a stage to be reached, either when society becomes sufficiently modern or when people gain consciousness of their state of oppression.[88] Expressions of nationalism,

---

[86] It has become fashionable for political scientists to dismiss grievances as too
ubiquitous to explain rare outcomes such as mobilization and conflict. See,
for instance, Collier and Hoeffler (2004); Fearon and Laitin (2003b); Kocher
(2004). For opposing views, see Gurr (1971) and Petersen (2002).

[87] Hechter (2000) offers an explanation for variation in nationalist responses to
empire that is relevant to grievances. He argues that direct rule prompts nationalist mobilization, but indirect rule thwarts nationalism because it reduces the
demand for sovereignty and raises the costs of collective action. He argues that
this explains differences in nationalism across the British and French empires,
but as Wallerstein (1961, 66) points out, the extent to which colonial rule was
direct or indirect varied within empires and even within colonies Evaluating
the spatial implications of his argument requires examining whether nationalist mobilization occurred where the colonial power had more direct control
over the population. I consider this hypothesis in the empirical sections, particularly in the subnational discussion of Morocco in Chapter 5. However, like
the explanations discussed here, this one provides few predictions for timing;
type of rule tends to be fairly stable.

[88] One example of this language is Haas (1993, 545).

in this view, are not unpredictable or surprising but are instead the natural end point of an evolutionary process. Colonies were on an inexorable path to nationhood; progress would produce independent nation-states. These understandings of nationalism essentially treat it as an apolitical phenomenon: a gradual, almost organic process. This developmental depiction of nationalism has been surprisingly tenacious, despite a growing literature that has pointed to the need to consider the specific historical factors that give rise to nationalism.[89] This book takes a different view, adopting an approach that emphasizes the dynamics of nationalist mobilization in space and time. It points to the contingent, fluctuating, and sometimes surprising nature of public expressions of nationalism. These expressions cannot simply be taken for granted as the next stage through which colonized peoples had to pass, for puzzles remain regarding how, where, and when people came to organize for nationalist ends. Focusing on gradual processes such as modernization or the growth of consciousness about colonial injustice cannot address these puzzles. Instead, this book identifies moments of rupture that can account for the shift toward nationalist mobilization, moments where previous organizing idioms failed and the political space opened up for a specifically nationalist form of opposition to colonial rule.

The chapters that follow focus on the ruptures that served to trigger nationalist mobilization, but they also touch on arguments about modernization and colonial injustice, using some empirical evidence to consider their contribution to understanding nationalist mobilization. It is worth restating that these are not rivals to the arguments of this book; my focus on understanding nationalist *action* requires a different kind of explanation. Further, my arguments are often compatible with insights from these literatures. Specifically, I agree that experiences of injustice were crucial for producing nationalist mobilization. Demonstrating a causal relationship between experiences of

[89] Duara (2004, 6) states that the challenge in thinking about the history of decolonization is to avoid a "misguided, evolutionary framework." McDougall (2006, ix) suggests that in North Africa in particular, discussions of nationalism are still dominated by tropes of awakening and consciousness.

colonial injustice and nationalist mobilization, however, requires more specificity. The right story is one that is capable of explaining both why mobilization would be framed in nationalist terms and why it varied over time and place. Rather than discussing a broad array of colonial injustices, the next chapters focus on the consequences of a particular French decision: to deny political equality to the majority of colonial subjects while granting it to only a few. This policy altered the discourse of political opposition in the empire and heightened the boundaries between the French and the populations in most of the colonial territories.

Caveats: The Scope and Limits of the Research Question
This book's focus on the timing and location of nationalist protests in the French empire leaves many worthy questions unaddressed, two of which I mention here. First, although the book seeks to address why nationalism became the dominant discourse of opposition, it does not explain why one version of the nation is adopted over another. Why Moroccans should come to organize as Moroccans, and not as Berbers, or as members of a Maghreb or Arab nation, is not a question I engage, but is a puzzle others have addressed in compelling ways. Despite the availability of pan-African, pan-Arab, and pan-Muslim ideologies that could connect peoples across the French empire, along with ethnic identities that could have served as a basis for nationalist organizing within colonies, French colonial boundaries turned out to be decisive in determining the unit that would become the postcolonial state. These boundaries defined the political space, enclosing the institutions that nationalists could use to mobilize. Although identities that spanned colonial territories were discussed and debated, and alternative versions of the nation were proposed, the colonial borders proved nearly unassailable.[90] In

---

[90] Foltz (1965) describes at length the difficulties in uniting across colonial boundaries in his analysis of the attempt at unity in French Africa. There, activists such as Senghor proposed an African national identity, rather than one based on the territorial boundaries of Senegal or Ivory Coast, even while seeking to retain French citizenship. See Young (2004, 12–13). Young (1994, 241) notes that territorial boundaries in Africa were accepted as definitive in

what follows, I do not investigate why actors defined the nation according to colonial borders in ways that privileged some identities but excluded others.

A second question that this analysis sets aside is who participates in nationalist protests. I discuss the circumstances that provided openings for people to publicly challenge colonial rule and I discuss how those circumstances motivated some to begin taking action, but I do not provide an explanation for which people mobilize and which do not. In most social movements, only a subset of the population that could be mobilized participates in public demonstrations; mobilization reflects only a minority of the affected population. The question of why some participate and others do not is one that scholars of collective action have addressed in a variety of contexts, but it is one that I do not attempt to answer here. I concentrate on asking why political activists began making nationalist demands and what opportunities induced people to take to the streets and voice those demands.

Plan of the Book

Chapters 2 and 3 investigate movements for political equality in the French empire and the French response to them. Chapter 2 explores the tensions between nationalist aspirations and calls for political equality and stresses the conceptual distinctiveness of these aims. It does so by examining movements for equitable reforms in Morocco and Algeria. These movements tend to be portrayed either as the initial stage of nationalism, or as a temporary precursor to the nationalist movement. This chapter argues that calls for equality constituted an *alternative* to nationalist mobilization, a different way to address the ills of colonial rule. The chapter thus disaggregates opposition to the colonial power,

the Organization of African Unity's 1963 charter. Colonial boundaries have been disputed in the Levant, but have remained in place. Roeder (2007) demonstrates the importance of prior boundaries for determining which nations achieve statehood; he argues that most successful nation-state projects were previously associated with an institution he calls segment-states.

pointing to the existence of alternative ideologies of opposition. It argues against the commonly held belief that opponents in the colonies had a stable preference for independent nation-states throughout the colonial period and advocates taking calls for political equality seriously.

Chapter 3 asks what would have happened if the French had decided to treat colonial subjects as equals. It makes the argument that the denial of political equality was a crucial cause of nationalist mobilization. It draws on two different streams of evidence to evaluate this claim systematically. First, it examines variation across the empire to consider the consequences of French decision making. Although the French denied political equality to Algerians, Moroccans, and most other colonial subjects, in places such as Martinique and Guadeloupe, erstwhile subjects became citizens. This chapter considers the effects that citizenship had on political organizing, examining the impact of the decisions made in the 1946 French constitution. Second, the chapter takes advantage of subnational variation in Senegal. The French granted citizenship to some Senegalese towns and denied it to others, a policy that provides a way to see the consequences of citizenship within one setting. The chapter demonstrates that calls for political equality were not destined to turn into demands for independence. Where the French lived up to their promises of equality, nationalist mobilization did not follow.

Chapter 4 addresses the timing of nationalist mobilization. Once political equality was denied, leaders still required opportunities to act. This chapter argues that disruptions in imperial authority provided a critical opportunity for nationalist organizing. When France's authority was compromised, nationalist demonstrations erupted in places where political equality had not been granted. The chapter looks across the empire at two crucial moments: post–World War I and during World War II, when imperial rule was most precarious and many nationalist movements were active. The chapter also looks at two case studies, Vietnam and French West Africa, tracing nationalist mobilization over time.

Chapter 5 provides a subnational test of the arguments by examining nationalist mobilization in Morocco. It explores variation along two dimensions. First, the chapter compares nationalist mobilization in Spanish Morocco and French Morocco. The division of the protectorate into two zones ruled by different European powers provides useful leverage for considering competing explanations for nationalist activity. Although the zones were similar in many ways, they differed in their respective levels of modernization and colonial injustice, and the impact of these differences can be evaluated. Further, the French and Spanish experienced disruptions to the control of their zones in different time periods. I study the consequences of these disruptions for nationalist organizing. The second source of variation is temporal. The chapter examines surges and ebbs in nationalist activity over time in French Morocco using monthly data on nationalist protests from the start of public protest in Morocco in 1934 through independence in 1956.

The book is thus organized by both place and theme. It begins and ends in colonial Morocco: Chapter 2 examines political action in Morocco from 1930 up to World War II; Chapter 5 emphasizes nationalist organizing from World War II through independence. The comparative case-study analysis is contained between these bookends. The theme of Chapters 2 and 3 is political equality; Chapters 4 and 5 study the disruptions that prompted the onset of nationalist protests.

The conclusion considers the implications of this study for postcolonial states and our broader understanding of nationalism. Political scientists, policymakers, and the media continue to take nationalist responses to foreign rule for granted. In part, this tendency has been shaped by impressions of what happened in the colonial empires. A better understanding of how colonial rule led to nationalist mobilization can speak to current debates about the causes of ethnic and nationalist conflict and the mobilizing power of nationalism.

Conclusion

The final scenes of Gillo Pontecorvo's critically acclaimed 1966 film *The Battle of Algiers* leave the viewer with two dramatically opposing perspectives on nationalist opposition. On one side are the bewildered French, inexplicably taken by surprise when mass protest erupts in Algiers. In the final minutes of the film, a journalist dictates his report: "We don't know the motive; we don't know the pretext ... but after two years of relative calm ... disturbances have erupted and nobody knows why or how." On the other side are the Algerians: the camera cuts to crowds of women and men confronting French tanks and snipers, waving flags, and demanding freedom for Algeria. Their voices and ululations continue on through the smoke of French gunfire; they cannot be stopped any longer. The inability of the French to comprehend or predict these actions appears absurd, and the cries for independence as the film ends leave the viewer with a sense of the inevitability of the nationalist movement's triumph.

This book seeks to undermine both of these views: nationalist mobilization is neither entirely inexplicable nor completely obvious. Nationalism did not simply happen when colonized societies reached a particular stage. Nationalist mobilization was *political*; it began only after other attempts to reform and reshape the very nature of imperial rule failed to generate results. It was then contingent upon opportunities for political organizing, which were hard to come by for those confronting imperial rulers. These arguments help explain the sporadic nature of nationalist protests across and within colonial territories. They shed light on why mass protest can seem simultaneously surprising and predictable. They provide an explanation for variation in anti-colonial activity across the French empire, helping make sense of differences in the timing and nature of opposition to colonial rule. In making these arguments, my hope is that the pages that follow will illustrate both the contingency and complexity of responses to colonial rule.

The Battle of Algiers depicts two mutually incomprehensible peoples engaged in a conflict seemingly about foreignness and difference. This portrayal reflects a widespread understanding of nationalist struggles as rejections of rule by the "other." Nations require self-rule, the logic goes, and nations imply a degree of homogeneity. This focus on the identities of the actors in conflict, and the cultural and ethnic distance between them, misses a crucial motivation underlying anti-colonial movements in the French empire. These movements did not begin as struggles for the recognition of difference. On the contrary, activists in the empire initially invoked a universal right: to be treated as equals, with the rights, duties, and privileges of citizens. They rejected the subordinate status of colonial subject, which placed their interests beneath those of full citizens. They concentrated not on who ruled, but on how they ruled. Political inequality lay beneath these struggles. Its persistence ultimately reinforced national differences and made them the primary cleavage of conflict. As Immanuel Wallerstein (1961, 50) put it, national independence became the alternate path to equality, as opponents of imperial rule came to demand equality not as individuals, but as nations.

2

Indigènes into Frenchmen? Seeking Political Equality in Morocco and Algeria*

"A good law is good for all, just as a sound proposition is sound everywhere."
– Marquis de Condorcet, 1819.

In the mid-1930s, Moroccan elites living under French protectorate rule petitioned French officials for a number of liberties and reforms. In Algeria, demands for reform were extensive: Algerian elites asked for political equality with French settlers and criticized the French for failing to assimilate Algerian Muslims. But within a decade or two, Algerians and Moroccans no longer advocated reform. In Morocco, the Hizb al-Istiqlal (Independence Party) was formed in 1944, and unlike earlier organizations, began demanding independent statehood. In Algeria, Ferhat Abbas issued the "Manifesto of the Algerian People," which called for the creation of an Algerian state.[1] As in other parts of the French empire, demands for national independence began supplanting calls to reform the injustices of colonial rule.

---

* Portions of this chapter were previously published in 2012 as "Rethinking Moroccan Nationalism, 1930–1944." *Journal of North African Studies* 17 (3): 475–490.
[1] See Horne (1977, 43); the demand for a state was made in a supplement to the manifesto.

The historical literature has largely treated demands for both reform and independence as instances of nationalism. Historians have described the early demands for equitable treatment and better provision of services in Morocco and Algeria as "proto-nationalist" or "early nationalist" activities, suggesting that these kinds of demands represent an early stage in an evolutionary process toward nationalist resistance aimed at liberating Morocco and Algeria from French rule. In their memoirs, nationalists also claimed that calls for reform were merely a first step in the nationalist project of separation from the empire, and spoke of their intention to demand independence all along. Colonial administrators likewise called the reformists nationalists and accused them of secretly harboring separatist goals. Nationalism is primary in these accounts: the foremost form of opposition.

This chapter argues against the grouping of demands to reform imperial rule and demands to end it under the same conceptual umbrella: nationalism. Instead, I offer an interpretation that sees these mobilization platforms as distinct challenges to colonial rule. Efforts to reform colonial rule and make it more equitable emphasized the authoritarian nature of French rule rather than its foreignness. Reformers criticized the inequalities of a system that provided rights and privileges to French citizens and settlers but denied them to colonial subjects. Demands for reform implied a desire for inclusion and access. Proponents sought to be treated as Frenchmen were treated: they asked to be regarded as political equals. Whereas reformists sought accommodation with colonial rulers, nationalists considered accommodation unthinkable. Nationalist discourses stress the right of nations to rule themselves. Nationalists thus focused on challenging the foreign nature of imperial rule, rather than specific injustices of colonial policy. Nationalists sought to capture the state, while reformists strove to democratize it.[2]

[2] Labeling the quest for political equality "nationalism" would be akin to likening the Civil Rights Movement in the United States to Marcus Garvey's Back to Africa Movement. Both of these movements constituted responses to systematic, institutionalized racism, but to see them as one and the same movement makes little sense given that the solutions they proposed were radically different.

Through rethinking the implications of each set of demands, I take seriously the reformists who sought to alter and improve imperial governance. I argue against assuming a static preference for independent nation-states among political organizers in Morocco and Algeria, and suggest that their goals shifted over time. I propose a dynamic understanding of anti-colonialism, one that recognizes that goals are not given in advance, but are shaped by the political context.

In drawing a distinction between these two sets of demands, my intent is not to suggest that they had nothing in common. Both proponents of reform and nationalists seeking independence opposed the existing colonial system and claimed to speak on behalf of oppressed people. Further, these goals were not necessarily incompatible: in some places, activists made hybrid demands that reflected concerns for both equality and national identity, asking for federation, for instance, instead of either independence or full inclusion as French citizens.

But conceptualizing these demands as components of one larger, nationalist agenda obscures important differences between them. Political equality and nationalism are analytically distinct concepts; the desire for equality is not reducible to nationalism, even though particular empirical cases may involve combinations or transitional phases from one discourse to another. Demands for political equality reflected aspirations and ideological commitments that were often in tension with nationalist aims. In the conclusion to this chapter, I explain why it is important to distinguish between these anti-colonial discourses. Calling different kinds of anti-colonialism "nationalism" puts disparate phenomena in a single analytic category, confounding an investigation into the conditions that promote specific modes of political opposition. Acknowledging the diversity of reactions to colonial rule matters because it forces a rethinking of the causes of nationalist protest, pointing to new questions and explanations.

The reform movements in Algeria and Morocco are two examples of anti-colonial opposition that have been subsumed into a larger nationalist narrative. By investigating these movements, I join a growing group of scholars who have suggested that nationalism is not the only organizing idiom for populations living under foreign rule.[3] The attention to nationalism and the relative neglect of other forms of anti-colonialism stems from the tendency to "do history backward," as Frederick Cooper (2005, 18) put it. In hindsight, it is tempting to dismiss alternative forms of anti-colonialism that often failed to achieve results. Yet privileging nationalism means failing to see the full range of options that colonial subjects considered when responding to imperial rule.

This chapter is divided into two parts: one on Morocco, and one on Algeria. In both parts, I examine the movements for reform, paying particular attention to activists' stated aims. I discuss and criticize conventional understandings of each of these movements, demonstrating the concern for political equality that reformists expressed. I then consider the implications of differences and similarities between the two cases. The colonial period in Algeria and Morocco, neighboring countries, differed in important ways. Algeria experienced 130 years of colonial rule; it had a large settler community; and the goal of assimilation supposedly guided colonial policy. There was no recognized Algerian nationality that

---

[3] See, among others, F. Cooper (2005), who criticizes the historiography of the period, saying, "We do not need to romanticize anti-colonial movements in their moment of triumph or treat colonial history as if the actions of the colonized never changed its course up to the final crisis" (32). See also F. Cooper's (2002) examination of labor movements in French West Africa, which demonstrates that people in the French empire asked for reform and political voice within the imperial unit right up until decolonization. In his study of the *salafiyya* movement in Algeria, McDougall (2006, 5) calls into question the determinism of histories that focus solely on nationalism and contributes to "the task of dismantling the linear certainties of foundational master-narratives" by focusing on one of the neglected alternatives to nationalism. See also Thompson (2000b), who examines religious, labor, and youth groups in Syria and Lebanon, and Clancy-Smith (1994) on responses to occupation in Algerian and Tunisian oasis towns. This chapter contributes to the trend of emphasizing the diversity of responses to colonial rule. In addition to labor, religious, and equality movements, there were other forms of political opposition in the colonial world: communist movements, feminist groups, pan-Arab and pan-Islamic movements, to name a few. These movements challenged imperial rulers and sought to reshape the boundaries of political communities. Here, I focus on one widespread form of opposition in the French empire – calls for political equality – but political opposition was not limited to nationalism and calls for equality.

predated the colonial period. It was, in fact, the French settlers who claimed a distinctive Algerian identity that set them apart from the metropolitan French. The native Algerian population was differentiated in religious, not national terms; they were called Algerian Muslims or Algerian Jews. In contrast, Morocco was a protectorate for only forty-four years, during which the sultan remained the official head of government. Assimilation was not protectorate policy, and a Moroccan national identity existed before the French conquest. Despite these differences, people in both countries mobilized for reform within the context of French rule *and* for national independence. I rely on these two cases to illustrate how demands for political equality differ from demands for national independence.

Chapter 3 widens the empirical analysis. Movements for political equality were not limited to Morocco and Algeria. Across most of the empire, elites asked for political equality before seeking independence. As for Morocco and Algeria, the literature tends to portray both sets of demands as nationalist in character. Chapter 3 investigates the relationship between movements for political equality and nationalist movements for independence across the French Empire, studying how the latter came to replace the former in many locations.

Reforming Imperial Rule: Demands for Political Equality

Before describing the reform movement in Morocco and Algeria, several caveats are in order. First, my focus on political activists should not be taken to imply that they were representative of the wider population in either country. Demands for political equality were made largely by elites who differed in many ways from the majority of the population. The Young Algerians or *évolués* (Westernized elites) had privileges most Algerian Muslims did not have.[4] They were well educated, well traveled, and most spoke and wrote in French. Their desires may have differed from

---

[4] Here I follow the French categorization of referring to the largely Muslim Berber/Arab population in Algeria as Algerian Muslims, to differentiate them from French settlers, who were largely Christian, and Algerian Jews.

those of the wider population, but they were an important political group, and received attention from both sympathizers and opponents in the metropole and Algeria. In Morocco, the elites calling for reform came from diverse backgrounds: some were educated in French schools, but many received training in Arabic schools in Morocco or the wider Arab world. Still, although they claimed to speak on behalf of all Moroccans, they constituted a small group of well-educated men. Their movement was significant, however, in a place where political organizing was limited. Neither the Moroccan reformists nor the Algerian évolués were involved solely in the reform movement; both also played key roles in the nationalist movement for independence.

Second, by focusing on groups advocating reform, I do not wish to imply that these reformers were the only active political groups. In Morocco, there were fewer alternatives to the reformers I describe, but there were groups with communist leanings, workers' groups that sought to associate with French socialists, and religious organizations. A majority of the leaders of the political reform movement were initially part of a religious reform movement. Opponents of the French in Algeria were more diverse, and I describe the major trends, but I focus on the Young Algerians who sought reform. The purpose here is not to fully describe all existing political currents in either setting but to single out one influential set of demands.

Finally, although I argue in this chapter that the contents of demands for equitable reforms and those for separation are distinct, the lines between the two movements are not. Generally speaking, calls for independence were characteristic of the post–World War II era in both Morocco and Algeria, whereas demands for equality were dominant before the war, but this characterization is imperfect. Organizations and individuals within the colonies were not part of homogenous, disciplined groups. Some called for independence earlier than others. In Morocco, mobilization in favor of independence did not begin until World War II, when elites who had previously advocated reform within the protectorate structure began advocating independence. In Algeria, some began advocating independence before World War II, when others were still mobilizing for political equality. Algerian organizations represented distinct political currents, but the proponents of political equality dominated in the pre-war era. Some continued to ask for equality beyond World War II, particularly when separation seemed unlikely, whereas others proposed compromise arrangements such as federalism and home rule. Eventually, many of those advocating political equality in the pre-war period came to support the idea of separation, particularly after the Algerian War of Independence began in 1954. By characterizing these two discourses of mobilization as separate movements, I mean to stress the general change over time from one set of goals to another, rather than to do justice to varying preferences and demands by individuals.

From Reform to Rejection in Morocco (1930–1944)

In 1930, protests over the Berber *Dahir* (decree) led elites to begin organizing for reforms.[5] The Berber Dahir was an attempt by the French to codify the administration of Berber customary law. It officially enshrined customary law, rather than *shari'a*, in the Berber tribal areas. Arab elites argued that the law was an attack on Islam and an attempt to divide Berbers and Arabs. Rumors circulated that the intention was to convert Berbers to Catholicism. Protests were organized against the statute in multiple towns, and the prayer of *latif* (said in times of great calamity) was recited in mosques throughout the country.[6] French authorities shut down the protests, but the events prompted a small group of young men

[5] In choosing to begin in 1930, the intention is not to imply that this is the onset of opposition to colonial rule. The reform movement did not start from a blank slate. In 1930, resistance to the French conquest was ongoing in rural areas; "pacification" would not be achieved until 1934. Moreover, many reformists were initially part of the salafiyya religious movement that constituted another response to foreign incursion. Both Arab nationalism and the salafiyya movement helped shape the specifically Moroccan brand of nationalism that became dominant in the post–World War II era. For more on the religious reform movement, see Eickelman (1985); Munson (1993).

[6] See Hoisington (1984); LaFuente (1999); Pennell (2000); Zade (2001). These protests did not occur in the Berber tribal areas affected by the law; Landau (1956, 146) notes that some Berber tribes welcomed the Dahir because they opposed the extension of the sultan's rule.

to organize. They set up an underground society and founded *L'Action du Peuple* in 1932, a newspaper that drew on French leftist ideals (Pennell 2000, 152).

The reformist platform was first articulated in 1934, after the formation of the Kutlah al-Amal al-Watani, known in French as the Comité d'Action Marocaine (CAM).[7] The CAM unified smaller religious groups and literary clubs under one umbrella. The CAM initially consisted of approximately ten elite individuals, primarily from Rabat and Fes. They presented a lengthy platform to the government in 1934.[8] The Plan of Reforms did not discuss independence; in fact, it demanded a stricter application of the Protectorate Treaty. The plan asked for separation of powers vested in *pashas* and *caids*, the unification of administrative and judicial systems, the appointment and promotion of Moroccans in all branches of the administration, freedom of the press, freedom to assemble, improvements to the educational system, and the establishment of municipal councils and a national council elected by the population. The plan thereby proposed that Moroccans gain the same kinds of democratic rights that French citizens enjoyed. Reformers made appeals to the democratic nature of the French state and argued that republican institutions were likewise suitable for Moroccans. The plan was designed to improve government accountability, establish an independent judiciary, and give Moroccans more opportunities.

Contact with the French left and French political institutions influenced the drafters of the Plan of Reforms (Rézette 1955, 28).[9] In 1932, Ahmed Belafrej and Mohamed Hassan al-Ouazzani had

[7] Demands for reform were heard first in the Spanish zone of Morocco, where elites presented a petition for democratic reform to President Necito Alcala Zamora in 1931, after the republicans took power in Spain (Zade 2001, 25). They asked for reforms similar to those that the Moroccans in the French zone would advocate. For more on the Spanish zone, see Chapter 5.

[8] On the Plan of Reforms, see Abun-Nasr (1975); al-Fasi (1970); Halstead (1969); Lazraq (2003); Rézette (1955); Waterbury (1970); Zade (2001, 26).

[9] Moroccan elites were not only influenced by ideology coming from France and the West, but also by the salafiyya movement and Arab nationalism, although the former was not a particularly strong ideological candidate in a country with a large Berber population. I focus on the influence of the French left because of its specific impact on these demands for reform.

founded the journal *Maghreb* in Paris with the help of an editorial board composed of French and Spanish liberals; the journal criticized protectorate policy (Lugan 2000; Zade 2001, 25). A group of French supporters founded the Comité du Patronage and submitted the 1934 Plan of Reforms along with the members of the CAM (Rézette 1955, 95).

The protectorate administration reacted negatively. Administrators thought the CAM and its supporters should recognize the existing efforts and achievements of the administration. In response to the CAM's request that more Moroccans be given responsible positions in the administration, French officials complained that they needed more time.[10]

With the May 1936 parliamentary triumph in Paris of the Front Populaire, a coalition of socialists and communists, reformists in Morocco and across North Africa hoped that France would finally implement meaningful reforms. Moroccan nationalist Allal al-Fasi (1970, 25–26) wrote:

The formation of the Popular Front in France, and its victory in the elections, was widely acclaimed by the people of North Africa, particularly in Algeria. Our countrymen believed that these leftist parties, which had unreservedly disassociated themselves from all the oppressive acts of the reactionary imperialists, would not hesitate to meet the wishes of the people, at least within the scope of their self-proclaimed principles which had installed them in power.

Other leaders described their joy at the political victory of the Popular Front, which was "for us the equivalent of the Great French Revolution in which we all believe and of which we all hope to be the beneficiaries."[11]

The number of meetings to discuss reforms increased (Cherif 1971, 241). Meeting in Fes in May, Moroccan reformists decided to resubmit the plan of reforms, this time scaled down to "urgent" reforms. In October, the CAM presented a list of reforms to Resident General Nogues, the head of the protectorate administration,

---

[10] *Direction des Affaires Indigènes, Situation Politique et Economique, Période du 1 au 15 May 1935 ; Période du 16 au 31 Juillet 1935.* SHAT 3H1413.

[11] Abdeljalil and al-Ouazzani to Vienot, October 26, 1936, cited in Hoisington (1984), 42.

asking for, among other items: democratic freedoms; more primary schools; a unified code of justice; separation of legislative, executive, and judicial powers; the distribution of communal land tracts; more generous credit facilities for farmers; equality between Moroccan farmers and settler landowners; the abolition of some taxes and the equalization (between settlers and Moroccans) of others; the application of French laws for workers to Moroccan workers; and improved public health facilities (Cherif 1971, 241; al-Fasi 1970, 156–157; MAE DI343).

Despite the promises of the Front Populaire, substantial reforms never materialized.[12] Although the French Communist Party had passed a resolution to support revolutionary movements directed against French imperialism at its 1926 annual party congress, when it actually had parliamentary power, it asked only that French colonial policy be investigated (Betts 1991, 27). The Front Populaire had other pressing concerns besides colonialism: the civil war in Spain, the growth of fascism, and the ambitions of Hitler and Mussolini. Imperialism was low on the priority list.[13] The government also denied the legitimacy of the CAM's platform. Foreign Minister Vienot dismissed the CAM as unrepresentative, writing, "No political group, whether in Morocco or France, can pretend to act for the Nation as a whole."[14] Resident General Nogues referred to the reformists as "youngsters" and "rowdy children" (Hoisington 1984, 43).

Instead of implementing reforms to redress political inequality, the Front Populaire vacillated between policies of minor reform and repression.[15] In November 1936, several leaders were arrested

---

[12] See Thomas (2005) for a discussion of reform movements in French overseas territories from the perspective of the metropole and the French government, particularly the chapter "Reform Frustrated: the Popular Front Experiment and the French Empire." See also Cohen (1972) for more on Front Populaire policies and a history of the attitudes of its composite parties toward colonialism.

[13] Colonel Olié, "Les mouvements nationalistes en Algérie." Report of the General Residence of France in Morocco, July 1949. SHAT 3H1417.

[14] Sic, quoted in Hoisington (1984, 43).

[15] A progressive minority in France critiqued the "state of gangrene" at the Quai d'Orsay, and the heavy-handed actions of protectorate administrators, demanding immediate reforms, including the right to unionize, reorganization of the justice

when a CAM meeting turned into a demonstration after attendees learned that the sultan had forbidden the meeting from taking place. But early the next year, Vienot told Nogues that "Morocco must be governed for the Moroccans ... Native policy presently is more important – much more – than all the rest."[16] Nogues thus decided to release some of the jailed leaders and to allow freedom of the press. But when the leaders decided to transform the CAM into a political party – the National Action Party – they met with repression, and the party was outlawed in March 1937.

The outlawed party re-established itself secretly as the National Party for the Realization of the Plan of Reforms (al-Hizb al-Watani li Tahqiq al-Matalib) under Allal al-Fasi.[17] The party began holding meetings in major cities and sending representatives to rural areas to recruit and gather information on grievances.[18] French reports suggest the party was gaining influence in a number of tribal regions (Hoisington 1984, 60).

The French ultimately silenced the opposition with repression, not reform. After riots in Meknes over water rights in September 1937 – organized with help from party representatives – and demonstrations in the towns of Marrakech and Khemisset in September and October, Nogues arrested Allal al-Fasi, Ahmed Mekouar, Omar Abdeljalil, and Mohamed Lyazidi. Protests broke

---

system, and improved public health facilities. Chaignaud, Paul, "La Question Marocaine." Rapport présenté au Congrès de Marseille, 1937. CAOM.

[16] Quoted in Hoisington (1984, 56).

[17] At this time, there was a split within the leadership of the CAM between Allal al-Fasi and Mohammed Hassan al-Ouazzani, who founded the Mouvement Populaire. This split has often been characterized as one between "traditionalists" and "Westernists," however, Zade (2001) questions this characterization and demonstrates that both groups contained traditional and Western elements. The most persuasive arguments suggest that the split had more to do with personality differences and disagreement over the structure of leadership (Rézette 1955; Rivet 1999, 363; Zade 2001).

[18] Tracts distributed by the CAM and the new party aired grievances about policies such as the collection of new taxes during times of economic depression (MAE DI343). Efforts to recruit began, and new recruits swore an oath of allegiance to God, the nation, and the party (Rivet 1999, 369). By the time it was banned, the party was reported to have a membership of 6,500 (Abun-Nasr 1975, 371). Others say it was more popular at an earlier date (Ghallaab 2000).

out in Fes, Sale, Casablanca, Oujda, and Taza, witness to the growth of the organization. The French moved to occupy the Fes medina (native town) militarily. The CAM leaders were imprisoned or sent into exile and the quest for reforms came to an end.

The demise of the reformist movement was disappointing. Leaflets distributed in 1938 by CAM members still at large decried the banishment of their leadership and began to discuss independence. Graffiti on the walls of the French neighborhood in Casablanca in October 1938 stated, "May God curse colonialism. It is better to die for the Nation than to live as slaves."[19] Although discussions about independence began to occur, there was almost no significant mobilization for several years. At the outset of World War II, the French received numerous vows of loyalty and support, even from their erstwhile critics.[20] Writing just after the fall of France, protectorate officials noted that the continuation of normal administration through their intermediaries was "the irrefutable sign of the durability of our protectorate."[21]

Yet within a year of the Allied invasion of North Africa, the ex-reformists had founded the Hizb al-Istiqlal (Independence Party), and the population had begun to engage in mass demonstrations calling for an end to French rule and the recognition of Morocco as an independent nation-state. Writing in February 1944, protectorate officials admitted that "the ideas of nation and independence are henceforth commonly acknowledged."[22] Allal al-Fasi, a leader of the newly formed party, wrote of the switch from calls for reform to calls for independence: "The real driving force behind the new approach has been the bitter experiences of the nationalist movement.... [which] had caused it thoroughly to despair of the protectorate rulers, who would receive all its sincere offers for cooperation

[19] Tracts 1938, MAE DI360.
[20] See the sultan's appeal to support the French at war time in Levisse-Touze (1994, 211).
[21] *Bulletin de Renseignements Politiques et Economiques du 7 au 13 Juillet 1940*, SHAT 1414.
[22] *Rapport Mensuel sur la Situation Politique en Milieux Indigènes*, February 1944. *Commandement Superieur des Troupes du Maroc*, SHAT 3H249.

with disdainful colonial arrogance" (al-Fasi 1970, 213–214). Although calls for reform continued alongside calls for independence in the postwar period, nationalist demands dominated political discourse in Morocco until independence was attained in 1956.

Conventional Understandings of the Moroccan Reform Movement

The case that reform was a real alternative to mobilization for independence is not obvious for Morocco. Scholars of the era have called the reform period "proto-nationalism," "early nationalism," or "incipient nationalism."[23] Although mobilization during the mid-1930s did not include calls for independence, scholars see the quest for reform as a step on the path toward separatism; before elites try to overthrow colonial rule, they first ask for minor changes.[24] Moore (1970, 36) describes three modes: activists first seek equality, activists engage in traditional anti-colonialism, and finally modern nationalism, when they "achieve full consciousness of their mission."[25] For some, seeking reform

[23] See Abun-Nasr (1975); Bernard (1968, 12); Clayton (1994, 24); Damis (1970, 77, 78); Entelis (1980, 33–34); Ghallaab (2000); Halstead (1969a, 265); Landau (1956, 149); Pennell (2000); Tessler et al. (1995); Waterbury (1970, 35); Zade (2001); Zisenwine (2010); Zniber (1984). Rivet (2002, 337) calls the years from 1930 to 1945 the "the beginning of the end." For some, nationalist activity began even earlier, in the pre-protectorate era or the first years of the conquest. See especially Burke (1976); Joffé (1985); Laroui (1977); Abu-Lughod (1980). Burke (2000) later acknowledged that labelling pre-protectorate activity "nationalism" was mistaken.

[24] One exception is Rézette (1955), who puzzled over the shift from reform-oriented demands to mobilization for independence. He concluded that ideology was simply not very important to elites. This explanation is not terribly satisfying, as it implies that elites did not care much about their own goals, but Rézette's main purpose is to describe the structure of the nationalist parties, not to explain their preferences. In response to Rézette, Halstead (1969a, 264–165) argued that elites were serious about reform and not yet concerned with taking power. Zisenwine (2010, 29) also notes the shift in demands (and the inattention to this shift) and attributes it to the war and international norms of self-determination that were taking root during the war.

[25] He refers to the quest for equality as "liberal assimilation," or the adoption of the values of the ruler. This discussion concerns the period of reform in

counts as nationalism because nationalism is the inevitable response to colonialism (Bidwell 1973, 7; Maxwell 2000, 158). Waterbury (1970, 35) states that pacification and the establishment of colonial rule "elicited their 'dialectical opposite,' the nationalist movement."[26] Moroccan scholars working on the period also stress the inevitability of the nationalist movement and treat activism in favor of equality as part of the larger struggle for independence (Essakali 1983).[27]

One reason for the dominance of this understanding stems from a desire to date the origins of the nationalist movement. Historians of the era describe nationalism almost as something organic, which has "roots" or an "embryonic stage" and a "birth" and then "grows" and reaches "maturity" or "ripeness."[28] Many studies were written prior to historical work on the constructedness of nations and nationalism, and they fail to recognize that the development of national consciousness takes continual work and may not, in fact, grow like a living organism.[29]

Morocco, but the term "assimilation" may be confusing in this context as assimilation was a policy explicitly applied elsewhere in the French empire but not in Morocco.

[26] The idea that colonialism confronts its dialectical opposite implies that there is only one response to colonial rule. Waterbury here borrows the term from Moore (1960, 265).

[27] For a critique of the tendency for Moroccan scholarship to portray Moroccan history as a series of successive victories, see Zade (2001, 10). He writes that "Moroccan historians, without exception, have remained prisoners of their anticolonial vision, and because of this have not been able to form the basis for a Moroccan school of history." His work documents the failures of the nationalist movement as well as its successes, although like European scholars he considers the reform movement to be a stage in the process of nationalist mobilization.

[28] See, for example, Abun-Nasr (1975, 372); Ageron (1991b); Deschamps (1954); Gallissot (1989); Halstead (1969a); Landau (1956, 149); Laroui (1977); Maxwell (2000, 170); Ruedy (1992); Zade (2001); Zisenwine (2010, 9).

[29] For work that criticizes conceptions of nationalism as latent, or "waiting-to-be-realized," see Comaroff (1995). See also Brubaker (1996), who develops a critique of accounts that treat nations as entities, and recommends studying "nationness" as a conceptual variable. Suny (2001b) defines identity as a provisional stabilization of a sense of self or group, thereby pointing to the more tenuous and contingent nature of national identity. See also Burke (2000, 29) for a criticism of "progress-oriented narratives" in nationalist and colonial historiography of North Africa.

The desire to pin down the origins of Moroccan nationalism has led to debates over the date that nationalism can be said to exist and who can be accurately called a nationalist. Looking back, it makes considerable sense to treat the reform movement as nationalistic. The reformist leaders had Moroccan nationality, even during their quest for reforms, and they later articulated demands for a separate state on behalf of the nation. But the very task of seeking the origins of nationalism in the early activities of political leaders tends to homogenise political mobilisation and obscure differences in the movement's goals and activities over time. Moreover, scholars run the risk of being biased by their knowledge of the outcome. Scholars know that nationalist movements eventually became dominant, not only in Morocco, but elsewhere in the colonized world; that is precisely why they are interested in identifying the beginning of the nationalist movement. But by reading back into history with this nationalist 'lens,' they may fail to take seriously other political currents because they already know that they were ultimately unsuccessful. In the search to locate nationalism's origins, it is tempting to depict the reform movement as simply a period of apprenticeship, but at the time, its fate was unknown.[30]

Another reason for labeling the reform movement 'nationalist' or 'proto-nationalist' is that many believe the quest for equitable reforms was masking a more genuine desire for independence. A number of pieces of evidence support the view that leaders in Morocco hid their true preferences when seeking reforms. This argument is a serious alternative to the interpretation I propose here; if independence were the goal in both periods, and the demands for reform purely rhetorical, there is little need to sharply distinguish the two periods. I therefore evaluate the evidence that leaders were dissimulating.

---

[30] Gelvin (1998, 5) suggests that historians are affected by nationalist history, but describes how scholars of nationalism in the past twenty years have sought to "deflate the teleological pretensions of state-supported nationalisms that represent themselves as the inevitable and singular historically inscribed expressions of national destiny" (10–11).

First, many of the leaders of the nationalist movement for independence were the same leaders who initially sought reform. Since they eventually expressed a desire for separation, it is plausible that they would never have been satisfied with reform, and always intended to ask for independence. In their memoirs, nationalists typically articulate this view. They explain the reform movement by saying that independence was not feasible at the time, so they asked only for change within the system. In his memoir, al-Fasi (1970, 169) calls the proposed reforms "minimal," and says that asking for reforms was part of a policy of gradualism, implying that reforms were intended only as a first step.

One problem with this claim concerns the reliability of the sources. Relying on nationalist memoirs is problematic because they were written after the movement for independence began, when elites were engaged in the project of constructing nationalist history. al-Fasi's (1970, 7) introduction exemplifies this project; he begins by asserting that "[n]ationalist consciousness existed in al-Maghrib before and after the advent of Islam." His memoirs depict nationalist mobilization as an obvious and inevitable stage for Morocco. His description of his preferences at the time of the reform movement cannot be separated from the political project of nation-building that he is engaged in at the time he describes those preferences.[31] Because al-Fasi did not publicly speak of a desire for independence during the reform movement, there is no way to know reliably whether he earnestly believed in reforms for their own sake or already wanted independence at that time. Nationalist writings typically say that separatism was always the main goal, but these are post hoc writings that seek to invoke a deeply rooted sense of nation.[32] At the time of the reform movement, leaders insisted that they did not seek

---

[31] His book was published in Arabic in 1948, during the process of mobilizing the population in favor of independence.

[32] If the reformists were dissimulating, we might expect to find some records of private conversations or correspondence that would reveal their true preferences, but the evidence is lacking.

separation, but sincerely desired meaningful change within the structure of French rule.[33]

Another reason to doubt nationalists' accounts is their explanation for why they did not speak of independence during the reform movement. They claim that independence was not feasible at the time, but they do not explain why this is the case, or why independence became more realistic later on (see Landau 1956, 155). In fact, most nationalist histories suggest that when the independence movement began, France had no intention of departing, independence required a struggle, and the nation had to rise up against an imperial power reluctant to leave.

Furthermore, this argument implies that reform was more realistic than independence. In fact, the requested reforms were extremely far-reaching. The movement essentially asked the Front Populaire to alter the form of government from an authoritarian one to one in which there would be lower inequality, representation of Moroccans in democratic institutions, universal education, public health, and land redistribution. The reformists challenged the French to follow through on their civilizing mission, and pointed to the failures of the French to live up to their promises. Their demands were not insignificant, nor do they seem to have been particularly feasible. If they were a first step, they were an audacious one, as they involved entirely changing the character of French government in Morocco.

The second piece of evidence that the Moroccan leaders advocating reform truly wanted independence comes from colonial sources. The French themselves, writing at the time, called members of the CAM 'nationalists', and speculated that activists were not really seeking reform, but were 'radicals' who wanted to oust the French from Morocco. In 1936, socialists charged that Moroccan activism was really a power struggle among the bourgeoisie who wanted to replace the French and were using the quest for reforms as a device to gain support (in Halstead 1969, 264). At the time, Moroccan

[33] To take an example, one letter from Moroccans in Paris during the fall 1937 unrest insisted, "The nationalists and Moroccans in general are not against France, but against the French colonial administration, which cannot possibly represent the true French spirit." MAE DI343.

activists denied the charges; the CAM asserted its reformist nature and its recognition of the authority of the protectorate in a March 1937 issue of *L'Action Populaire* (Rézette 1955, 105). But after unrest in the fall of 1937, Nogues wrote that he suspected CAM nationalists of harboring desires for separation, saying, "[I]f the real intentions of the leaders of the Moroccan national movement have escaped us for the past several years and prompted us to follow a liberal policy, these last events should leave no doubt as to their bad faith and the anti-French nature of their activity."[34] In a November 1937 report, Nogues insisted that the CAM had changed: despite its stated attachment to France, he thought the CAM now sought to create a theocracy.[35] But Nogues's statements at this time are suspect, given that his main objective was to stop ongoing protests. He made these statements immediately prior to arresting the CAM leadership, a move that required a justification.

Further, Nogues's evidence that members of the CAM could not be satisfied with mere reforms comes from his belief that France had indeed followed a liberal policy, and yet the CAM continued to mobilize. The idea that French policy in 1930s Morocco was liberal, however, is demonstrably inaccurate. Whereas Nogues made some reforms during his tenure as resident general, he also used repression, and he never implemented the kinds of reforms the activists sought. His conclusion that the CAM would not have been satisfied with the reforms they sought is unknowable, as the French never implemented serious political reforms.

Again, the problem with using evidence from French reports is the reliability of the sources. French officials used the term nationalist to describe any kind of opposition to French policy, without reflecting on the meaning or implications of the term.[36] It is worth considering why they might have preferred to call any and all opposition nationalist. Like the nationalists, the French were motivated by their own political goals, which

---

[34] Quoted in Hoisington (1984, 66).
[35] Report by General Nogues to the Ministry of Foreign Affairs, November 5, 1937. MAE CDRG212.
[36] In the Spanish zone of Morocco, the high commissioner maintained in a 1934 article in *El Sol* that it was possible for Moroccans to be both nationalist and

compromises their usefulness as sources for the preferences of the reformers. French administrators wanted to portray opposition as more extreme than it really was; they sought to convey that all was well with colonial policy to the government in Paris, and that the only opposition was from a noisy, extremist minority who rejected French rule, no matter how equitable it might be. By calling the reformists nationalists with separatist aspirations, the French avoided taking demands for reform seriously.

Moreover, French administrative reports are not good sources of evidence because they had no reliable way to know the motivations of the Moroccan leaders. There is little reason to believe they had privileged insights into these men's private thoughts. Indeed, French reporting on the motivations of the native population contains obvious contradictions. Although they wanted to understand the preferences of the Moroccan population, and devoted numerous special reports as well as sections of their monthly reports to indigenous public opinion, their analyses generally wavered between two stark poles. Either they described the population as completely loyal, or they called them anti-French. Mobilization for change was often interpreted by protectorate administrators as anti-French, even when it resembled the kinds of political mobilization commonly organized by students, workers, or other social groups in metropolitan France.

I have suggested that both the French administration and Moroccan leaders had reasons to call the reform movement nationalist even if they understood that it was not. They may also have been aware of movements outside the French empire that framed their demands on behalf of a distinctive nation – as did the CAM in Morocco – but also explicitly asked for

---

pro-Spanish, saying, "I believe that Moroccan nationalism has at its base a sincere love for Spain." His view that nationalism can entail love for another nation (and a conquering one at that) is a curious one, but it may reflect the fact that the Moroccan political activists in the Spanish zone were promoting a reformist agenda rather than the nationalist view that Morocco should govern itself separate from Spain. *Direction des Affaires Indigènes, Situation Politique et Economique, Période du 1 au 15 Septembre 1934*. SHAT 3H1413.

separation – which the CAM did not. Thus, both the French and Moroccans may have been following an emerging convention in their terminology while simultaneously understanding very well the differences between these two mobilization platforms.

The third piece of evidence regarding Moroccans' true goal comes from descriptions of political protest in the 1930s. During mass protests in the cities, anti-French slogans were common. During the 1937 Meknes water riots, crowds expressed hostility toward the French, shouting, "Water or death!" (Landau 1956, 140). In Rabat, graffiti on the city walls protested the arrest of CAM leaders with statements such as, "Demonstrate, reclaim your rights!" and "France is the enemy of Islam!"[37] These statements document anti-French sentiment, but they do not reflect a pro-independence stance. This kind of rhetoric is compatible both with demands for decolonization and with demands for better government.[38]

A final piece of evidence that leaders may have had nationalist aims in mind is that they interacted with other known nationalists. In France, student groups and workers had already spoken of independence for North Africa, and Moroccan leaders made contact with these groups during trips to France. Moroccan leaders also met with Arab nationalist Chakib Arslan, who traveled to Tetouan in 1936.[39] Arslan influenced many of those who would eventually lead the nationalist movement (Thompson 2000, 11).[40] Arslan was less interested, however, in encouraging local nationalisms than in promoting the unity of Arab countries. He supported pan-Maghrebism, or the unification of Algeria, Tunisia, and Morocco (Julien 1972, 34). Contacts with Arab

---

[37] MAE DI43.

[38] Abun-Nasr (1975) argues that mass agitation itself was a sign of nationalist mobilization, because he did not believe the population was interested in reform. He does not explain why he thinks that the masses acting in protest events wanted independence, however; he simply assumes they do.

[39] Tetouan was the capital of the Spanish protectorate. Chakib Arslan also had a key role in the Berber Dahir protests of 1930. In his journal *The Arab Nation*, he publicized the protests surrounding the Dahir.

[40] Leaders Mohamed Mekki Naciri and al-Ouazzani studied with him in Geneva (Rézette 1955, 62; 94).

nationalists such as Arslan and others in the East were undoubtedly important for the thinking of Moroccan leaders. But again,
this contact, far from meaning that leaders were already seeking Moroccan independence in the early 1930s, might have
dissuaded them from developing the particularistic Moroccan
nationalism that came to dominate in the postwar era in favor
of focusing on regional Arab ties. Alternatively, the ideas of Arab
nationalism and Moroccan independence may also have come
to matter to these leaders only once they realized that reforms
would not be granted. The adoption of nationalist objectives
does not occur automatically upon exposure to nationalist ideas.
Moroccan leaders interacted with leftists, nationalists, and other
politicians in Morocco and abroad. The clearest way to evaluate
their ideology is to observe their actions and statements.

Equitable Reform: A Distinctive Agenda

I have laid out criticisms of the conventional approach to understanding the reform movement, arguing against the view that
leaders in the 1930s already had the goals they would espouse in
the postwar era. There are three further reasons to believe that
reforms constituted an alternative to separation, not a stage of
nationalism.

The first piece of evidence is that the sultan's attitude toward
the reformers was sharply different from his attitude toward
nationalists seeking independence. During the unrest in 1936
and 1937, the sultan opposed the proponents of the Plan of
Reforms. The sultan expressed anger that French administrators
had allowed the activities of the CAM to expand. He was outraged to learn that organizers had claimed to have his approval
for a meeting in Casablanca planned for November 14, 1936.
Speaking to French administrator Thierry, he said, "I could not
tolerate it. I let my subjects know that they have been misled
and I forbade any demonstration. What is more, I ordered the
arrest of the principal organizers." The sultan described CAM
leaders: "They are usurpers. Have they received their authority from the sultan, from the protector state? Or even from a
fraction of the Moroccan people? Are they *ulema*? For my part,

I think it is necessary to deal severely." He asked the delegate, who reproduced the sultan's phrases for the Ministry of Foreign Affairs: "Now I want to know what you plan to do. I am ready to punish those who not only are agitators but have outraged their sovereign. The evil must be destroyed while there is time."[41] In his communication to Paris, Thierry stressed the importance of maintaining good relations with the sultan. He wrote, "For the moment [the sultan] depends on us, but if he perceives some hesitation on our part, he will quickly lose confidence [in us] and completely change his position" (Hoisington 1984, 47). Vienot answered that although he was glad to see the sultan take a stand against the "separatist nationalists," he thought punitive measures should be avoided, arguing that it was important to remember many of the nationalists' demands "inspired moreover by [the Popular Front's] own program" were "justified."[42] He decided to reassure the sultan of France's support, and ask him to avoid making martyrs of the CAM leaders.

The sultan's overt hostility to the CAM is noteworthy, given that he later worked with nationalist leaders and became the undisputed leader of the movement for independence. The goals of the Plan of Reforms were quite different from the goals of the independence movement, however. The sultan's political authority was guaranteed by the protectorate, and he worried that challenges to that system, even if they were accompanied by professions of loyalty to him, threatened his authority. The Plan of Reforms did not directly call for a constitutional system of government, and al-Fasi later explained that the reformers wanted to gradually prepare the people for democratic life while maintaining a relationship of trust with the sultan (in Zade 2001, 27). But the democratic government envisioned in the Plan of Reforms left no clear role for a sultan. "He realized that a Morocco molded in the image of the Plan of Reforms would be a state wherein his power would

---

[41] Quoted in Hoisington (1984, 45).

[42] Vienot appears contradictory, calling the CAM separatists but maintaining that they had an agenda that was justified and inspired by the French government.

be severely curtailed" (Hoisington 1984, 47). Members of the CAM tried to woo the sultan and reassure him that the plan would not threaten his position.[43] They ran a series of articles to this effect in *La Voix du Peuple*, and also organized the annual Fête du Trône, which began in 1933 (Waterbury 1970, 48). But an alliance with the sultan was not achieved until World War II, when the platform had changed.[44] The goal of independence was compatible with a ruling monarch or a constitutional monarchy. The sultan himself saw a big difference between the mobilizations of the 1930s and the nationalist movement of the postwar era.[45]

The sultan was not the only actor to participate in just one of the two mobilization efforts. The differing social composition of the two movements is a second reason to see them as distinctive. Whereas many French settlers opposed both the

[43] al-Fasi, however, openly admired the Turkish republican Mustafa Kamal Atatürk, suggesting that he may have been more anti-monarchy than he later admitted (in Moreau 2003, 65).

[44] Rivet (1999, 369) suggests not only that the CAM come into existence without the sultan, it was also initially opposed to the sultan. The oath that new pledges to the CAM took contained no mention of the sultan, but after its formation, the Istiqlal party added a vow of loyalty to the sultan. Some saw the Istiqlal's relationship with the sultan as evidence that the party had developed an autocratic bent (381).

[45] The sultan's statements regarding his views of the reformers (quoted in Hoisington in Footnote 41) come from French sources, particularly from the report of Thierry to the minister of foreign affairs, November 16, 1936, in Nogues's papers. An opposing account in Moroccan histories holds that the sultan never opposed the CAM, but was unable to openly support it because of the limits placed upon him by the French (see Essakali 1984). This account points to acts of loyalty by members of the CAM, such as their establishment of the annual Fête du Trône in his honor. In weighing the validity of these contradictory accounts, the French one appears much more likely to be accurate. The French account comes from documentation written at the time; moreover, the reports were drafted because the French were not happy with the sultan's attitude, but worried that he would be excessively punitive toward the CAM leaders. The Moroccan interpretation comes long after these events, when the sultan had become the recognized head of the independence movement and there were political reasons for the sultan to claim that he had always supported the nationalists. As Hoisington (1984, 55) notes, "It was good politics for the nationalists to portray the sultan as the unwilling instrument of the French – the *machine à dahir* – and much later for the partisans of the monarchy to accept that version of history."

reform movement and the nationalist movement, prominent French leftists mobilized for reform alongside Moroccans. In addition, French and Moroccan workers participated in a number of strikes during the 1930s, jointly asking for higher wages and better working conditions.[46] Joint mobilization efforts took place during the quest for reforms, but after 1944 the boundary between Moroccans and French was sharper, and common protests became less feasible. The nationalist agenda delineated two sides, while during the reform period, nationality did not fully determine attitudes toward reform.

A third reason to differentiate these movements is the sharp time distinction between the two. Moroccan reformers avoided speaking openly about independence before the collapse of the Popular Front. French reporting suggests a marked shift during World War II from complaints about particular protectorate policies to mobilization for independence, even among some traditional elites who ruled rural areas on behalf of the protectorate.[47] A French report from early 1944 states that the then-ubiquitous nationalist activity had little in common with mobilization during the mid-1930s, as the latter did not call the protectorate into question.[48] The absence of claims about independence in the interwar years supports the view that these were distinctive mobilization platforms.

The Movement for Inclusion in Algeria

For Algeria, it is relatively easy to make the case that demands for political equality constituted a distinct alternative to the movement for independence. Mobilization for political equality occurred throughout the colonial period, whereas demands for statehood were not dominant until the mid-1940s or later. French historians writing as late as 1953 did not foresee widespread separatism in Algeria (Keris 1953). Algeria was a department of

---

[46] MAE DI456.
[47] *Rapport de la Direction des Affaires Politiques,* January-February, 1944. SHAT 3H1417. The war's impact is discussed in Chapter 5.
[48] Ibid.

France, and the official policy in Algeria was assimilation, meaning "the progressive integration of natives (*indigènes*) into the French collective."[49] The reform movement invoked the policy of assimilation as a justification for their claim to political equality. A group of elites in Algeria pointed out the injustices of French rule in Algeria, and the failure to extend the same rights and privileges to Algerian Muslims that the French enjoyed. They asked the French government to carry out its promises to integrate the population and allow Algerian political participation. Mobilization in favor of inclusion in the French Republic is well documented by historians of the colonial period

Citizenship in Algeria was governed by the 1865 *sénatus-consulte* legislation, which stated that Algerians were French (they had no other nationality), but were not citizens of France. To become citizens, they had to renounce their Muslim civil status. Only about 2,000 Algerians gained French citizenship in this way.[50] The French then suggested that Islam, not French policy, stood in the way of assimilation.[51] However, even those who chose to renounce Islam were not assured of attaining citizenship; local administrators could and did hinder applications, and an Algerian who renounced his religion but failed to gain citizenship risked exclusion from both communities.[52] Collective naturalization of Algerian Jews took place in 1870, and set them apart from the Muslim community .

The movement for political equality began at the close of the nineteenth century, with the activities of the Young Algerians, who dominated Muslim political mobilization in Algeria until the mid-1930s (Ruedy 1992, 133). They were French-educated intellectual and commercial elites who openly demanded citizenship.[53] Although a minority spoke of the need to preserve

---

[49] Colonel Olié, "Le mouvements nationalistes en Algérie." Report of the General Residence of France in Morocco, July 1949. SHAT 3H1417.

[50] Ruedy (1992), 75–76.

[51] Colonel Olié, "Les mouvements nationalistes en Algérie." Report of the General Residence of France in Morocco, July 1949. SHAT 3H1417.

[52] Stora (2001, 10).

[53] Scholars debate the date at which assimilation was no longer feasible. Lorcin (1995) claims it was already a pipe dream by the end of the nineteenth century; for others it was possible until World War II (Grimal 1985, 8; Halstead 1969a,

Muslim and Arab heritage, the majority desired acceptance by the French body politic (Ruedy 1992, 106–107). Assimilation, however, did not mean an abandonment of Islam; the Young Algerians sought the acceptance of Muslims by the French state. They called themselves Algerians, but portrayed that identity as *"franco-musulman,"* and envisaged a multiracial future for France (Gallissot 1989, 20). Liberals in France likewise supported assimilation and dreamed of a France that would be a "better and younger" America (Singer and Langdon 2004, 300–301).

In their first political action, the Young Algerians addressed a pending proposal to draft Algerian Muslims into the French army. Many settlers did not want Algerians conscripted because they did not want them to gain easy access to arms; likewise, many Algerian Muslims did not want to fight France's wars.[54] The Young Algerians saw an opportunity to push for reform. A delegation met with Prime Minister Clemenceau in October 1908, and expressed their opposition to conscription unless Algerians were granted full civil rights. Clemenceau made one concession. He accorded Muslims the right to elect the Algerian members of the general councils, who had previously been appointed.[55] This reform was not terribly significant, as the only population qualified to vote for them were the 5,000 who chose the members of the financial delegations (Ruedy 1992, 107–111).[56]

96). "Association" became the new favored term to describe French policy in much of the colonial world, but as Chafer (2002, 30) points out, debates over whether French policy was assimilationist or associationist miss the reality that both policies prevailed at different times and places. Regardless of the term used, French liberals and intellectuals, along with Algerian Muslim elites, continued to discuss the extension of rights to Algerians until the war of independence broke out in 1954. My view is that for elites in Algeria and France, the feasibility of assimilation and meaningful reform varied over time, depending on the circumstances. Algerian participation in World War I, the advent of the Front Populaire, and the collapse of French authority in World War II are examples of events that changed what many people thought possible.

[54] Some 200 notables emigrated in 1911 to Turkey, Tripolitania, and Syria because they feared the consequences of the conscription law (Stora 2001, 11).

[55] There were three general councils, one in Algiers, one in Constantine, and one in Oran.

[56] The *délégations financiers*, the most important electoral body in Algeria for most of the colonial period, decided budgetary matters for Algeria. Decisions were subject to approval by the French Parliament, prime minister, and

Prior to World War I, the Young Algerians published a number of newspapers and journals. *L'Islam,* a French-language journal, was the most influential and called itself "the democratic organ of the Algerian Muslims." In April 1911, the Young Algerians published a list of demands for reform in l'Islam; some of which would benefit them as a group while others were intended to improve the lot of all Algerian Muslims. They asked for the unification and equalization of the tax codes, the elimination of the Native Code[57] and *tribuneaux répressifs,*[58] the broadening of the municipal voting rolls, and the reform of Muslim representation in elective bodies in such a way as to "reserve a preponderant place for the intellectual elements of the country able to collaborate effectively."[59] They also sought the same direct access to the French government that the settlers had, requesting either parliamentary representation or membership in a special council in Paris. Their goal was liberation through political equality (Gallissot 1989, 19).

The Young Algerians made another attempt at reform in 1912, traveling to Paris to ask Prime Minister Poincaré for equality before the law in accordance with the assimilation policy (von Albertini 1975, 4). Several sessions of parliament were devoted to debating reforms for Algeria in 1913 and

president, but these authorities seldom intervened. The assembly was composed of forty-eight elected Europeans and twenty-one Algerian Muslims, some of whom were appointed. The Muslims met separately and had little impact on the allocation of resources (Ruedy 1992, 87).

[57] The Code de L'indigénat or Native Code was imposed in 1881 as an emergency measure, but it survived until World War II. It contained a list of infractions that were not illegal under French law, but which were illegal in Algeria when committed by Muslims. Offenses included: speaking disrespectfully to or about a French official; defaming the French Republic; failing to answer questions put by an official; traveling without a permit; begging outside one's own home commune; shooting weapons in the air in celebration; avoiding the *corvée* (forced labor); and forgetting to declare a family birth or death. The maximum penalty was five days imprisonment and a fifteen-franc fine, but these punishments were applied frequently, particularly when the code was new (Ruedy 1992, 89).

[58] Courts empanelled to try natives accused of crimes more serious than those in the Native Code; there was no jury, just a judge assisted by a European and Muslim appointee.

[59] Quoted in Ruedy (1992, 109).

1914. The end result was a reduction in the penalties of the Native Code, exemption from its provisions to certain categories of évolués, and an increase in Muslim representation in the municipal councils (from a quarter of each council to a third). Most French politicians, uninterested in colonial policy, did not attend these parliamentary debates, and those representing settler interests were able to ensure that the reforms were minimal.

After World War I, Clemenceau resolved to reward Algerian Arabs and Berbers for their support during the war. One hundred and seventy-three thousand Algerians had served as soldiers during the war, and 119,000 were requisitioned to replace French labor in the metropole (Stora 2001, 12). The bulk of the reforms came in the Jonnart Law of February 1919, which expanded the Muslim electorate to 400,000 for the *douar* (communal) councils and 100,000 for the general councils (Stora 2001, 247).[60] The law also instituted a separate college for non-French voters. The maximum number of natives permitted in the municipal councils was still limited to a third of the total number in the council, and a quarter of the number in general councils. Thus, "this newly qualified electorate was invited into a world of political activity designed to assure that most of its goals could be systematically frustrated by the representatives of the minority" (Ruedy 1992, 112). The law also annulled the Native Code, although it was reinstated a year later (Abun-Nasr 1975, 317). No significant concessions were made concerning the extension of citizenship to Algerian Muslims.

French settlers disapproved of the reforms, which they thought went too far, but many of the native population thought France had delivered little in exchange for their sacrifices during the war. The Young Algerians accepted the reforms as a sign of progress, but one of their group, Emir Khaled, broke with

---

[60] Those empowered to vote in communal elections included: all honorably discharged veterans; owners of land or businesses; active or retired civil servants; recipients of French decorations; graduates of elementary school; and members of chambers of commerce or agriculture. Muslim municipal councilmen could now participate in the election of mayors (Ruedy 1992, 112).

them.[61] He demanded more extensive reforms that would extend French citizenship to Algerians while allowing them to retain their Muslim personal status. In addition, his proposed reforms would allow Muslim representatives in the French Parliament, provide compulsory and free bilingual education, and abolish the mixed communes.[62] On this platform, the Emir's ticket swept the municipal elections of 1919, making him the most influential leader of Algerian opposition (Ruedy 1992, 113). During French President Alexandre Millerand's 1922 visit, Emir Khaled declared:

The people of Algeria are all, without distinction as to religion or race, equally children of France ... the desire we have to create within the bosom of France a status worthy of us and worthy of France is the best proof that we are good Frenchmen and wish only to strengthen the bonds that attach us to the mother country (quoted in Ruedy 1992, 130).

In 1924, Emir Khaled went into exile.[63]

Ferhat Abbas, a longtime advocate of assimilation and equal rights, is the most well-known leader of the Young Algerians. In his writings and speeches, he exposed the contradictions between colonial rule and republican values. He asked France to extend democracy to Algeria and force the settlers to respect the natives. For Abbas, a person could be French and Muslim simultaneously (Stora 2001, 17). In 1927, the newly formed Fédération des Élus Musulmanes, made up of the so-called évolués who worked in

---

[61] Emir Khaled, or Khaled Ibn Hashimi ibn Hajj `Abd al Qadar, was a graduate of the French military academy at Saint-Cyr and had served in the French army for twenty-seven years, attaining the rank of captain. He affirmed his loyalty to French Algeria, but considered settlers and the colonial government the main impediments to reform.

[62] Mixed communes were transitional regions in which a few colonists had settled, but the majority was Algerian Muslims. Under the Third Republic, they were governed by civilian officials, who were advised by a commission made up of elected Europeans and appointed Algerian Muslims. These appointees came from those the French considered dependable; both Algerians and the French referred to them using the derogatory nickname *Beni oui-ouis* (essentially "yes men").

[63] There is some question about whether he was forced into exile or whether he went voluntarily. He may have been pressured, or he may have made the decision himself. He was deeply in debt, and the French may have offered to pay his debts if he left (Abun-Nasr 1975, 318; Ruedy 1992, 131).

the French administration or liberal professions, held its first congress in Algiers. This group called for equal rights for Muslims in Algeria. In 1931, Abbas (1931) published a series of articles written by évolué leaders called "De la colonie vers la province: le jeune Algérien," which expressed the desire that Algeria be fully integrated and Muslims granted French citizenship.

As in Morocco, the victory of the Front Populaire increased political activity among those seeking meaningful reform. The victory was followed by a wave of strikes in both Algeria and France. The Young Algerians along with the *ulema* (religious leaders)[64] convened an Islamic congress in June 1936. The resolutions made by the congress asked for: the suppression of all special legal restrictions on Muslims; the total administrative assimilation of Algeria into France, including the abolition of the position of governor of Algeria; the preservation of Muslim personal status; and universal suffrage. In a speech at the congress, religious leader Abdelhamid Ibn Badis said, "When French liberty was sleeping, we kept silent. Liberty has revived in France, and we intend to follow it."[65] Following the congress, a new group – the Youth of the Muslim Algerian Congress – was founded, and also sought rights for Algerians.

[64] In 1931, a group of ulema from Constantine created the Association des Oulemas Réformistes d'Algerie. Abdelhamid Ibn Badis and Tayeb al-Oukbi were the founders of the group. The association drew on the salafiyya movement, Wahabism, and the writings of Egyptians el-Afghani, Mohamed Abdou, and Rachid Rida. It sought religious freedom, the return of confiscated *habous* (communal religious) lands, and the recognition of Arabic as the national language (Entelis 1980). Ibn Badis (1889–1940) was the president of the association, and although he was an avowed nationalist, and the association of ulema was among the first to articulate an argument for the existence of an Algerian nation, he and other ulema saw the advent of the Front Populaire as an opportunity for progress, and collaborated with the Young Algerians to advocate reforms that would make possible "the pure and simple integration of the Muslim collectivity into the great French family" (quoted in Stora 2001, 17). The ulema advocated independence after the reform movement failed (Notice sur les Mouvements Politiques Indigènes en Afrique du Nord, Mars, 1940. Théâtre d'opérations de l'Afrique du Nord, Etat-major, Bureau Politique. SHAT 3H1417). See McDougall (2006) for a discussion of the relationship between the association of ulemas and the nationalist movement.
[65] Quoted in Abun-Nasr (1975, 322).

The hopes placed in the Front Populaire were founded on the colonial platforms of the parties that composed it. French socialists had previously openly supported assimilation; Lagrosillière stated at the 1926 congress of the Section Française de l'Internationale Ouvrière (SFIO, French Branch of the Workers' Internationale): "There can be only one formula to represent and characterize the Socialist colonial policy, and that is assimilation!"[66] SFIO leader Georges Nouelle had likewise promised that colonial peoples would be "liberated" when socialism came to power in France, by which he meant that they would be freed from the repressive aspects of colonial rule, not granted independence from France (in Cohen 1972, 373). The French Communist Party (PCF) initially supported independence, helping to found the anti-colonial Étoile Nord Africaine (North African Star), an association of immigrant workers and students living in France, which asked for independence for the three North African states in 1927 (Pervillé 1991, 72), but relations between the PCF and the Étoile became hostile in the early 1930s. During the campaign that led to the victory of the Front Populaire, the PCF dropped the term "national independence." In February 1939, French communist leader Maurice Thorez seemed to advocate assimilation when he characterized Algeria as "a nation in formation in the melting pot of twenty races."[67] But for the PCF, fighting fascism came before anti-colonialism.

The Front Populaire gave Maurice Violette responsibility for Algerian affairs, and he drafted a plan of reform for Algeria, the Blum-Violette Bill. This legislation would have offered French citizenship to a small proportion of the population – about 25,000 Muslims – without requiring them to renounce Islamic personal law. It was to be extended gradually to the rest of the population. The bill thus eliminated the incompatibility of religious identity with membership in the French political community (Stora 2001, 18). It was a cautious, moderate approach to assimilation. When the Blum-Violette Bill was proposed, the évolués and the communists welcomed it, and the ulema called it a good step forward.

[66] Quoted in Stora (2001, 15).
[67] Quoted in Stora (2001, 16).

The settlers opposed the bill, and ultimately it was defeated in 1938. The bill's rejection was a great disappointment to the proponents of equality and reform (Horne 1977, 37). Its failure has been called the final defeat of the Young Algerian movement (Ruedy 1992, 144).

During the interwar period, there were two other important political movements besides the Young Algerians and the ulema. First, a nascent nationalist movement began to compete with the assimilationists. Messali al-Hajj, with support from the PCF, was the founder of the Étoile Nord Africaine. At the time, this group was the only one demanding independence for Algeria (Stora 2001, 17). Messali was imprisoned in 1933 for his actions with the Étoile Nord Africaine, and released in 1935. After his release he went to Switzerland, where he met Chakib Arslan, who influenced him in a nationalist rather than Marxist direction (Abun-Nasr 1975, 320). In 1936, he was allowed by the Front Populaire to return to Algeria; he then went to France to found the Parti du Peuple Algérian (PPA) in 1937.[68] He subsequently opened branches in Algeria and recruited new members, particularly in the Kabyle and Constantine regions. French reports suggest that the PPA's initial membership was weak.[69] Messali opposed the Blum-Viollette Bill and advocated independence. This position created hostility between his group and the Front Populaire, and he was arrested and imprisoned in August 1937 for two years. Following his release, the party was banned and a number of other leaders arrested. This repression may explain why the party was unable to grow substantially before World War II.[70]

[68] The PPA was similar to the Étoile Nord Africaine in its program, except that the PPA had no ties to the Communist Party, and it focused on political activity in Algeria, rather than in France. For a more extensive discussion of the PPA, see Kaddache (1982) and Saadalla (1975).

[69] Deschamps (1954, 107) reported that the PPA had 3,000 members in 1938, but it is hard to know the basis for this figure. It may include Algerians or Frenchmen living in France. French reports do not contain reliable membership figures. Messali claimed to have 11,000 supporters in October 1936 (Ruedy 1992, 142).

[70] Notice sur les Mouvements Politiques Indigènes en Afrique du Nord, March 1940. Théâtre d'opérations de l'Afrique du Nord, Etat-major, Bureau Politique. SHAT 3H1417.

The second political movement was the Algerian Communist Party (PCA), founded in association with the PCF in 1935, and led by two French militants, Barthel and Deloche. Members were initially mostly European. When recruitment of Algerian Muslims began, some Europeans left the party. When the PCF joined the Front Populaire, Europeans began to return. In 1937, the PCA had more than 5,000 members.[71] The PCA condemned the nationalist aims of Messali's organizations (Ruedy 1992, 139). It was ordered dissolved in 1939, when the PCF was also banned in France.[72]

During World War II, the platform of the évolués began to shift toward independence, although some continued to advocate reform, if not assimilation, rather than separation. In 1943, Ferhat Abbas issued his "Manifesto of the Algerian People," demanding immediate participation of Muslims in government. In a supplement, he called for a separate Algerian state. After French authorities placed him under house arrest, he recanted and reaffirmed his loyalty to France (Horne 1977, 43). In 1944, Abbas organized the group Friends of the Manifesto of Freedom (Amis du Manifest de la Liberté), which aimed to create an Algerian republic federated with France (Abun-Nasr 1975, 323). This was a clear shift away from inclusion, an intermediate solution that pointed to nationalist aims as well as equal rights, although Abbas did not speak of full independence. Writing in 1946, Ali Maalem (1946, 320), another Algerian francophone, argued that it was not too late for France to change its policy and find a solution within the existing system. Speaking of the new turn to nationalism, he wrote, "Nationalism is not virulent, nor exclusive, and even if it opposes the colonial idea, it could be perfectly compatible with a new [colonial] attitude." Like Abbas, he advocated a move toward federation, rather than complete separation.

---

[71] Notice sur les Mouvements Politiques Indigènes en Afrique du Nord, March 1940. Théâtre d'opérations de l'Afrique du Nord, Etat-major, Bureau Politique. SHAT 3H1417.

[72] Colonel Olié, "Le mouvements nationalistes en Algérie." Report of the General Residence of France in Morocco, July 1949. SHAT 3H1417. For more on leftist political currents in Algeria, see Nouschi (1979) and Tlili (1984).

After WWII, nationalist mobilization became a more important part of the ideology of Algerian activists. During the Algerian War of Independence, nationalist separatism was indisputably the dominant ideology of Algerian politics. The move from seeking reform to independence is outlined in Chapter 3.

Understandings of the Algerian Reform Movement

The argument that the reform movement was quite different from the independence movement is less controversial for Algeria than it is for Morocco. Historians represent the two movements as ideologically distinctive, and note conflict between the organizations involved in each. Assimilation and separation appear ideologically opposed to one another, and it is less clear that one could be a first step toward the other. Still, some of the same arguments put forth to demonstrate that the Moroccan reform movement was a manifestation of nationalism are also present in historical work on Algeria. There is a similar tendency, in some accounts of Algerian history, to "do history backward," to look through the lens of the later nationalist success, and to assume that all other alternatives were either nationalism in disguise or doomed to failure. As one historian puts it, the literature on Algeria suffers from "too much reading the present into the past and too little consideration of the past on its own terms" (Prochaska 1990, 1). Algerian nationalist historiography insists that assimilation was never a reasonable alternative because the two national cultures were too different. In these accounts, Algerians were destined to recover their national identity.[73]

Other historians do not accept such historical inevitability, but they still write Algerian history with the expectation of the dominance of the nationalist movement. There is a tendency to see all forms of political contestation in Algeria as contributors to nationalism (McDougall 2006, 15). An example from von Albertini (1975, 4) shows the kind of subtle wording that

---

[73] For an account that sees nationalism beginning with the conquest, see Lacheraf (1965). For a discussion of this literature, see McDougall (2006, 6–8) and Ruedy (1992, 144). For a critique of the problems with both colonial and nationalist historiography, see Burke (2000).

privileges nationalist mobilization over other failed movements: "[In the years before World War I], [n]ationalist organizations and parties began to demand, if not immediate independence, at least a relaxation of authoritarian rule and an increasing share in government and administration." He suggests implicitly that requests for representation and the "relaxation" of authoritarianism are intermediate steps on a continuum that ends at independence, although there is little evidence that the organizations he describes were concerned with independence at all at that stage. In their summary of the nationalist movement in Algeria, Entelis and Arone (1995, 396) minimize the importance of the reform movement by implying that it was short-lived: "Algerian activists initially called for equality with the Europeans in Algeria, but their demands soon turned into calls for independence." They fail to explain that calls for reforms lasted for more than thirty years, longer than mobilization for independence if we date its origin from the appearance of Messali's PPA. This kind of wording suggests an approach that is affected by the historian's knowledge of the outcome. Work that implies that alternatives to nationalism were always less meaningful to proponents and less realistic than nationalist separatism suffers from a post hoc reading of history that fails to take seriously the contemporaneous goals of political actors.

Like scholars of Moroccan nationalism, historians of Algeria are often preoccupied with pinning down the origins of nationalism, and read history with the aim of identifying the first nationalists. But as McDougall (2006, 45) points out, asking who the first nationalists were may be the wrong question; instead, it is more productive to discuss the conditions under which different nationalist enunciations were produced.

The Young Algerian movement is often categorized as a nationalist movement simply because all native political organizing tends to be organized in chapters and articles on Algerian nationalism. But scholars do distinguish between the Young Algerians, PPA, Association des Oulemas Réformistes d'Algerie, and Algerian Communist Party. For the most part, analysts do not call the sincerity of the Young Algerians into question in the way that historians of Morocco have doubted the sincerity of the CAM leaders. But again, the French called the Young Algerians nationalists and troublemakers in an effort to brand them as extremists. Algerian nationalists also later claimed some of the assimilationists as nationalists. For example, despite Emir Khaled's pro-assimilation stance and his claim that he wished to be a good Frenchman, both Algerian and French authors have called him the first Algerian nationalist (Julien 1972, 100–101; Kaddache 1982, 182; Koulakssis and Meynier 1987). Ruedy (1992, 130) says that this unlikely portrayal of Khaled originated with the French administration and the PCF, both of which labeled him a nationalist. Here we can see that the French imposed the nationalist label for political purposes, just as they did in Morocco.

Morocco and Algeria in Comparative Perspective

This chapter has drawn on the history of Morocco and Algeria to illustrate the differences between demands for political equality and independence. Both cases experienced political movements for equitable reform during the years before World War II. These movements resembled each other in some ways, but there were important differences, as well.

Moroccans asked the French to fulfill the promises made in the protectorate treaty, including the development and general advancement of the country. They sought a role in governance and improvements in their relative economic and political status. Although indirect rule was supposed to guide colonial policy, in reality the French controlled the government and made the important policy decisions. Moroccans contested this state of affairs. They called attention to the abusive aspects of colonialism and asked for many of the rights and privileges enjoyed by French citizens. They sought the kinds of political institutions available to French citizens in France and Morocco; but ironically, the French defended the traditional rule of the sultan and other traditional elites. Assimilation was never a serious option for Moroccans and reformers did not ask for French citizenship. Nor did they question the French presence.

Like the Moroccan reformers, the Young Algerians who sought reform criticized the nature of French rule without demanding an end to it.[74] They, too, asked France to keep its promises. Unlike Moroccan reformers, the Young Algerians sought to eliminate inequality via incorporation. They asked France to assimilate Algerians in accordance with France's stated policy, but for them, assimilation was political and did not entail the abandonment of their religion or culture. A concern for political equality underlay both Moroccan and Algerian opposition to French rule in the 1930s, but these movements proposed somewhat different solutions.

The claim that demands for reform differ in important ways from nationalist objectives is more intuitive for Algeria than Morocco. The calls for assimilation in Algeria appear easily distinguishable from calls for independence. For Morocco, scholars have had good reasons to contextualize the attempts at reform in the 1930s within a broader nationalist framework: the leadership was similar, claims were made on behalf of the same people, and the opponents were the same. Yet this chapter has pointed to similarities in the content of the demands made by Moroccan and Algerian reformers, emphasizing their shared criticism of the authoritarian, unequal nature of colonial policy. It is striking that these movements should resemble one another at all, given that assimilation was never held out as an option for Moroccans. Moreover, even though Moroccan reformers thought of themselves as having a distinctive nationality, they still found the idea of implanting democratic French institutions appealing. We might expect nationalist demands for independence to predominate in Morocco, but Morocco, like Algeria, did not have only one kind of anti-colonialism.

Similar movements occurred across the French empire, although not all at the same time. Demands for assimilation began in Guadeloupe and Martinique in the mid-nineteenth century. Tunisians began asking for equitable reform and respect for

---

[74] I refer here to the reformists covered in this chapter, not to Messali, of course, who did demand independence.

Islam in the late nineteenth century.[75] Madagascar, like Algeria and Morocco, saw elite movements for reform during the interwar years. In much of French Africa, movements for inclusion only gained momentum after World War II.

Calls for reform across the empire were similar because activists expressed a commitment to equality and political rights, but they were not identical. I have emphasized the similarities, but the solutions proposed to the problems of empire varied from place to place. For instance, reformists in the protectorates of Indochina and Tunisia were closer to the Moroccan model because they did not call for assimilation. But calls for the extension of French republican institutions were common across the empire before nationalist mobilization began. Chapter 3 discusses reform movements throughout the empire.

Conclusion

"The creation of a nation forms a consensus without concerning itself with the ambiguities of real history."

- Stora (2001, xii).

This chapter sought to unravel the assumption that requests for political equality constituted a stage of the nationalist movement for independence. Rather than subsuming all political opposition into the nationalist narrative, I have stressed the distinctiveness of these mobilization platforms. By doing so, I pointed to the diversity of responses to imperial rule: anti-colonialism had multiple forms. But what exactly is gained by conceptualizing these demands as separate movement platforms? Although scholars and participants called the reform movements nationalist, they typically did not fail to recognize that demands for independence

---

[75] On early anti-colonial movements in Tunisia, see Perkins (2004), along with Moore (1970) and Government of Tunisia (1969). Demands for independence became common earlier in Tunisia than in Morocco or Algeria, but demands for reform also emerged. Like Morocco and Algeria, demands for equitable reform were heard in the interwar years; Tunisians called for a constitution and also a parliament that would contain both Tunisian and French representatives. The Destur Party, founded in 1920, takes its name from one of its core demands: a constitution.

were different from demands for reform, and they discuss the shift from one platform to another. So what is the harm in categorizing both demands for political equality and independence as instances of nationalism? I maintain that inattention to the distinctions between the two has produced three related consequences for the study of nationalist movements.

First, broadly categorizing both sets of demands as nationalist obscures the tensions between them. The goals of the reform movements were different from, and in many ways opposed to, the goals of the nationalist movements in favor of separation. Proponents of political equality argued that the democratic principles of the French Republic were universal, and ought to be extended to French colonies, regardless of race, language, or religion. They invoked the French Revolution and claimed that the principles of *egalité*, *fraternité*, and *liberté* ought to prevail outside France.[76] As Frederick Cooper (2005, 12) put it, they used the "logic of equivalence" to claim for themselves the same privileges that French citizens took for granted. This demand was revolutionary in its own right. Pro-assimilation elites who maintained that inclusion did not require the abandonment of Islam or indigenous culture did not seek to become Frenchmen, but to change what it meant to be French.[77] They argued that political inclusion in a single state was compatible with distinct identities, a claim that challenges the nationalist tenet that sovereignty implies shared nationhood. They believed a citizenry could include multiple peoples. They asked France to expand its boundaries, erase the distinctions between citizens and subjects, and treat the people of the colonies equitably.

---

[76] The gaps between French republican principles and actual colonial practices have been widely discussed. See Thompson (2000b) on the ideological commitments of colonial administrators.

[77] In Algeria, reformists sought to remove the stipulation that French citizenship could only be obtained through renouncing Islam. In Africa, Césaire and Senghor led the negritude movement, which emphasized Africanness and forms of the African personality and culture, but maintained that negritude was compatible with French citizenship (F. Cooper 2002, 25).

The shift from movements for political equality to movements for national independence entailed a move away from universal principles to particularistic identities. As Duara (2004, 12) writes, "The ideals of egalitarianism, humanitarianism (or universalism) and the moral and spiritual values represented by the twin pillars of socialism and civilization discourse were frequently in tension with the program of nation making." Instead of emphasizing equality between Frenchmen and colonial subjects, nationalists emphasized the incompatibility of local and French culture in order to support the claim that colonial territories were nations in need of their own states. Their allegiance was no longer to French democratic principles, but to their co-nationals in the colonial territory. Nationalist movements rejected the fusion of different peoples and nations within one polity that the reform movements sought.[78] Both movements wanted to end the inequality of imperialism, but in different ways. The reformers wanted to alter the nature of imperial rule, whereas the nationalists wanted to eject imperial rulers and build nation-states.[79]

A second consequence of treating the reform movement as a stage in the nationalist movement is that it produces an elite-focused history. Throughout the empire, reform movements were primarily elite initiatives and popular participation was limited. If the elites' reform-oriented activities count as the beginning of nationalism, there is no need to look beyond elites to analyze the onset of nationalist mobilization. The literature has often focused on the leadership; less attention has been paid to how and why other segments of the population became involved. Instead, nationalism is presumed to expand among the population

---

[78] For more on nationalism as exclusionary, see Wimmer (2002). See also Pratt (2007, 35–37) on the exclusionary nature of nationalism in the Arab world.

[79] See Suny (2001a), who suggests that hierarchy and unequal rule define empire; an empire no longer constitutes an empire once the distinctions and privileges of the imperial center are gone. In his study of French West Africa, Chafer (2002, 76) distinguishes decolonization through assimilation from decolonization through independence, but he persists in calling the former nationalist. He adopts the term "assimilationist nationalism" to describe the democratic reform movement, a term that again shows the conceptual contortions required to label all political action in the colonies as nationalist in nature.

through underspecified mechanisms. Distinguishing between the elite movements for reform and the nationalist movements generates new areas of inquiry about how participation in nationalist movements transpired.

Third, the shift from advocating reform to demanding independence is under-theorized in a literature that sees both sets of demands as aspects of one phenomenon. When no distinctions are made between different kinds of political opposition, the question of why nationalist movements in particular arise is either not posed or there is a presumed teleology in which nationalist movements seeking independence naturally follow demands for reform. Gelvin (1998, 12) states that "it is necessary to step outside the nationalist narrative and to focus on those factors that prompted the transition from a social system that was not conducive to nationalism to one that was apposite to the ideology." The conditions that promote nationalist mobilization for independence may be quite different from those that facilitate reform movements. Moreover, the relationship between movements for political equality and nationalist movements may be causal, not constitutive, a possibility I analyze in Chapter 3. Instead of finding that demands for reform evolved into demands for independence, I demonstrate that it was the success or failure of calls for equality that mattered. The fate of the reform movement led to nationalist mobilization in the French empire, as reformists came to see independence as the only remaining way to redress the inequalities of colonialism.

3

Political Equality and Nationalist Opposition in the French Empire

> At the request of the Italians, [Livius Drusus] promised to put forward once again legislation on the subject of citizenship, because this is what they most wanted, and they thought that by this single thing they would immediately become masters instead of subjects ... Drusus too was killed during his tribunate ... and the Italians, learning of Drusus's fate and of the excuse for sending these men into exile, considered it intolerable for those who were politically active on their behalf to be treated in this way any longer, and as they saw no other method of realizing their hopes of gaining Roman citizenship, decided to secede from the Romans forthwith and make war on them to the best of their ability.
>
> – *Appianus* (1996, 20–22), *The Civil Wars 43–31 BC, Book 1, Chapters 35–38*.

Chapter 2 argued that the demands for political equality made by colonial subjects were qualitatively different from nationalist demands: proponents of political equality sought inclusion in the French system and access to political power, whereas nationalists demanded separation on behalf of a distinct, sovereign people. This chapter takes the distinctiveness of these objectives as given, and examines the relationship between them. Conventional accounts of the colonial period treat the quest for political equality as a rehearsal for the nationalist mobilization that followed. Movements for equality built organizational capacity and strengthened opposition to colonial rule, which was then fully realized in the form of movements for independence. In this view, demands for equality lead to demands for independence; they are the first stage of the nationalist movement. As Chapter 2 discussed, one reason both movements are understood to be manifestations of nationalism is the (sometimes implicit) conviction that demands for political equality would eventually morph into nationalist demands for separation. This logic implies a uniform prediction: political equality movements should give way to nationalist movements.

This chapter argues that movements for political equality were consequential for nationalist organizing, but in a different way. Demands for political equality did not give way to demands for national independence as movements matured. Instead, it was the response to these movements that prompted nationalist mobilization. Exclusion produced nationalism: the *failure* of movements to achieve political equality led elites to begin expressing nationalist goals. Thwarted aspirations diverted politics from a framework of equal rights to one that increasingly emphasized national distinctiveness and the need for independence. Successful mobilization for political equality, in contrast, did not lead to nationalist mobilization.

Similar arguments have been invoked to explain other conflicts, going as far back as the Social War in Rome, which began when the Romans rejected Italians' demands for Roman citizenship.[1] Under French rule, this argument was proposed by activists in the colonies seeking greater political rights, French

---

[1] This argument has also been made about African-American social movements in the United States. McAdam (1999, 107–108) asserts that support for Garvey's separatist movement in the early 1900s reflected pessimism among blacks during those years about the feasibility of equal rights. According to Wilson (1976, 97), we observe "a push for integration during periods when blacks are optimistic about meaningful assimilation and a drive for separatism during periods of disillusionment and resignation." Note, too, that prior to the American Revolution, Americans first attacked "taxation without representation" before they declared the colonies independent. See Klooster (2009), chapter two. Roeder (2007, 73) argues more generally that exclusion from a central state creates grievances in the periphery, although his foremost objective is to evaluate why proponents of a nation-state project succeed or fail, not why they come to seek independent statehood. He sees the institutional framework and bargaining incentives as the key factors shaping elite preferences.

leftists who opposed the authoritarian nature of imperial rule, and various scholars. For instance, scholars and observers of the nationalist movements in Algeria and Morocco maintained that the failure of France to rectify political inequalities was a key factor motivating elites to begin advocating separation.[2] In the "Manifesto of the Algerian People," issued in 1943, Algerian advocates of inclusion stated:

Politically and morally, this colonialism can have no concept other than that of two societies, one foreign to the other. Its refusal, systematic or disguised, to give French citizenship to Algerian Muslims has discouraged the partisans of the policy of assimilation extended to the autochthones. This policy appears today in the eyes of all, as an inaccessible thing, a dangerous device placed at the service of colonialism – *Manifeste du peuple Algerién* (quoted in Hahn 1960, 143)

Moroccan nationalist Allal al-Fasi likewise agreed that the failure of assimilation mattered for nationalist organizing. He praised France for rejecting demands for political equality because it protected Algerian national identity: "What is interesting for our purpose is the fact that the colonials and the local French administration in Algeria supported the correct view: that it was the duty of France to preserve for the Algerians their national character; that she should not integrate them into France or attempt their assimilation" (al-Fasi 1970, 28–29).

French supporters of increased political rights in the colonies likewise spoke of the potential consequences of continued exclusion. In an address to the French national assembly in 1937, Maurice Violette warned, "When the Muslims protest, you are indignant; when they approve, you are suspicious; when they keep quiet, you are fearful. Sirs, these men have no political nation. They do not even demand their religious nation. All they ask is to be admitted to yours. If you refuse this, beware, lest they do not soon create one for themselves" (quoted in Horne 1977, 37). Anti-colonial activist Charles-André Julien (1972, 591) was among those who argued that meaningful political reform would

---

[2] See Abun-Nasr (1975, 322); Ageron (1968); Berque (1962); Halstead (1969a, 6); Julien (1972); Keris (1953, 24); Maalem (1946, 267); Rézette (1955, 29).

reduce the desire for separation; he describes French policy in North Africa as a series of lost opportunities. Even those who opposed the political inclusion of colonized subjects recognized the dangers of rejecting their appeals for equality; a 1943 army report on public opinion in North Africa described the strong wave of support for independence that was sweeping the region, blaming colonial policy because the French "did not know how to satisfy the legitimate aspirations that French culture had awakened."[3]

The claim that a denial of political rights would lead to nationalism was intended to influence policy, but its advocates rarely provided evidence in favor of the thesis.[4] Since the end of the colonial era, this argument has lost much of its appeal.[5] In hindsight, and particularly given the consolidation of the nation-state system, it seems implausible that France could have continued to rule vast territories outside of Europe without engendering nationalism, even if significant political rights had been granted. Nationalists and historians beholden to nationalist accounts contend that colonial subjects would never have been satisfied with reform, and would eventually have turned to nationalist opposition. That a state could have included Africans, Asians, and French seems unlikely, given the norm of self-determination and the increasing emphasis on the link between nation and ethnicity in the international arena. As Emerson (1960, 43) puts it, "The simple truth is that, once a certain stage of development is passed, colonial peoples will not accept good government as a substitute for self-government."

These claims remain largely unevaluated: if the French had treated colonial subjects as political equals, would they have forestalled nationalist organizing, as the proponents of equal

---

[3] *Note sur l'évolution de l'opinion musulmane de l'Afrique du Nord, de 1920 à nos jours.* Commandement en Chef, Etat-major, Inspection des Affaires Militaires Musulmanes, June 1943. SHAT 3H249.

[4] Some proponents of equality may have been acting strategically to obtain concessions, and were thus employing this argument rhetorically without considering its empirical validity.

[5] Some scholars, particularly in Europe, continue to connect the failure of assimilation to nationalism. See, for instance, Brunschwig (1986, 51).

rights asserted? Or were the movements for political equality simply a step toward nationalist mobilization, as nationalists and historians sympathetic to them later maintained?

Any attempt at answering these questions must confront a host of problems that bedevil inference-making. In places such as Morocco and Algeria, political equality was never granted. The counterfactual we would ideally want to observe is an alternate Morocco, where Moroccans were given rights equivalent to those French settlers enjoyed, or an alternate Algeria in which the French National Assembly voted to enfranchise Muslims in 1938. We could then compare political organizing in an Algeria composed of French citizens to mobilization in an Algeria made up of French settlers and Algerian Muslim subjects. But history provides us with no such counterfactuals, and no straightforward route to reliable causal claims. Instead, we have to look for alternative sources of variation and consider the implications of these arguments for how individuals with and without political equality ought to behave.

The rest of this chapter does just that. I begin by further developing the logic of the proposed argument and its mechanisms through considering what might have happened had the French chosen to be more equitable in Algeria and Morocco. This counterfactual discussion is followed by an examination of actual macro-level variation across the French empire. France did not uniformly deny political equality to its colonies. They implemented three main policies: they denied political rights to some; promised political equality and took limited steps toward it for others; and incorporated a final group as full citizens with the same rights as the people of metropolitan France. After comparing across the empire, the third section exploits intra-colony variation. The French gave citizenship to the Four Communes in Senegal, denying the rest of the colony any rights. This policy provides a unique opportunity to compare the beliefs and behavior of those with and without political rights. The fourth section assesses the main determinants of French decisions to grant some people and places political equality while others were denied. The fifth section considers alternative arguments, with the aim of evaluating the potential for endogeneity.

The evidence provided to assess the argument here is, by necessity, imperfect. But although this is true about the argument I propose, the evidence supporting the conventional understanding of the relationship between movements for political equality and nationalism is much thinner. The view that demands for political equality would evolve into nationalist demands regardless of what the French did is difficult to substantiate empirically. The conclusion shows the difficulties of reconciling the conventional view with the historical record and discusses the importance of considering the effects of political equality and inequality.

Imagined Alternatives: The Potential Effects of Political Equality

The French did not ultimately offer political equality to Moroccans, Algerians, or the vast majority of their colonial subjects. But if they had, what would the results have been? What was the effect of refusing political equality?

Consider first an alternate Morocco in which significant political reforms were implemented. The proposed reforms aimed at reducing settler privileges by allowing Moroccan political participation and changing taxation laws so that Moroccans did not pay a disproportionate share. Reforms would thus have reduced the political and economic distance between colonial subjects and settlers.

Had they been implemented, they would have opened up the possibility of alliances between Moroccans and groups in the French population of Morocco. These alliances are not just hypothetical; history shows that such efforts were underway during the period when Moroccans sought equitable reforms. The French administration itself acknowledged the potential for alliances across national boundaries, and feared political mobilization by a combined French-Moroccan organization. For example, by 1937 there were 68,000 Moroccan workers employed in the principal industries of the French zone. Moroccans were forbidden from joining French unions, but some joined anyway, encouraged by French workers. A June 1936 strike in Casablanca included both Moroccan and French workers; about 1,400 of the 2,000 strikers were Moroccan (Hoisington 1984, 99). This coalition frightened French businessmen: "Their overriding fear was of Moroccans and Europeans marching arm in arm in the streets and together occupying the factories" (Hoisington 1984, 100). Had the reforms been carried through, Moroccan workers would have had the right to join French unions and might then have been more tempted to seek alliances with French workers than to ally with the small group of elites who eventually led the nationalist movement. Instead, laws were enacted that punished them for joining unions, and the incipient alliance was crushed.[6]

Class cleavages would also have been affected if the elected municipal councils Moroccan leaders asked for had been created. Elections might have made class more salient had Moroccans become tied to sister parties in the metropole and voted along class lines, as voters did in other parts of the empire where there were branches of French parties. Shared ideology, rather than nationality, might have become the politically salient identity.

Moroccan elites asked for access to administrative posts. If they had been able to hold important positions, they might have felt that their interests lay in the continuation of the regime, rather than in an alliance with poorer segments of the population. Instead, the elites who asked for reform came to believe that the only way they would obtain access to political power was via an independent state.

The Algerian case further illustrates the potential effects of political reforms on nationalist organizing. If the 1937 Blum-Violette Bill that would have enfranchised a small number of Algerians had passed, it might have tied them more closely to France, rather than prompting opposition to French rule. The Algerian pro-assimilation

---

[6] The administration's desire to prevent ties from forming between Moroccans and French settlers can also be observed in their policies regulating housing and marriage. See Abu-Lughod (1980) on efforts to segregate the populations. Some French settlers wanted to move into the native medinas, but were prevented from doing so. Administrative records indicate that the administration sought to police romantic relationships, as well, confiscating love letters and listening in on phone calls between French and Moroccan youths. See *Politique Musulman au Maroc*, 1943–1952. MAE DI341.

elites were already the most likely among the indigenous population to express an allegiance to France. They were typically well educated; many had traveled or studied in Europe, and they came into contact with foreigners more often than most of the population. Some *evolués*, including Ferhat Abbas and Messali al-Hadj, were married to French women. Many of those who would have qualified for citizenship under the Blum-Violette Bill were concerned with the lack of opportunities for educated Algerians. If the French had passed the Blum-Violette Bill, the new citizens would have had an incentive to work within the system. After all, citizenship would have removed the legal barriers to their advancement; a stake in the administration might have made these elites partners, not enemies, of the administration.

After the bill passed, elites would have had three possible courses of action. They might have: worked to expand citizenship to the rest of the population, sought to retain their privileges and stopped advocating further reform, or moved toward nationalist demands. The first two courses of action would have forestalled nationalism. Enfranchising the entire population might have reduced the demand for independence by giving Algerians a stake in the government. Alternatively, if the bill's beneficiaries instead sought to guard their privileges, they might have been enlisted on the side of the French in discouraging the nationalist aspirations of the un-enfranchised.[7] Instead, the failure of the bill made it clear that Algerian elites would not be treated as political equals in a French-run system, and the elites who had previously advocated assimilation increasingly began to articulate nationalist aspirations.[8]

---

[7] In this scenario, nationalist mobilization might have been delayed rather than foreclosed; the un-enfranchised would be expected to organize, but with greater difficulty given that they would need to confront the French plus a satisfied Algerian elite.

[8] On Abbas's move toward favoring separatism after the failure of assimilation, see Keris (1953, 24), as well as his own statement in the beginning of this chapter. Abbas's eventual support for nationalist goals did not come as an abrupt departure from his pro-assimilation stance. Faced with repeated disappointments, particularly in 1937, Abbas modified his proposals. In the 1946 French Constitutional Assembly, he advocated a relationship that would reflect both a

These alternative scenarios point to several hypotheses. If granting political equality produces the results I have suggested, we would expect to see individuals with political rights working to build and strengthen ties with French actors. We might expect to observe demands to deepen democratic institutions and increase Algerian or Moroccan involvement in public affairs, but within the existing system. We might expect to see attempts to eliminate persistent racism and inequality, although we might not see alliances forming between those with political equality and those without it. If the argument is right, we would not expect those with political equality to emphasize national differences between the French and themselves or support those making nationalist claims. If recipients of political equality do shift toward nationalist demands, the conventional view that movements for political equality set the stage for nationalism would be supported.

These predictions cannot be evaluated in the context of Algeria and Morocco, where we can only speculate about how political equality might have affected its proponents. The following sections consider whether or not these predictions were borne out in other places within the French empire.

The Consequences of Exclusion and Equality across the Empire

Calls for political equality were widespread in the French empire, and in some places they were successful. Coding the success or failure of demands for political equality is, however, somewhat tricky

particular Algerian identity and the desire for equality. In his final comments, he lamented a missed opportunity to link Algeria, with its own identity, to France in "a policy of loyal and egalitarian association," which could only come about via an abandonment of centralization and the creation of greater federal powers (see Assemblée Nationale Constituante, Débats, September 28, 1946, 4230–4233). Abbas's history of activism shows the possibility of hybrid demands; whereas I have stressed the conceptual distinctiveness of political equality and national independence, activists such as Abbas proposed solutions to empire that combined elements of both goals. After the Algerian War for Independence began, the National Liberation Front (FLN) rejected such solutions.

because the French deliberately tried to obfuscate, continually declaring good intentions and promising that equitable reforms were on the way, but often failing to make meaningful political changes. Deciding when exactly the quest for political equality can be said to have definitively failed is thus difficult because we do not always know when proponents of political equality in the colonies decided that French promises were no longer credible. Indigenous leaders went through intense mobilization for reform when left-leaning governments in France expressed sympathy with their claims. Just when they decided to give up is not always clear; it varied both across cases and within them, as some persisted in demanding equality after others had ceased. Moreover, in the cases where full citizenship was ultimately extended, success was often piecemeal, as laws granting increased rights were passed at different times. Likewise, the failure to achieve equality did not typically occur at a single, obvious point in time; in some cases, advocates of reform won significant concessions and made considerable progress toward equality before their proposals were rejected.

Although the outcome of calls for political equality was not always easy to foresee, it is useful to take a definitive moment when French policies were clearest and study the downstream consequences across the empire. The aftermath of World War II provides a key decision-making moment when the French took stock of their empire. Specifically, at their postwar constitutional assembly in 1946, the French decided how they would administer the empire in the postwar era. The passage of the 1946 constitution provides an opportune moment to determine French policies because the constitution supplies clear indicators. Prior to its passage, elites in particular territories may have had a sense of whether or not the reforms they wanted were feasible. Indeed, in some places the shift from calls for reform to calls for independence had already occurred. But studying this decision-making moment provides some advantages over evaluating the outcome of reform movements on a case-by-case basis: the constitution sent each territory a clear message about the prospects for political equality, thereby providing a way to compare French policies toward different colonial possessions; studying one moment allows us to hold the international environment constant; and this approach does not require intuiting what elites in the colonies might or might not have been thinking about the prospects for reform.

At the most basic level, the postwar French decisions differentiated possessions whose inhabitants were legally political equals of Frenchman from places whose inhabitants were not.[9] In six territories, France granted full citizenship: Martinique, Guadeloupe, Guiana, Reunion, Polynesia, and New Caledonia.[10] The rest of the empire did not gain the same rights. If political exclusion encourages nationalist aspirations, we would expect the places that were denied full citizenship to begin nationalist organizing, whereas those with full citizenship should not turn nationalist. If, on the other hand, movements for political equality produce nationalist organizing regardless of their outcome, there should be no observable difference in political activity between places that were granted political equality and those that were not.

Table 3.1 suggests that political exclusion was consequential for nationalist activity. It shows that where political equality was not granted in 1946, nationalist movements began opposing colonial rule within a decade.[11] Where full citizenship was granted, no nationalist movements were active in the decade following the extension of citizenship.[12] Contrary to claims

---

[9] France's two Middle Eastern mandates, Syria and Lebanon, became independent at this time. Movements for political equality were absent in the Levant under French rule, largely because nationalist mobilization had already begun prior to the arrival of the French, during the breakup of the Ottoman Empire. Reform movements occurred during the period of Ottoman rule.

[10] Martinique, Guadeloupe, Guiana, and Reunion became departments, with the same legal identity as any department in metropolitan France; Polynesia, New Caledonia (and later Mayotte) became overseas territories with many of the same rights as French citizens.

[11] The twenty-three colonies in Table 3.1, column 3 include the territories of French Equatorial Africa (AEF), French West Africa (AOF), and the protectorates and mandates. Excluded from the table are Djibouti, Mayotte, St. Pierre and Miquelon and Wallis and Futuna, as their status was not conferred until later.

[12] The time period is limited to ten years because the extension of citizenship should not prevent nationalist organizing indefinitely; there are other paths to nationalism within multiethnic states. Indeed, some of the places that were granted citizenship have experienced sporadic nationalist unrest since the 1946 constitution. New Caledonia is a case in point; the Kanak independence movement became active there in the 1980s, and in 2014, voters who have lived in the archipelago for at least twenty years will be asked to vote on the question

TABLE 3.1. *Nationalist Movements by Political Equality*

Nationalist Movement*	Political Equality?	
	Yes	No
Yes	0	23
No	6	0

*within 10 years.

that movements for political equality were a stepping-stone to nationalist demands, in places where demands for equality were met, nationalist demands did not follow.

This test is imperfect because building nationalist movements requires more than just a change in goals; opportunities to organize and act are also needed. Ideally, to get at the consequences of granting or denying political equality for the mindset of political organizers, it would be preferable to have systematic measures of elite opinion so that we could observe whether it changes over time. But such measures are difficult to come by, although there is ample anecdotal evidence that elites became frustrated when reforms repeatedly failed to materialize. Looking at the existence of nationalist movements is a rough indicator of ideological change; Table 3.1 does not tell us whether the absence of nationalist movements among those colonies that received citizenship is due to a lack of nationalist aspirations or simply the inability for these cases to experience an independence movement.

Incorporation and Citizenship in the New Departments
A closer look at several of the cases where full citizenship was granted can alleviate concerns that these new citizens lacked the capacity, but not the will, for nationalist organizing. The extension of citizenship resulted not in talk of independence, but in demands for further incorporation. Inhabitants welcomed the 1946 extension of French citizenship enthusiastically (Bruné 1996, 15). After Martinique and Guadeloupe became French departments,

of full independence. For more on New Caledonia, see Trépied (2007). For nationalist perspectives from the Antilles, see Moutoussamy (2000), and on postindependence politics, see Descamps (1981).

assimilationist trends strengthened (Blérald 1988).[13] The expansion of the education system and the spread of French television and newspapers brought the two departments closer to the metropole. Political activists made social welfare demands and encouraged the government to do more to integrate the departments. The change in political status prompted further demands for equality, not demands for separation (Hintjens 1995).

Given the active reformist mobilization that occurred in the wake of incorporation, it is hard to sustain the position that politicians in the new French departments and territories wanted to mobilize for national independence but were unable to do so. Political activism was facilitated by the new democratic context; as citizens, these populations now had the right to participate in politics. Politicians were capable of, and indeed actively engaged in, mobilizing constituencies to participate in the institutions of the Fourth Republic. Had these new citizens wished to advance nationalist demands, it would have been easier for them than for French subjects in other parts of the empire who lacked the same rights and protections. In the new departments, now shielded by French democracy, there were fewer obstacles to free expression and political organization.

Nationalist movements failed to arise despite ethnic and cultural differences between mainland France and the overseas departments. These cleavages were politically salient, even if they did not produce nationalist movements. Many decried persistent French racism. The *négritude* movement was, in part, a reaction to racism.[14] Led by Leopold Senghor from Senegal and Aimé Césaire from

[13] The quest for citizenship in both Martinique and Guadeloupe has a long history. Nicolas (1996, 396) examines why Haiti experienced a movement for independence after slavery was abolished in 1848 but Martinique did not, concluding that the bourgeoisie in Martinique instead sought citizenship and equality. In Martinique, the abolition of slavery was seen as a move toward recognizing blacks as equals. See Glissant (1989, 7), who laments the absence of nationalist mobilization in Martinique. For more on political trends in overseas French departments and territories, see Aldrich and Connell (2006). Blérald (1988); Bruné (1996); Guillebaud (1976).

[14] See Wilder (2005) on the emergence of the negritude movement, as well its relationship to reform efforts on the part of both colonial subjects and administrators articulating a discourse of cultural humanism.

Martinque, it sought to affirm the value of African art and culture. As Senghor put it, negritude was "the manner of self-expression of the black character, the black world, black civilization."[15] In his *Discours sur le Colonialisme*, Césaire (1955) reacted to French racism by emphasizing the positive attributes of blackness, but as Cooper (2005, 41) notes, few later scholars noted that Césaire did not demand independence. Despite his focus on African identity, Césaire advocated for Martinique's transformation into a French department. Pride in identity was not absent in the cases that achieved political equality, but this pride did not preclude French citizenship. Political assimilation, leaders such as Césaire argued, did not have to entail the abandonment of culture. France could, by embracing pluralism, include diverse peoples. A commitment to Martinique's or Guadeloupe's distinctive character did not imply a nationalist commitment to the right of self-governance.

The Fourth Republic's Promise of Citizenship: The French Union and the Indivisible Republic Divided

The cases where full citizenship was granted do not support the view that nationalist demands superseded demands for political equality. Differences among the other cases – those excluded from full citizenship – also point to the effects of political equality and exclusion on nationalist organizing. Table 3.1 emphasizes the distinction between the six incorporated territories and the rest of the empire, but French postwar decisions produced a further division. The 1946 constitution established the French Union, which differentiated the "associated states" (the protectorates of Morocco, Tunisia, and Indochina) from the other territories of the empire.[16] Whereas assimilation was foreclosed for the associated states, the

---

[15] Quoted in Chafer (2002, 16).
[16] The French had already begun combating nationalist movements in the protectorates of Morocco, Tunisia, and Vietnam when the French Union was created; these states declined to participate in the institutions of the French Union, but remained part of it as "associated states." The former colonies, including French West Africa and French Equatorial Africa, became "territories" within the French Union. Algeria, already a department but without equal rights, was also a core part of the French Union but with a special status. Unlike the protectorates,

promise of citizenship within a federal structure was held out to the rest of the French Union. The 1946 *Loi Lamine Guèye,* named after the Senegalese delegate who sought political rights for Africans, did away with the distinction between subjects and citizens, calling all of the former colonial subjects "citizens," with rights to be specified.[17] The term was ambiguous; they were citizens but it was not clear exactly what they were citizens of (Cooper 2009, p. 101).[18] Citizenship, according to the new constitution, did not mean equality with citizens in France; it was not accompanied by proportional representation in the French National Assembly or universal suffrage.[19] Had proportional representation been the rule, representatives from the colonies would have swamped delegates from the "hexagon," as the population of the colonies outstripped the population living in France.[20]

---

all of the former colonies were understood not to have distinct national identities, but were parts of the French Republic. For an online text of the 1946 constitution, see: http://www.conseil-constitutionnel.fr/conseil-constitutionnel/francais/la-constitution/les-constitutions-de-la-france/constitution-de-1946-ive-republique.5109.html.

[17] Article 80 of the constitution that followed the law stated, "All inhabitants of the overseas territories have the quality of citizen, on the same bases as French nationals of the metropole or of the overseas territories. Specific statutes will establish the conditions under which they will exercise their rights as citizens."

[18] Person (1982) describes the law as "theoretically" extending citizenship. The populations of the associated states became "citizens of the French Union," a designation that never became clear in practice.

[19] The French Overseas Ministry claimed that "the legislature wanted to mark the perfect equality of all in public life, but not the perfect identity of the French of the metropole and the overseas French" (quoted in Cooper 2009, p. 101).

[20] Representation at the center was highly unequal for members of the French Union. Togo, for example, had a population of 972,000 in the late 1940s, but was granted only 2 deputies at the French National Assembly. Furthermore, one of these deputies was elected solely by Europeans and the "assimilated" (approximately 1,080 people). Representation in other African colonies followed a similar pattern. In contrast, Guadeloupe and Martinique, now French departments, each had 3 deputies at the French National Assembly, although their populations in 1950 were 210,000 and 222,000, respectively. The African delegates to the constitutional assembly did not necessarily see this as a problem; they did not seek "one citizen, one vote" but proposed a federal system in which each component could exercise powers over its own affairs (Cooper 2009, 100).

The newly created French Union also lacked strong federal structures. The constitution established assemblies for the Union, and these were supposed to make up for the lack of a proportional say in French assemblies, but they had few powers.[21] The individual territories also lacked strong elected executive authorities.

Although the new law did not make French Union citizens the political equals of French citizens, it had important consequences. First, the colonies had representation in the French parliament, which prompted political party formation. These parties were often tied to sister parties in France, although local parties were also created. The inclusion of African politicians in French institutions made Paris an important political arena; African delegates had a significant minority voice, which gave them some parliamentary power (Young 1994, 194). Second, the law gave the new "citizens" the right of *libre circulation*: they could migrate to and live in any part of the French Union, including France. Third, and most important for evaluating the argument here, the Loi Lamine Guèye prompted mobilization in favor of more equitable reforms across Africa (Cooper 2009, 102–103). To African leaders, the symbolic extension of citizenship was a step toward recognizing their rights and treating them as Frenchmen; they regarded it as a success (ibid.). The law encouraged demands to deepen the French commitment to equal rights for erstwhile colonial subjects and make more meaningful democratic changes.[22]

Politicians in Africa thus did not turn to nationalist mobilization in the wake of the 1946 constitution.[23] French Union citizenship

---

[21] For more on the debate in France on the French Union and Loi Lamine Guèye, see Chafer (2002); Grandhomme (2001); Lakroum (1992); Morgenthau (1964); Young (1994). African leaders pushed not just for greater individual rights, but also for more powerful federal institutions (Cooper 2009, 104). As associated states, Tunisia and Morocco declined to participate in the main federal institutions.

[22] For more on movements for equality in postwar Africa, see Cooper (2002; 2005).

[23] See Young (1994, 194–196) on the African elites elected to the parliament. He suggests that the benefits of holding these positions led African leaders to support cooperation with France while pushing for increased rights. Félix Houphouët-Boigny, the representative from the Ivory Coast, stated his opposition to nationalism when he said, "To the mystique of independence we oppose the reality of fraternity" (on 196). Ageron (1986a, 8) also maintains

led instead to demands to provide the same rights to citizens of the French Union that French citizens enjoyed. Nationalist mobilization in Africa began only a decade after the Loi Lamine Guèye passed. In 1956, France devolved authority to the individual territories and away from the federal structure. At this point, "... [I]ntellectuals turned to where others had started, the alternate path to political equality: political separation, that is, national independence. Here the demand was not that individual Africans be placed alongside individual Europeans in equal status, but that Africans as a group be equal to Europeans as a group, both being organized into sovereign nations" (Wallerstein 1961, 50).

The granting of greater autonomy in 1956 sparked discussions of nationalism and independence, but it did not mark an abrupt shift toward mobilizing for independence, as Wallerstein claims. African movements espoused a variety of aims. Politics throughout the 1950s was often about seeking institutional forms that would combine French citizenship, which Africans retained until independence in 1960, with recognition of an African national identity.[24] Some politicians favored remaining in a French federation or confederation right up until 1960; others proposed an independent African federation, and still others sought independence for their particular territory.[25] For some territories, nationalist mobilization occurred primarily after independence.

that concessions to elites blunted nationalism in Africa. One interpretation is that elites were co-opted by the French; their stake in the existing system prevented more radical demands. But this interpretation is unnecessarily simplistic; by thinking of non-nationalist goals as evidence of co-optation, we are again forced into seeing politics in the colonial world as a binary in which one is either a nationalist or a collaborator. As Maghraoui (2000, 52) notes, history has been focused almost exclusively on resistance and the rise of nationalism, neglecting those willing to work within the system. African politicians pushed a radical, non-nationalist agenda. They did not act as co-opted elites seeking merely to maintain their privileges.

[24] At independence, Africans could remain citizens if they chose to reside in France; the specific rules differed for some of the former colonies.

[25] On the respective proposals of Senghor and Houphouët-Boigny, see Cooper (2009, 104). He writes, "People tried to figure out, unsuccessfully in the end, institutional mechanisms for the expression of distinct national personalities and destinies within a greater France that remained egalitarian (ibid., 116).

The impetus that led the French to pass the Loi Lamine Guèye and extend a form of citizenship constitutes further evidence in favor of the importance of political equality. The law suggests that the French understood its significance for colonial subjects. At the Brazzaville conference in 1944, René Plevan, who presided at the conference said, "In the Great French Empire, there are neither people to liberate nor racial discrimination to abolish. There are peoples who feel French, who wish, and to whom France wishes to give, an ever greater part in the life and in the democratic institutions of the French community."[26] These rhetorical claims aimed at showing France's good faith toward the colonies. By calling the populations of the French Union citizens, the French hoped to preempt nationalism. As Overseas Minister Marius Moutet told the National Assembly in 1946, "A nation – ours in particular – will only maintain its influence over the overseas territories with the free consent of the populations that inhabit them."[27] Granting citizenship was a way to get that consent. But when the rhetoric of citizenship failed to translate into equal rights for Africans, elites began issuing nationalist demands.

This section has looked broadly across the French empire and demonstrated a correlation between political equality and the absence of nationalist movements demanding an end to French rule. This correlation rests on a comparison of places that differ from one another along multiple dimensions. The next section makes comparisons within one colonial state, presenting intra-colony evidence of the consequences of political equality and exclusion.

Subnational Evidence: Political Equality and Exclusion in Senegal

Senegal was unique among the African colonies of the French empire because the French actually implemented their stated

---

[26] Quoted in Young (1994, 183). This speech is not evidence of the absence of racism, of course, nor does it convey the true wishes of the French, but it reflects the intent to show movement toward equality.

[27] Quoted in Young (1994, 194).

policy of assimilation there, although never for the entire territory. During the French Revolution, and again after the abolition of slavery in 1848, France granted citizenship to the Four Communes – Dakar, Rufisque, Gorée, and St. Louis.[28] These communes were the oldest African territories in the empire. Citizenship was automatic and did not require naturalization. In the wake of the 1848 decree, people flocked to the cities (Johnson 1971, 78).[29] As citizens, inhabitants of the Four Communes elected municipal councils, a grand council, and a delegate to the French National Assembly.

Outside the Four Communes, the Senegalese were subjects, not citizens: they could be drafted into forced labor brigades; they lacked representative institutions; and they could be detained without charge, tried without a lawyer, and sentenced without the possibility of appeal for any number of infractions (Johnson 1971, 84; Morgenthau 1964, 127). The secretary-general for French West Africa reported that people outside the Four Communes resented the privileges of the communes (Johnson 1971, 132–133).

Most of the new citizens differed little from those in other parts of Senegal; the majority was illiterate, poor Africans (Conklin 1997, 152). Initially, Africans participated little in the political life of the communes; politics was dominated by a mixed-race French-Creole elite in St. Louis who sought the support of African voters, but saw them as children to be manipulated (Johnson 1971, 36, 102). The mayors of St. Louis and Gorée were typically Creole at the turn of the century, and the mayors of Rufisque and Dakar were typically French. Then, in 1909, Galandou Diouf – an independent African candidate from

[28] See Grandhomme (2001); Wallerstein (1961, 65). The 1889 edition of the *l'Annuaire du Sénégal* reads: "The natives born in the territory of the communes of full exercise are all French citizens" (Coquery-Vidrovitch 2001, 289). However, the law did not define citizenship (Lakroum 1992, 172). Some thought it only conveyed the right to vote; others interpreted it as full citizenship. Its meaning remained unclear until the Blaise Diagne Law in 1916.

[29] Three to five percent of the total Senegalese population were African citizens of France; in 1936 there were 78,373 African citizens in Senegal, including women and children, who could not vote (Morgenthau 1964, 128).

Rufisque – won election to a municipal council, inaugurating African participation in Senegalese politics.

The French administration in Senegal saw the extension of citizenship to the Four Communes as a mistake, the result of actions by politicians in France who knew little about Senegal. At the turn of the century, Governor General Roume warned, "The Ministry should be aware that the real power in an election for deputy in Senegal lies in the hand of the black voters, who are mostly illiterate" (in Searing 1985, 375). An inspector general sent to Senegal in 1905 argued that the electoral rights of the Four Communes were the result of "accidents" and "errors" on the part of the administration, and asked to limit citizenship to Africans considered "evolved" (ibid.) Administrators made various attempts to revoke the acquired rights.[30] Roume, for instance, wrote to the Minister of Colonies in France to ask that the municipal councils be disbanded:

[I]t seems impossible to allow Dakar and Gorée to continue to be administered by municipal assemblies elected almost entirely by native voters, the majority of whom are still primitives, incapable of understanding the serious projects of general interest which will be submitted to the municipal councils of these two localities.... If we find among the natives a few intelligent men, relatively educated, whose interests are tied to the prosperity of the colony and who are predisposed to collaborate with us, the vast majority is, on the contrary, hostile to any improvements which threaten to disturb the population's ancestral customs. It is unacceptable that the future of Dakar, on which so many hopes have been founded, can be compromised or even delayed by the ill-will or the ignorance of assemblies elected by natives, or composed in majority of natives (quoted in Searing 1985, 382).

The government in Paris refused to abolish the municipal councils, so the administration turned to the courts in 1912, seeking

---

[30] Administrators unsuccessfully attempted to convince Creole politicians that the rights of African citizens should be limited. Carpot, a Creole representative, noted that France's approach to governing Africans was to treat them as citizens each time it was a question of obligations and duties, and as subjects each time it was a question of rights and privileges (Conklin 1997, 145).

to acquire a ruling that French citizenship could only be attained by naturalization (Conklin 1997, 152).

Africans from the Four Communes reacted to these attempts to curtail their rights by becoming more politically active. Diouf organized protests to the proposed naturalization law in the Grand Council, and in 1912, the African French citizens – called *originaires* – established the Young Senegalese Party to defend their rights (Searing 1985, 387–388). This party encouraged Blaise Diagne to run for office; he became the first African deputy in 1914. Diagne – originally from Gorée – had spent most of his life outside Senegal, serving in the colonial service in Réunion, Madagascar, Guiana, and Dahomey. Diagne and other members of the Young Senegalese were impressed by the participation of blacks in local politics in Guadeloupe, Martinique, and Guiana. At a meeting in March 1914, Diagne spoke:

Friends, they want to diminish our claim to French citizenship so that in another fifteen years there will be no more voters among us. From Cape Blanco to the remotest limit of our African colonies, your fathers, your brothers, and yourselves have stood beside the French to conquer this vast domain. What kind of recompense is this for all the devotion we have shown toward France? ... I ask myself, do we really belong to a democracy? We're no longer slaves. We're French citizens with the same rights as anybody else (quoted in Johnson 1971, 162–163).

Diagne set about clarifying the legal status of the *originaires* by proposing amendments to laws governing military service. Up until 1915, only noncitizen natives were subject to military recruitment; those from the Four Communes were exempted. After his election, Diagne brought a proposal before the Chamber of Deputies to allow *originaires* into the French army. In a cable to Diouf, Diagne argued: "We must show that we are no longer inferior to our brothers in the Antilles, Guiana, and Réunion in the sense of responsibility that we bring to our patriotism.... This is a chance to prove to the many Negrophobe functionaries in French West Africa that we are truly worthy of our status as voters and French citizens" (quoted in Johnson 1971, 184). The proposed legislation would incorporate them into regular French units, not the *tirailleur* units in which noncitizen Africans served. Diagne and his supporters were insistent on this point. Although authorities in the colony were unenthusiastic (arguing that the law reinforced inequality among Africans), Diagne's oratorical skills, combined with the continued need for soldiers at a time of war, led to the law's passage.[31]

This law was followed up by one that was intended to clarify the first, and which read: "The natives of the *communes de plein exercise* of Senegal and their descendants are and remain French citizens subject to the military obligations laid down in the law of October 19, 1915"(Searing 1985, 421). This law was presented as a technical extension of the first and passed without discussion, but its language effectively settled the citizenship status of the Four Communes.

During the interwar period, the Young Senegalese continued to seek increased rights and opportunities. In the weekly newspaper *La Democratie,* they asked for more important administrative positions, better salaries, and more educational opportunities both in Senegal and France (Johnson 1971, 150–151). Colonial authorities sought to portray Diagne and the Young Senegalese as radicals who wanted Africa for the Africans, but the party's platform endorsed assimilation. In the 1919 election, Diagne's platform advocating full equality with Europeans for the *originaires* and the gradual extension of rights to the rest of the colony again led to victory (Searing 1985, 453).[32] Local French officials sought "to confine the disease to the Four Communes in order to stamp it out later ...

---

[31] The authorities were correct in asserting that the law codified inequality among French Africans. *Originaires* who joined the army received a premium of 500–800 francs, but tirailleurs received only 50 francs; pay for a corporal was 6.5 francs per day for an *originaire*, but only 1.15 for a tirailleur. *Originaires* also received better housing, family benefits, and retirement benefits (Searing 1985, 420). Note that the colonial authorities never proposed addressing the inequality between Senegalese citizens and subjects by elevating African subjects to the status of citizen; rather, they supported reducing the status of the *originaires* to that of colonial subject.

[32] Other *originaires* opposed drawing parallels between *originaires* and other Africans. Amadou Duguay Cledor speaking in the Counsel in November 1922 stated:

We have shown as much as possible a generous spirit of conciliation. But every time that you ... wish to reduce us to the same level as the new colonies, which were conquered and civilized by us or with our aid, you will create an prevent at any cost the extension of the right to vote beyond its actual limit,"[33] and ultimately Diagne quietly dropped the demand for full assimilation for all of Senegal, limiting his agenda to maintaining the communes' privileges (Searing 1985, 526).

Opponents accused him of selling out, and others took up the cause. Among them were Lamine Guèye, the first African to earn a doctorate in French law, and Galandou Diouf, who advocated full rights for Africans until his death in 1941.[34] Guèye established the Senegalese branch of the French Socialist Party in 1936. His party was antifascist, pro-women's rights, and pro-assimilation for all Senegalese, although its constituents were mainly privileged African citizens (Morgenthau 1964, 132–133).

World War II marked the end of the special status of the Four Communes. During the war, the *originaires* lost their privileges under Vichy rule. After the war, the French revisited colonial policy, and as discussed previously, Lamine Guèye drafted the law that would extend citizenship to all French colonies. In the Four Communes, reaction to the law was mixed; many supported the extension of political rights, but some regretted the loss of their special privileges (Roche 2001, 68). The Loi Lamine Guèye erased the legal distinction between the *originaires* and the rest of the

unbridgeable gap between us.... Is it for us the conquerors, the pacifiers, and the civilizers of the young colonies to submit to the rule of those who were civilized only yesterday? No! It is not going to be said that we, the elected members, the real representatives of the population, have relinquished the rights and the prerogatives of this country, which has ... a legitimate right to be part of the *grande famille française* (in Searing 1985, 515).

[33] Merlin's plan in reaction to Diagne, quoted in Searing (1985, 511).

[34] Guèye's dissertation endorsed the rights of the *originaires*. Diouf defended his principles in a letter to his son from his deathbed in 1941:

When it comes to working themselves to death for France, the blacks are good Frenchmen and good brothers. But when it is a question of granting them certain advantages enjoyed by their white brothers, we are dirty niggers [sic, in French, *sales negres*] good for nothing.... I am certain that we, the blacks, will be the last to defend the Tricolor.... Luckily, in addition to bastards of this stripe, there are good Frenchmen who think differently. I no longer want to think of those other Frenchmen, because it increases the pain in my chest. Those who live will see what comes. In any case, we are ready to disappear with the Tricolor because we are French. It is not the color of the skin that makes a good Frenchmen (quoted in Searing 1985, 472–473).

Senegalese population; ultimately it failed to include political rights equivalent to those the Four Communes held during the first half of the twentieth century.

The case of Senegal is instructive in several respects. First, those with citizenship rights did not articulate nationalist aspirations. From the initial extension of citizenship in the nineteenth century through its codification in 1916, and in the decades that followed, the dominant theme for African politicians in the Four Communes was political equality and incorporation. Blaise Diagne never spoke of independence (Johnson 1971, 213). He de-emphasized differences between Africans and Frenchmen and spoke of universal republican values. In 1936 he stated, "France, in my person, surprises the world by staying true to the principles of the Revolution of 1789. The unity of our country is above differences of skin color, so much that it stupefies with admiration or horror foreign peoples ... a lesson of high moral probity which only France is capable of giving."[35] Other proponents of assimilation likewise pointed to the potential for Africans to participate as equals. Some sought political equality for *originaires* only; others desired the extension of political rights throughout Africa. But as in Martinque and Guadeloupe, the extension of citizenship in Senegal did not produce a demand for separation, but instead prompted further mobilization for inclusion. The Senegalese reacted to French citizenship in the same way as those in the territories that were departmentalized in 1946.

Nationalist responses occurred only when political equality appeared to be threatened. When a rumor spread through Dakar in 1946 that the Loi Lamine Guèye might be reversed, unions and parties of the left organized a protest, the message of which was that if citizenship rights were revoked, immediate separation should follow (Roche 2001, 69–70). Nationalism did not spread when equitable reform seemed likely.

The Senegalese case is also important because it serves to cast doubt on an alternative argument. The French only extended citizenship to a few select populations; it is therefore possible

[35] Quoted in Young (1994, 226).

that those who were given citizenship were precisely those who were least likely to cause trouble and issue nationalist demands. According to this argument, it is not the extension of citizenship that prevents nationalist aspirations but the absence of nationalist aspirations that leads to citizenship. In Senegal, however, those with political equality were the most demanding in West Africa. Citizenship was not extended to those least likely to mobilize; the inhabitants of the Four Communes were the most politically active Africans in Senegal. The Four Communes were a thorn in the side of the colonial administration throughout the twentieth century; the administration described them as hostile troublemakers. It is difficult to believe that the *originaires* were incapable of nationalist mobilization given their active political agenda. Colonial officials saw the extension of rights as an accident of history, not a reward to a particularly compliant population. The following section discusses French decision making further, considering why some colonial populations got citizenship and others did not.

The Causes of Political Equality and Exclusion

The conqueror, by nature and by function, and whether he wishes it or not, is an aristocrat. His government, by duty and by necessity is a despotic government ... and cannot be otherwise. Democratic institutions, founded on equality and liberty, cannot be transported to the dominations, and universal suffrage, in truth, is there a monster.

– François-Jules Harmand (1910, 339–350)[36]

Very few people in the empire became the political equals of French citizens in metropolitan France. In the majority of their colonial possessions, France ultimately refused demands for political equality; subsequently, nationalist movements arose and independence followed. If the causal logic I have proposed is correct, and nationalist movements resulted from the denial of political rights, the logical question to ask is why the French refused to grant equality to the majority of their empire. Were

---

[36] Also quoted in Martin Lewis (1962, 148–149). See Lewis for more on Harmand's views; Harmand proposed association rather than assimilation.

most places denied political rights precisely because they were already on the path to nationalist mobilization, or was the denial because of other factors? What characteristics set apart the minority of places that were folded into the French Republic from the majority that were not? Were they unlikely to experience nationalist mobilization regardless of French policy?

If the French decision to grant political equality was influenced by the risk of nationalist opposition, the argument I have proposed here would have the logic backward: the success or failure of movements for political equality would have resulted from nationalist opposition, rather than causing it. To some extent, this alternative can be addressed through careful process tracing, as in the Senegalese case previously discussed. In studying the history of these movements, I have paid particular attention to timing, evaluating when the discourse shifted from the demand for political rights within the empire to calls for separation from it. Where nationalist demands became common only after the French had made their refusal clear, we can reasonably suppose the causal logic works in the direction I have proposed, as the French themselves would have had difficulty anticipating a nationalist movement where nationalist claims had not yet been articulated.

Moreover, the debates in France about colonial policy cast doubt on the idea that expectations about nationalism affected decision making. There is little to suggest that the French anticipated widespread nationalist resistance when they were discussing the extension of political rights to their colonies. Although some did argue that nationalist resistance would result if such rights were denied, fear of existing nationalism was not a factor. Indeed, the reason the French were reluctant to reject calls for equality was because they sought to reward colonial populations for their loyalty during the Second World War. There is little direct evidence that the French thought people from Martinique, Guadeloupe, New Caledonia, or the Four Communes ought to become citizens because they were unlikely to engage in nationalist revolts. Nor did French politicians state that Algerians and Africans were being denied citizenship because of the prospect of nationalist opposition.

What did affect French decision making? As I stated previously, some colonial officials thought decisions about political equality were made haphazardly by politicians in Paris with little connection to the colonies. Policymakers were influenced more by ideology and political competition in France than by conditions in the colonies. Even left-leaning parties who were more ideologically sympathetic to the plight of colonial subjects failed to provide reliable support for political equality, largely because colonial policy did not take center stage in French politics. Colonial administrators were correct in their complaints that policy was often formulated or laws passed by officials who cared little about the empire: imperial concerns were never high on the agenda. Domestic issues and conflicts within Europe were far more important to politicians in France and their constituents.[37] Still, at times, French politicians emphasized universal principles rather than nationalist ones and supported increased rights for the colonies, particularly after the two world wars, when they recognized the empire's contribution to France's defense.

Because the colonies were of minor interest to most French delegates, an informal pro-imperial faction was often able to exert a stronger influence on colonial policy than its numbers warranted (Spruyt 2005). This colonial party represented settler interests and opposed equitable reform. To take an example of settler viewpoints, Victor de Canières, the publisher of *La Tunisie Française*, insisted that equal treatment was impossible for Tunisians who were, "after all, just Arabs" and hence "a race that a depressing religion and a long atavism of laziness and fatalism have rendered manifestly inferior."[38] Settler opposition to reducing their own privileges vis-à-vis colonial subjects constituted a serious obstacle to proponents of reform; the colonial party uniformly opposed elevating the status of natives. Where settlers were a numerous minority, it was difficult to make any headway toward equality. Additionally, as de

---

[37] For more on colonial policy, see Betts (1991, 18); Cohen (1972); Keris (1953, 9); Pervillé (1991).

[38] Quoted in Perkins (2004, 66). On settlers and the use of repression in the French empire, see Lawrence (2010a).

Canières's statement suggests, prejudice and racism also affected French willingness to assimilate imperial subjects.[39]

French decisions to extend citizenship were neither random nor dictated entirely by the prejudices of the colonial lobby, however. The places where political equality was granted were systematically different from other places in the empire in two ways: they were smaller and generally had a longer history of French control than the places where political equality was denied. The size of the population was particularly crucial for the feasibility of political equality. The French overseas departments and territories (DOM-TOMs) have about 2.57 million inhabitants today, or about 4 percent of France's population. Discounting Antarctica, their landmass is about the size of Pennsylvania.

Extending citizenship to these territories was far less costly and disruptive to French political institutions than it would have been to do the same for more populous colonies.[40] The economic costs of democratizing the empire have been well documented. In the postwar era, the obligations of the French state expanded, as citizens came to expect the state to provide more welfare benefits than ever before. The potential cost of fulfilling those obligations for overseas populations as well as citizens at home was staggering. These costs were not hypothetical; in the aftermath of World War II, France abandoned the requirement that colonies should pay for themselves and began assuming the cost of some public programs. In comparison with earlier times, massive public funds were invested in France's colonies, even as France received aid under the Marshall plan.[41] Economic development became

[39] Race does not explain the variation between places with and without full citizenship, however, as the new departments were also racially and culturally different from France. Race and prejudice toward Muslims in particular may have informed the overall reluctance to treat colonial subjects as equals, however.

[40] The territories and departments that were incorporated into France remain a drain on the treasury; in 1985, social security taxes from the DOM-TOMs covered only 30 percent of what the state paid out to them (Rosenblum 1988, 10, 56). But the small size of these territories makes the burden far lighter than it would be if they were as populous as Algeria or Senegal, for instance. Brunschwig (1986, 51) states that imperial expansion made assimilation unfeasible.

[41] See Young (1994, 213–215) on the dramatic jump in public appropriations to the colonies in the postwar era, largely through the Fonds d'Investissement pour le

the new raison d'être of the empire. This willingness to expend significant funds probably increased the sense in the colonies that real citizenship was feasible. But the costs of incorporation would have dwarfed even these vastly increased outlays. Edouard Herriot famously warned in 1946 that extension of citizenship would make France "a colony of its former colonies."[42] Another statesman said:

The policy of assimilation pursued to its logical conclusion would give the overseas deputies the majority in the French parliament, because the metropole includes 43 million inhabitants against more than 50 million in the external territories. This would only be acceptable if the 50 million ex-colonial natives were truly assimilated, if their mentality had become as close to that of a metropolitan French man as an Aubergnat or a Provençal. If not, the French could never accept being governed by the deputies of their old colonies (Duverger, quoted in Yacono 1971, 75).

If overseas deputies constituted the majority in parliament, they would have been able to redistribute resources away from metropolitan France to its colonies.[43]

Government leaders spoke of these costs to justify the 1956 decision to amend the postwar assimilation policy. One speaker at the national assembly stated:

When you speak of assimilation to our compatriots in the overseas territories, they understand it, first and foremost, as economic and social assimilation in regard to standard of living. And if you say to them that France wants to realize assimilation overseas, they reply: Well, give us immediately equality in wages, equality in labor legislation, in social

---

Développment Economique et Social. See also Chafer (2002), particularly chapter 2. The French did not justify their empire on economic grounds the way that the British did; French colonies were not known for being lucrative or resource rich, but were largely seen as strategic assets contributing to France's power projection capabilities.

[42] Another well-known saying about the costs of overseas governance was uttered in the French National Assembly much earlier, in 1889: "Il y a deux choses dans la politique coloniale: d'abord la joie des conquêtes et ensuite la carte à payer!" (There are two things in colonial policy: first the joy of conquest and then the bill to pay!") quoted in Ansprenger 1989, 16).

[43] See Acemoglu and Robinson (2006) and Boix (2003) on how inequality impedes democratization.

security benefits, equality in family allowances, in brief, equality in standard of living (quoted in Cooper 2005, 228).

The French thus worried that making concessions to demands for equality would embolden social movements in the empire and lead them to increase their demands. Africans, as Wallerstein (1961, 48) puts it, "came to demand equality, and equality not only in the political arena but in all aspects of life: economic equality, educational equality, religious equality, cultural equality," although political equality was the core demand. Because the standard of living in the colonies was vastly inferior to the standard of living in France, economic and social assimilation would have been incredibly expensive. As Cooper (2005, 228) states, the French government could not shoulder the burden of an "empire of citizens." By granting reforms only to the smallest pieces of the empire, the French avoided the economic and political upheaval that would have accompanied a general policy of democratizing the empire.

The length of time under French control is another potential determinant of political equality, but the overlap is imperfect. Parts of Senegal had been under French control since the early seventeenth century – just as Guiana, Martinique, and Guadeloupe were – but Senegal did not become a French department. Algeria was conquered before the French gained New Caledonia and French Polynesia, but Algerians were not made full citizens. Size better differentiates those places that gained political equality from those that did not, but the timing of conquest is also potentially important, largely because the policy of assimilation was taken more seriously early in the colonial era. Many of the places that were ultimately granted citizenship had had rights extended early on, making them more likely to achieve equality in later years.

Additionally, and more speculatively, it may be that the longer the French held a territory, the more likely they were to see it as an integral part of France and therefore to treat its inhabitants as Frenchmen. Prior to the twentieth century, Frenchmen appeared better able to imagine a multiethnic political community whose boundaries exceeded those of mainland France. Over time, as elsewhere, the contours of national identity became more rigid. Thus, it may have been that French national identity restricted the extension of citizenship, rather than national identity in the colonial territories.

Political equality for the empire thus turned out to be exceedingly difficult to bring about. It would have exhausted France's resources, broken France's own fragile domestic social and political compact, and required the French to think differently about race, religion, and their own national identity. Proponents of equality understood that the obstacles were immense and offered proposals that would mitigate them. African leaders proposed federal arrangements that would limit the electoral impact of African voters at the center, thereby addressing fears that incorporation would necessitate redistribution. In other cases, political equality was proposed only for segments of a population. The Blum-Violette Bill was one such proposal; it would have incorporated a small number of Algerians, much as the citizenship in Senegal was extended to four locales rather than the entire territory. Political equality thus could have been extended in more cases than it was, or it could have been extended in different cases. It was not inevitable that political equality would succeed only in the cases where it did succeed. France could have chosen (and nearly did choose) to be more egalitarian or establish institutional rules that would reduce the costs to the center.

What is noteworthy is that the impediments to political equality originated in France. It was not the nationalism of the colonial population that stood in the way – they were willing to embrace political equality. It was the French who did not offer it.

Alternative Arguments: Assessing Omitted Variables

The size and age of colonial territories were thus the main determinants of the success or failure of movements for political equality. The relationship between the size and age of a territory and the outcome of demands for political equality is only relevant for the argument here if these factors have an independent effect on nationalist mobilization. If smaller, older French territories were less apt to experience nationalist movements in general, then size or age may explain both the decision to grant political equality and the absence of nationalist mobilization. Next, I consider whether small size or an early date of colonization might directly impede nationalist organizing. Then, I evaluate whether modernization might be the omitted variable that accounts for both nationalist organizing and decisions about political equality.

Size, Age, and Nationalist Mobilization

One possibility is that national independence was less appealing to older, smaller possessions because they were economically and strategically dependent on France. Smaller places in particular may have relied heavily on French trade and security guarantees. This argument, however, does not explain the distribution of nationalist movements, because other territories in the empire were similarly dependent on France. Colonies in French Africa continued to require economic aid from France after independence. They did not have the resources to fund effective national defense forces, and they relied on French security guarantees, permitting French bases well beyond independence.[44] Dependency was not incompatible with sovereignty, and the French could and did provide resources even after their colonies became independent states. There is no reason why small, dependent islands could not ask for independence along with security and aid guarantees.

Moreover, in general, smaller places appear at least as likely as larger places to experience nationalist mobilization. A classic argument from the collective action literature is that mobilization is easier for smaller groups than larger ones (Olson 1971), suggesting that nationalist mobilization ought to be easier to achieve among small populations than large ones. In addition, there are multiple examples of nationalist movements that claim small portions of territories within existing states. Nationalist

---

[44] On France's polices in Africa postindependence, see Domergue-Cloarec (1995) and Gueriviere (2001), chapter 4.

movements in places such as Bougainville Island, Catalonia, the Comoros Islands, Haiti, Northern Ireland, and the Western Sahara suggest that size does not prevent nationalist organizing. Small size, although consequential for the decision to grant political equality, does not foreclose nationalism.

The length of time under colonial rule might have an independent effect on nationalist mobilization if a longer history of French rule resulted in populations with a weaker sense of identification with their own territory. However, the people of Martinique, New Caledonia, and Guadeloupe continue to articulate a sense of cultural distinctiveness. Ethnic and religious differences distinguished the DOM-TOMs from metropolitan France, and provided a potential platform for nationalist organizing during the era of decolonization, but nationalist claims were not common. Moreover, a long history of French rule did not prevent Algerians from developing a sense of national identity and engaging in a long battle for national independence, despite debates over whether Algeria counted as a nation.[45]

Ruling out all alternative pathways whereby size and duration of colonial rule might exert an independent effect on nationalist mobilization is difficult. There is no way to be sure that nothing about these characteristics mattered. The intra-colony analysis provides an important check; people with equal status in Senegal, like those in the smaller islands, also did not turn to nationalism, but instead sought the extension of equality. The impact of these factors on nationalism appears to work indirectly, via their effects on French decisions about political equality.

Modernization and Nationalist Mobilization

Another alternative argument to my own is that smaller possessions may also have been less modern, and that is why they did not turn to nationalism. Modernization, as Chapter 1 discussed, has been thought to facilitate nationalism. If modernization is also systematically associated with the granting of political

---

[45] Ferhat Abbas famously claimed that he had looked for an Algerian nation, but not found it. See Horne (1977, 40–41).

equality, the apparent relationship between political equality and nationalism may be spurious: less modern places might have been simultaneously more likely to be incorporated by France and less likely to experience nationalist opposition.[46]

One way to assess this hypothesis is to compare relative levels of modernization across the empire. Finding reliable indicators of the extent to which a territory could be considered modern, however, is notoriously difficult for this time period. Large-N cross-national work that uses income, one indicator of modernization, has relied on measuring gross domestic product (GDP) per capita after independence or extrapolating from known neighboring cases.[47] Measurement error is probable, because a territory's actual GDP per capita may be quite different from neighboring states or what it would be in the postwar world. Looking only at French cases provides an advantage, as the French collected data that allows comparisons across the empire. Specifically, in censuses carried out after World War II, the French enumerated the population living in towns of greater than 20,000 people.[48] These measures provide a fairly reliable indicator of urbanization, a phenomenon closely linked to modernization. I calculated the percentage of the total population living in these towns to gain a measure of overall urbanization for each territory.

Urbanization does not differentiate the cases that were granted political equality from those that were not. In fact, the incorporated cases are split right down the middle. Martinique, Réunion, and Guadeloupe were among the most modern territories, with 25 percent, 44 percent, and 15 percent of their populations living in towns and cities, respectively. From their

---

[46] It is difficult to see, however, why the French would choose to incorporate the least modern colonies.

[47] For cross-national work that includes measures of modernization for colonial territories, see Boix (2003); Boix and Stokes (2003); Fearon and Laitin (2003).

[48] The data for this analysis was found in the *Annuaire Statistique de l'Union Française Outre-Mer, 1939–1949*. Paris: Imprimerie Nationale de France. Ministere de la France d'Outre-Mer and Ministere des Finances et des Affaires Economiques, CAOM. These figures exclude Lebanon and Syria, which became independent after the war.

level of modernization, these places might be expected to be *more* nationalist than other parts of the empire, not less. New Caledonia, Guiana, and Polynesia, in contrast, are among the least urban, with virtually no large towns, but they, too, were granted political equality. Moreover, some of the places that were denied political equality had significant urban populations: Tunisia and Morocco at 20 percent urban, Senegal at 17 percent, and Middle Congo and Algeria at 15 percent. Modernization, measured using urbanization, does not explain which cases were incorporated by the French.

Nor is there an evident relationship between urbanization and nationalist organizing in the empire. Using the decade in which the first public demonstrations in favor of independence occurred, I considered whether more urbanized places experienced nationalist mobilization earlier than less urbanized places. Table 3.2 shows the average percentage of the population living in towns greater than 20,000 for the cases that experienced an onset in nationalist mobilization in each decade. The places where nationalist mobilization erupted in the 1930s were, on average, more urbanized, but the places that did not see nationalist mobilization until beyond the 1960s (or not at all) were also quite urbanized. Such a test is rough, however. For one thing, urbanization is measured for some cases after mobilization had already begun.[49]

Table 3.2 collapses variation among cases that mobilized in the same decade. In the 1930s, both Vietnam and Tunisia saw nationalist mobilization: 20 percent of Tunisia's population lived in towns and cities, whereas only 7 percent of Vietnam's population did. During World War II, Cambodia and Laos experienced nationalist mobilization despite the absence of large towns. After World War II, mass protests began in Morocco and Madagascar; their respective rates of urbanization were 20 and 6 percent. At the close of the 1950s, nationalist mobilization began in many of France's African colonies. Among these colonies, the majority

---

[49] To the extent that levels of urbanization are *relatively* similar in the 1930s, the 1940s measure remains useful for the purposes of comparing cases.

TABLE 3.2. *Nationalist Mobilization and Urbanization*

Onset of Nationalist Mobilization	Average percentage of population living in towns > 20,000
1930s	14%
1940s	8%
1950s	4%
After 1960s or no onset	10%

had low levels of urbanization, but there were some with fairly large shares of town dwellers, as Table 3.3 shows. Yet nationalist mobilization began in these territories around the same time – as independence approached – with the exception of Cameroon and Togo as well as Madagascar, which had some mobilization earlier on (Wallerstein 1961, 72–73).

Urbanization is not a good predictor of the order of nationalist mobilization in the French empire, nor does it appear to correlate with the refusal or granting of political equality. The relationship between modernization and nationalist mobilization can be very difficult to untangle at the cross-colony level, however, because French territories differed from each other along multiple dimensions. Chapter 5 looks at the impact of modernization on nationalist organizing by comparing different regions of Morocco. This subnational analysis provides further evidence that nationalist mobilization occurred even in places that were underdeveloped.

Relative levels of development across the empire may not be the relevant comparison. Instead, it may be the general difference between France and the empire. France was more modern than all of its possessions: its population was richer, more developed, and better educated. These differences were precisely the reasons given to oppose the extension of French citizenship; ultimately, the French incorporated the places that would cost the least. Overall, low levels of modernization mattered because they made political equality uniformly difficult to offer to colonial territories.

It is also likely that a degree of modernization is important for contentious politics in other ways. More modern places may be more likely to see greater numbers of people participating

TABLE 3.3. *Urbanization in African Colonies, 1940s*

Territory	Percent living in towns > 20,000
Gabon	0%
Mauretania	0%
Niger	0%
Chad	1.0%
Guinea	1.7%
Upper Volta (Burkina Faso)	1.9%
French Sudan (Mali)	2.6%
Togo	3.1%
Ivory Coast	3.3%
Dahomey	3.5%
Ubanghi-Shari (Central African Republic)	3.8%
Cameroon	4.2%
Madagascar	6.2%
Middle Congo (People's Republic of Congo)	15.4%
Senegal	16.6%

in politics in general. In addition, people in more economically developed societies may have an easier time organizing any kind of opposition, nationalist or reformist. Modernization may thus facilitate multiple types of mobilization, not just nationalism.

These cases also point to a general insight about the relationship between modernization and political activism: opposition is not foreclosed to societies at a low level of economic development. Opposition to colonial rule was widespread in the empire in a variety of forms. It occurred in some of the least urban cases, such as Ivory Coast, Guinea, and Cambodia. Politics was not absent anywhere in the empire.

Conclusion

Disentangling the relationship between movements for political equality and nationalist movements for independence is empirically challenging. I have drawn on the available evidence to make my case, but ultimately, any assertion about how colonial subjects might have behaved in alternate circumstances is subject to a degree of uncertainty. Although the evidence for my argument is imperfect, the evidence for the teleological view that movements for political equality are in fact evidence of "proto-nationalism" or "early nationalism," leading inexorably to nationalist movements for independence, is far more problematic. To rehabilitate this view, we would need to believe that those who gained political equality differed from those who were denied political equality. In this view, we cannot extrapolate from cases such as the Four Communes, Martinique, or Guadeloupe, because Algerians, Moroccans, and other Africans would have reacted differently had they been granted political equality. This possibility cannot be ruled out entirely, but it requires a theory about why we should expect political behavior to have varied among populations that are all ethnically and racially different from the French. Absent such a theory, we should be skeptical about this claim.

This chapter has argued that nationalist mobilization in the French empire occurred only after calls for political equality went unheeded. If political equality had been granted, political activists might never have advocated ejecting colonial rulers and establishing independent states. My argument suggests the need to consider the mobilizing power of ideologies other than nationalism, even in the context of foreign rule. Political activists in the French empire were able to imagine a variety of futures: as full French citizens; as autonomous members of a French community; and as independent states. With the benefit of hindsight, it is tempting to dismiss alternatives to independence as irrelevant and impossible. But doing so would be erroneous for three reasons.

First, one risks projecting certainty into an uncertain past. As Cooper points out, (2009, 92) "The spectrum of political possibility in the past was wider than people in the present – projecting backward their own positions – allow it to be." Political leaders across the colonial world did not know what we know today: that political equality would be denied to the majority of the empire. They took the prospect of political equality seriously, and they had good reasons to do so. Political equality seemed feasible at various points in time because of the politics of the metropole: in 1848, when slavery was abolished; in the mid-1930s, when the Popular Front was in power; and after World War II, when France revised its colonial relationships in the new constitution of the Fourth Republic and began pouring resources into the colonies. It was not only politicians who supported political equality; public opinion polls taken after World War II show that a majority of the French public favored treating colonial subjects as equals.[50]

Second, political equality cannot accurately be called infeasible, despite the obstacles outlined here, because it happened in some places. The granting of equality on a small scale contributed to the sense that it was a viable way to dismantle empire. Algerians and Africans saw Guadeloupe, Martinique, and the *originaires* in Senegal as examples of what might be. They invoked cases from outside the empire as possible models, as well: the British Commonwealth and the Austro-Hungarian empire, and the federal systems of the United States and Soviet Union. Africans made significant progress toward political equality themselves. The Loi Lamine Guèye established important democratic rights that provided a basis to pursue further equitable reforms. The law demonstrates that partial successes were possible. Although the promise of citizenship never led to equality with French citizens, activists achieved significant change. Political equality was not an impossible, all-or-nothing goal.

Third, thinking through the consequence of political equality and exclusion matters theoretically, even if the world provides many more cases of exclusion. Scholars need to consider the potential importance of political participation and equal

[50] A poll carried out in March 1948 found that 63 percent of French metropolitan citizens were in favor of "granting to the populations of the colonies the same rights as French citizens" (Ageron 1986b, 35). French respondents also seemed to know and care little about the politics of the empire, although they supported having one (ibid., 36–40).

treatment for alleviating conflict across deep cleavages. Political equality is typically overlooked on the grounds that it would be unacceptable to populations who differ from the politically dominant with respect to ethnicity, nationality, or religion, but as this analysis suggests, the problem may lie more with what the privileged are willing to offer than with what the less privileged are willing to accept. A more accurate understanding of the impediments to remedying inequalities within and between states can point to the underlying causes of ethnic and nationalist conflict.

Another reason that movements for political equality have been overlooked stems from distaste for the concept of assimilation, which is often taken to imply identity change. Opponents of assimilation decried the move to turn Africans into Frenchmen, with all that this transformation might imply. But the discourse of assimilation advanced by colonized subjects did not necessarily reflect a desire to change their own identity. Instead, activists were in effect suggesting a change in what it meant to be a French citizen. They advocated a French identity on the basis of shared principles, not on ethnic or cultural homogeneity.[51] The proponents of negritude exemplify this approach: they envisioned a shared political identity that would not require abandoning African cultural heritage. In so doing, they proposed a way to reconcile national differences with a shared commitment to political equality. Ultimately, it was the French who proved incapable of enacting an inclusive, multicultural republic.

Where calls for political equality went unheeded, discussions of independence became increasingly prevalent, but the shift to a new idiom is only part of the story. The desire for national independence cannot automatically produce active mobilization, particularly under authoritarian rule. The argument advanced in this chapter does not account for timing.

---

[51] French leaders considering assimilation, however, often thought identity change would be required. See Martin Lewis (1962, 133–136) for early debates on assimilation, association, and repression.

The absence of political equality was not a proximate trigger for nationalist mobilization. A full account of the causes of nationalist mobilization requires that we consider both motive and opportunity. Chapter 4 examines the eruption of nationalist movements seeking independence, identifying the openings that provided opportunities for nationalist activities and events.

4

Empire Disrupted

Nationalist Opposition Accelerates

"Revolutions are not made; they come"
— Wendell Phillips, 1852

France's failure to meet aspirations for political equality did not immediately bring about nationalist protests. The very fact that the French felt they could reject reformists' proposals suggests their confidence in their hold over the empire. As French settlers implied during the debates over reform, there was little reason to expect that French colonial rule could not continue on as it had before, policing opposition and repressing regime critics. The status quo did not appear unsustainable, and few anticipated widespread mobilization in advance. When nationalist protests occurred, they often arose suddenly. What were the triggers of mass nationalist action? What prompted people to take to the streets to demand an end to French rule and independence for their nations?

This chapter argues that nationalist protests in the French empire were prompted by *disruptions in imperial authority* at the level of the colonial territory. The imperial power's control could be disrupted by the invasion and occupation of the territory or by the very decision to grant autonomy or decolonize. These events produced a situation in which France's authority over a given territory was either partial or nonexistent and provided openings for political opponents to stage nationalist demonstrations.

This argument addresses variation in the timing and location of nationalist protest. It accounts for the sporadic, and often unexpected, outbreak of nationalist activity in the twentieth-century French empire. Further, it provides a counterargument to the claim that nationalist mobilization produced disorder and imperial collapse. The causal relationship was not so straightforward; in many instances, imperial authority had already been disrupted by the time mass protests peaked. Street demonstrations demanding an end to colonial rule then weakened the imperial power further. In these circumstances, France had two options: attempt to reestablish control or let the territory go.

The chapter is divided into four main parts. In the first part, I draw on the collective action literature to develop my argument. In the second and third parts I evaluate this argument by examining nationalist mobilization across the empire at two moments in time. The second part looks at the state of nationalist organizing in the interwar period. The third part examines the eruption of nationalist mobilization during World War II. Many scholars believe that France's defeat in 1940 was one of the major triggers of nationalist mobilization in the French territories. However, the war affected France's overseas possessions in different ways. I show that a focus on the war's effects within individual colonies and territories helps explain when and where nationalist movements began engaging in active opposition. The fourth part describes the onset of nationalist mobilization in two cases: Vietnam and French West Africa. Whereas Vietnam is the case that most clearly demonstrates the impact of a disruptive invasion on nationalist organizing, the evidence from French West Africa is more ambiguous and nuanced. But both cases show the consequences of continuity versus change in colonial authority for nationalist organizing.

Imperial Authority Disrupted: Opportunities for Action

Studies of social movements and collective action have addressed mobilization in a wide variety of settings, from protest movements in favor of civil rights to revolutions. Since the late 1970s, social movement scholars have asserted the importance of political opportunities for the emergence of collective action. McAdam et al. (1996, 8) synthesize nearly two decades of political opportunity theory affirming that "most political movements and revolutions are set in motion by social changes that render the established political order more vulnerable or receptive to challenge."

But what kinds of changes constitute political opportunities, and how can they be identified and measured? The difficulty is to find a way to measure opportunities ex ante, without simply looking back from a mobilization event and seizing on an apparent opportunity that preceded it. The key challenge is not just to identify opportunities, but to say where and when they do *not* exist. In response to concerns that the concept of political opportunity lacks conceptual precision, McAdam et al. (1996, 10) lay out four dimensions that indicate whether or not a political opportunity exists: the relative openness of the institutionalized political system; the stability of elite alignments; the presence or absence of elite allies; and the state's repressive capacities.[1] These four dimensions are made fairly general in order to accommodate diverse contexts, but they do little to advance conceptual clarity. The dimensions are challenging to measure, they are potentially endogenous to political mobilization itself, and the relative importance of each dimension is unknown. How crucial is it for elites to have allies? With whom must they ally for their movement to succeed? How open does the political system need to be to allow political mobilization? How repressive must a state be to prevent mobilization? The indicators designed for measuring political opportunities seem nearly as difficult to conceptualize and measure as the concept itself.

Further theorizing has continued to muddy the conceptual waters. In the same volume, McAdam et al. (1996, 8), suggest that

---

[1] This discussion draws on Lawrence (2010b, 97-98). McAdam (1994) further identifies four types of "expanding cultural opportunities" that increase movement activity: 1) the dramatization of a glaring contradiction between a highly salient value and conventional social practices; 2) suddenly imposed grievances; 3) dramatizations of a system's vulnerability or illegitimacy; and 4) the availability of a "master frame" for demands and grievances.

opportunities cannot be measured solely by analyzing structural factors, because perceptions of opportunities are also important: "No matter how momentous a change appears in retrospect, it only becomes an 'opportunity' when defined as such by a group of actors sufficiently well organized to act on this shared definition of the situation." This statement suggests that an opportunity for mobilization can only be judged an opportunity when groups have seized upon it and declared it to be the moment for action, implying that political opportunities for mobilization are defined by whether or not mobilization follows the opportunity. In their more recent work on contentious politics, McAdam et al. (2001, 45) reaffirm their contention that opportunities are not objective categories – an intuitive idea, but difficult to operationalize.

The problems of theorizing political opportunities have been pointed out by Gamson and Meyer (1996, 275):

> The concept of a political opportunity structure is in trouble, in danger of becoming a sponge that soaks up virtually every aspect of the social movement environment – political institutions and culture, crises of various sorts, political alliances, and policy shifts…. It threatens to become an all-encompassing fudge factor for all the conditions and circumstances that form the context for collective action. Used to explain so much, it may ultimately explain nothing at all.

Despite this criticism, political opportunity models have provided important insights into how the larger political context affects the likelihood of collective mobilization, and historical studies have identified specific changes that made it easier for political entrepreneurs to mobilize.[2] The insights of the political opportunity literature have been particularly important for theorists seeking to explain mobilization under authoritarian rule, where political opposition is difficult to mount.

The literature suggests the need to specify political opportunities precisely, so that their causal impact can be systematically investigated. Next I identify a particular kind of political opportunity,

---

[2] For recent examples, see Yashar (2005), who points to the importance of political associational space for providing opportunities for indigenous organizing in Latin America; see also the revolutions literature (Goodwin 2001; Kuran 1991; Skocpol 1979).

one that is easier to identify and measure ex ante than the broader concept of political opportunity: disruption in imperial authority.

Disruptions in Imperial Authority

Colonial powers ruled over distant territories for long stretches of time; periods of opposition alternated with periods of compliance. What prompted mobilization in some periods and not others?

I argue that public demonstrations in favor of national independence typically began when imperial authority within a given territory was disrupted. A disruption in imperial authority occurs when the colonial power's ability to govern and control the territory in question is seriously impaired. Specifically, the colonial power's authority was severely compromised when it was no longer the sole authority in the territory but shared control with another powerful actor or actors. Disruptions occurred only in a limited number of situations. International war was an important source of disruptions. Specifically, when a colonial territory was invaded and occupied by another state, the colonial power's authority was dramatically disrupted. Invasion compromised the sovereignty of a territory; the colonial power no longer had full administrative or military control. Another major cause of disruption stemmed from the colonial power's own decision to devolve authority over the administrative apparatus of the state to local leaders. It then no longer had full control over the territory, but shared power with local authorities. This voluntary ceding of colonial power often initiated a period of transition to autonomy or independence and marked a disruption in the colonial power's authority.

These disruptions have different origins: invasion and occupation is an unwanted, abrupt disruption to colonial rule, whereas autonomy or independence is a deliberate decision to cede power and is hence potentially less abrupt or disruptive.[3] Whether both types of disruption have a similar effect on nationalist organiz-

---

[3] Decisions to grant autonomy or decolonize could be quite abrupt, however, and were often not voluntary from the point of view of colonial administrators and settlers who resisted ceding power.

ing is an empirical question. I contend that both types created opportunities for nationalist mobilization.

There are several reasons why we might expect such disruptions to be consequential for nationalist mobilization. First, a disruption of imperial authority signals to colonial subjects that the likelihood of independence has increased. In an international context of declining imperial legitimacy, a reduction in the colonial power's authority suggests that the end of its rule may be in sight or at least plausibly attainable. The belief that the probability of independence has risen provides an incentive for participation in nationalist demonstrations: people prefer to join a movement that has a better chance of success. Further, they might estimate that the risks of participation have decreased, and they may join as they see others joining, producing a cascade effect.[4]

Second, discontinuity in imperial authority reduces the benefit of allying with colonial rulers. Where these rulers no longer controlled the territory, they had little to offer their collaborators. No longer assured of the benefits of cooperation, allies may switch sides and join the nationalists. Side-switching of regime intermediaries who assisted in governing the state made imperial authority appear even more precarious, and produced new movement leaders and participants.

Third, the disruption of imperial authority can reduce the colonial power's ability to closely monitor and police nationalist activity, leaving leaders freer to mobilize the population. It is

---

[4] These microfoundations resemble those of Kuran (1991), who posits that Gorbachev's reforms provided an opening for revolution in Eastern Europe; participation cascaded as the individual costs went down. Note, however, that Kuran assumes people had a private preference for regime change that they hid when the cost of mobilization was high. I am agnostic on this point; protest participants may have wanted independence and waited for an opportune moment, as Kuran argues, but preferences can also change as events unfold. For instance, those who are initially politically indifferent may participate because others are doing so and they wish to share the moment. They may become committed nationalists in the course of mobilizing. There is evidence that preferences may change after mobilization has begun; even those who previously supported the French regime sometimes changed their views as mobilization was underway. Nationalist mobilization may not solely reflect previously held commitments, but may also itself affect public opinion.

important not to overstate the effects of disruption on the colonial power's repressive capacities, however. A disruption does not necessarily decrease the use of repression. Even when the French cut their forces or willingly granted autonomy, they often retained significant coercive capabilities. But their reduced position could result in less discriminating repression, which may have increased the desire for independence and further motivated participation.

Finally, disruptions in imperial authority create conditions of uncertainty and insecurity, which can lead people to identify more strongly with the nation. Historian James Gelvin (1998, 12) suggests that periods of crisis "may effect a temporary reification of the boundaries separating self-ascribed national subjects from an external 'other' and induce those subjects to privilege the bonds of nation over other attachments." Wedeen (2003, 702–703) argues similarly that "experiences of collective vulnerability" in Yemen prompted people to make appeals to the "nation" and the "people," articulating idioms of collective attachment and communal solidarity in public. In the French empire, the experience of disrupted imperial authority, combined with the prior failure to achieve equitable reforms, led people to demonstrate their commitment to the nation at a moment when the future seemed highly uncertain.

In sum, I posit that disruptions in imperial authority prompt participation in nationalist action via four mechanisms: disruptions (1) create the perception that independence is more likely than it was under stable imperial rule; (2) reduce the benefits of collaborating; (3) decrease the policing capacity of the state; and (4) produce uncertainty that prompts identification with the nation. Taken cumulatively, these effects of disruption make nationalist mobilization more appealing and less dangerous than it is when the imperial authority's control is secure.

In the French empire, nationalist leaders seized on these moments of instability to mobilize opposition and channel participants into nationalist activities.[5] They used the means of communication they had available to funnel supporters into active

---

[5] Laitin (2001) posits similar mechanisms to explain ethnic conflict in Eurasia following the collapse of Communism.

participation, announcing events via radio, newspaper, and word of mouth – organizations even sent out scouts and messengers to get the word out about upcoming demonstrations.

These causal mechanisms provide a general explanation for the timing of mobilization, but they do not constitute a microlevel model of decision making aimed at explaining how an individual decides to attend a rally, boycott French products, or storm the French Residency. In the subnational study of Morocco in Chapter 5, I show that disruptions in imperial authority affected nationalist mobilization in the ways I suggest here. But even there, I do not directly develop and test a model of individual participation. This omission is only partly due to the absence of individual-level survey data on political beliefs during the colonial period, although that is certainly an obstacle. My goal is different: to understand when and where some individuals will be prompted to heed the call to action by identifying the triggers that provide opportunities for collective action. This approach allows for a variety of possible motivational microfoundations. Individuals may have multiple motivations for participating, and their motivations may change over time.[6] They may have varying degrees of commitment to the nationalist cause; they may be part of networks that are mobilized; or they may respond to selective incentives or personal goals. Nationalist movements, like most social movements, only turn out a fraction of the underlying

---

[6] One Moroccan nationalist gave several reasons for his decision to join a violent nationalist group at the end of the colonial period: fear, as a neighbor had issued a threat if he did not join; hatred of French policy in Morocco; and camaraderie, because his brother and close school friends were in the same resistance cell. There is no reason to suspect that any one of these motivations represents his uniquely true motivation; motivations can be multiple (Abderrahim Ouardighi, Interview with author, May 16, 2006, Rabat). Recognizing a multiplicity of motivations may help scholars put aside the debate over whether participants in collective action are motivated by self-interest, variously defined, or by emotions or selfless impulses. The debate is often framed as one in which these two categories are mutually exclusive: motives are either rational or not. Studies that examine how actors can be simultaneously or consecutively motivated by rational and nonrational impulses or how self-interested motives and selfless motives can be endogenous to one another may make some headway in demonstrating the kinds of motivations that affect individual choices to mobilize.

population for protest events. The story of how individuals are brought into nationalist movements is a different one.[7]

Disruptions in Imperial Rule and State Weakness

The argument advanced here builds on prior work in the collective action tradition focusing on changes at the level of the state that produce an opportunity for mobilization. Other scholars have looked at the consequences of state weakness or crises for mobilization. Some have argued that state weakness leads to civil conflict. Fearon and Laitin (2003a) find a relationship between reduced state capacity and civil war. One problem with focusing on state capacity and weakness is that it is easy to define weakness so broadly that nearly everything that might make opposition more likely counts as a weakness. State capacity can thus be as problematic a concept as political opportunity.[8] For Fearon and Laitin, state capacity is a continuous variable (proxied by GDP per capita), whereas I provide a more restricted definition, one that captures only major discontinuities in state control over time.[9] Focusing on disruptions sets up a hard test for the theory; mobilization is expected to occur only in moments of extreme weakness, when the state no longer has full control over the territory. By specifying a narrow set of circumstances that constitute an opportunity for action, my intention is to produce clear observable implications.

The importance of state crises has been emphasized in work on revolutions. Skocpol (1979) argued that social revolutions are triggered by political crises that weaken state control and reduce the state's capacity for repression. Goldstone (1991) outlines three components of state crisis: fiscal strain; elite conflict;

---

[7] For examples of work that provides a microlevel account of mobilization, see Gould (1991); Petersen (1993).

[8] On state capacity, see Kocher (2010).

[9] Using a general measure such as GDP to measure state weakness may also mean that short periods of state crisis are not captured by the independent variable because periods of state instability may have a variable affect on GDP, depending on the structure of the economy. For more on the inability of GDP per capita measures to account for temporal variation, see Lawrence (2010b).

and popular revolt. He sees population growth as a key driver for all three components, whereas for Skocpol, military strain is the primary cause of fiscal crisis. Collins (1999) adds that state breakdown can also come from defeat in war.

Skocpol and her successors challenged a literature in which revolutions were explained primarily by class divisions. Although class conflict remained important to Skocpol, she posited a state-based account of revolution. Explanations for conflict that focus on class have since declined in popularity, but many of the claims that used to be made about class are now made about nationalism. Nationalism is understood to motivate opposition to the state, particularly in situations of foreign rule. In studies of the colonial world, nationalist mobilization is frequently depicted as a cause of state crisis, not a result of it. I suggest here that the stability of the state also matters for nationalist organizing, extending the argument from the revolutions literature to a different set of circumstances.

I also provide several innovations. The first is conceptual: I disentangle revolt from revolution. The dependent variable in studies of revolution requires not only mobilization of at least some factions or groups in society, but also the destruction of the regime (and potentially the reorganization of society, if the dependent variable is social revolution). Less attention is paid to conditions that produce regime opposition that fails to topple the state.[10] The concept of revolution thus conflates the process with the outcome. By investigating mobilization, I set aside the question of whether or not the aims of mobilization are achieved. Instead, I focus on how the process gets underway. My outcome is why nationalist action occurs, not whether independence results. These are different issues; the causes of state collapse may be quite different from the conditions that promote mobilization against the state, and mobilization does not always (or even

[10] This issue is different from that of selecting on the dependent variable by examining only cases of revolution. Goldstone addresses this problem by looking at periods without revolution. But both Skocpol and Goldstone define revolution according to the outcome, and thus do not consider how their arguments relate more generally to the production of anti-regime mobilization.

often) result in a revolutionary outcome. Conflating nationalist mobilization with the attainment of independence in the colonial world would be a mistake, because nationalist movements encountered serious opposition and endured repeated failures prior to independence. Further, other factors besides nationalism led rulers to decolonize (Spruyt 2005).

In addition, I unravel the relationship between mobilization and crises in state authority by paying close attention to sequence. In the revolutions literature, the relationship between popular revolt, elite crisis, and state crisis is unclear: popular revolts and elite crises seem to both prompt state crises and result from them. Here, I consider the effects of crises in imperial authority that are exogenous to popular revolt. I then trace the onset of mobilization and the further consequences for imperial authority.

The remainder of this chapter looks at how well the evidence from the history of the French colonial empire supports my argument. I employ two strategies to weigh my argument against the dominant explanations for nationalist mobilization in the French empire. First, I examine two time periods: the early 1920s and World War II. Each time period provides a snapshot of the state of politics in the empire. For both periods, I look at the state of imperial authority across the empire, and study the downstream effects on nationalist mobilization. I hypothesize that in places where imperial authority is disrupted, we should observe active participation in nationalist movements. I selected these time periods because they provide variation on the independent variable: at these times, we see some places where colonial authority is in crisis. Next, I focus on two colonial territories: Vietnam and French West Africa. Vietnam experienced a lot of nationalist mobilization, including a war of national liberation, whereas French West Africa saw only a little nationalist mobilization, mostly at the end of the colonial period. I study the conditions that facilitated nationalist action in each case.[11] Chapter 5 considers the case of Morocco, employing a subnational research design to study nationalist protest over time.

---

[11] An alternative research design would look at nationalist mobilization from the 1920s through the end of the colonial period using a panel dataset that covers the entire French empire. Such a dataset is not currently available, although

The Empire after World War I

The years after World War I were largely characterized by stable colonial rule across the French empire. The empire had provided 587,000 troops during World War I, and the contribution of the colonies to the war was portrayed as a testament to the value of the empire and the loyalty of imperial subjects.[12] During the war, resistance developed in response to efforts to conscript – sometimes forcibly – soldiers from Africa and other parts of the empire, but it was not nationalist in nature.[13] In the years after the war, French rule was stable in Africa (Ansprenger 1989, 100). The interwar years provided few opportunities for organizing opposition and the threat of repression was real (Cherif 1971, 239). In his novel *Batouala*, for which he won the Prix Goncourt in 1921, French Guianese poet and novelist René Maran evokes the difficulties of organizing against the French in interwar Africa in a speech by one of his characters, an African elder:

There is nothing more to do. Resign yourselves. When Bamara the lion roared, no antelope in the area dared to make a sound. It is the same

Wilkinson (2004) is currently in the process of compiling data that may make such an analysis feasible.

[12] Albert Sarraut, minister of colonies in 1920, provided this troop total (in Thomas 2005, 11).

[13] See Conklin (1997), chapter 5, on resistance in West Africa during World War I. She suggests that revolts broke out not where recruitment efforts were most intensive and abusive, but where the government's control was weak and traditional elites had been eliminated. A letter to the French administrators in Upper Senegal-Niger written by local chiefs complained that collaboration had begun to seem unattractive. They wrote:

Not only have we not revolted, but at the moment when the entire region was getting ready to do so, we helped suppress the rebels.... Because we are your friends, you profit from us to ask for *tirailleurs* and cattle, which we promptly provide. We have the French school in our encampment, while the circles of Timboctou and Gao do not have one. We have accepted to be counted and given exact information, and now we are paying the price, while those who revolted go wherever they like and pay almost no taxes. There do not have to be many more measures of this type to make our people conclude that it is better to keep a distance from the French rather than to be their friends, because only in the former case do they leave you alone (Conklin, 149).

They thus suggest that in areas outside effective government control, there are incentives to resist.

for us as for the antelope. Not being the strongest, we can only remain quiet. Our peace depends on it. Besides, let me remind you that we are not here to curse our masters. I am old. My tongue has dried out during your harangues. We would do better to complain less about the whites and to drink more (Maran 1922, 77).

Some political ferment took place in the early 1920s in Togo and Cameroon, the territories acquired from Germany during the war, but opposition was limited, as an elite articulating nationalist goals did not yet exist in either place.[14]

In Algeria, colonial rule was stable. The postwar years saw efforts at reform; Algerian elites advocated citizenship and pointed to the contributions made by Algerians during the war in support of their claim. Messali al-Hajj founded the nationalist PPA in 1937, but its membership was small, and Messali was subsequently imprisoned for two years. As Chapter 2 showed, discourses of equality were dominant.

In neighboring Tunisia, French rule was likewise secure, and nationalist mobilization limited. Speaking at the second congress of his Neo-Destour Party in October 1937, Habib Bourguiba – who would later lead Tunisia to independence – spoke of continued French tutelage and denied nationalist aims, calling those Tunisians who spoke of independence "demagogues" attempting to stir up the population. He noted that nationalists were answered with tomatoes and stones from Tunisian crowds loyal to France (in Government of Tunisia 1969, 138).

Only three territories saw serious mobilization in favor of independence in the early 1920s: Syria, Lebanon, and Morocco. In these places, nationalist mobilization occurred in the absence of imperial authority.

[14] French and British troops invaded Togo in August 1914; the colony surrendered three weeks later. In Cameroon, combat lasted a bit longer before the Germans fled in 1916. See Manning (1988, 66) and Ansprenger (1989, 27–28). On the opposition that followed, see Hodgkin (1957, 104). The resistance that occurred supports the claim that switching colonial rulers can provide a disruption that prompts opposition, but this opposition need not be nationalist. In Togo, calls for reform characterized the interwar years and beyond. For an account of the development of nationalism at the end of the colonial period, see Lawrance (2007).

Nationalism in the Levant: Discontinuity in the Wake of the Ottoman Collapse

In Syria and Lebanon, nationalist mobilization erupted during the two years between the end of Ottoman rule and beginning of French rule. Ottoman rule collapsed in September and October 1918; the San Remo conference of the Allied Supreme Council established that France would govern Syria and Lebanon under the mandate system of the League of Nations in April 1920.[15] In the interim, a flood of nationalist activity began. Gelvin (1998, 295) summarizes the state of affairs after the Ottoman collapse: "[T]he interval separating the withdrawal of Ottoman forces from Syria and the beginning of the quarter-century French occupation marked a clearly bounded episode in the history of nationalism in the Arab Middle East during which the struggle over nationalist issues was especially manifest and contentious." Khoury (1987, 6) states further that the collapse of Ottoman authority was one of the factors that made nationalism the dominant political ideology in Syria. Nationalist mobilization was particularly contentious between the Ottoman collapse in 1918 and July 1920, when French military forces entered Damascus and Aleppo (Gelvin 1998).

Three strands of nationalist mobilization can be discerned. First, Amir Faysal, who had gained authority in Damascus with the support of the British after the invasion of British, Australian, and Arab troops in 1918, mobilized support for his regime. In 1919, he organized demonstrations and distributed anti-European sermons to be read at Friday prayers (Gelvin 1998, 34). Second, al-Fatat,

---

[15] France and Great Britain had concluded the secret Sykes-Picot Agreement in 1916, which defined their spheres of influence in the Middle East in the event that the Ottoman Empire was defeated; this agreement came as an unwelcome shock to the Arab nationalists seeking independence in the wake of the Ottoman collapse throughout the Middle East. The American King-Crane Commission, which toured Syria in 1919, confirmed the opposition of Syrians to French control, but allied agreements at the end of the war established that Syria and Lebanon were to be League of Nation mandates. Syria, including Lebanon, formally became a Class A mandate under the League of Nations in 1923. For an overview of this period, see Cleveland and Bunton (2008).

a nationalist organization with headquarters in Beirut, also mobilized. Al-Fatat was founded before the war, but its organization did not exceed seventy members during the 1911–1918 period (Gelvin 1998, 55–56). After the Ottoman collapse, al-Fatat changed from a secret society to a large patronage organization, and membership climbed. To accommodate new members, the executive committee of al-Fatat commissioned the formation of the Arab Independence Party (Gelvin 1998, 58–59). Third, in addition to al-Fatat, Syrians also joined popular committees that were independent of Faysal's government, and employed a discourse that conveyed an image of a community imperiled by foreign imperialists (Gelvin 1998, 288–289). By the time the French arrived to establish the mandate, an insurrection had broken out in Damascus and elsewhere in the Levant (Gelvin 1998, 1). The arriving French faced nationalist resistance in multiple locations.[16]

Nationalist activity in Syria and Lebanon from 1919 through the early 1920s conforms to the expectations of this chapter's argument. The Ottomans had decolonized; their forces had departed in 1918. Authority had been disrupted, and there was no effective imperial rule. Various actors took advantage of the political vacuum to organize nationalist movements and demand independence. The French would struggle against organized nationalist groups for much of the mandate period.

Nationalism in the Moroccan Rif Mountains

In Morocco, nationalist mobilization in the 1920s also took place in the absence of imperial authority. Technically, the 1921–1926 Rif War did not constitute nationalist mobilization in the French empire because it took place in the Spanish zone of Morocco, but the French eventually joined the Spanish in fighting the Rif insurgents, so it is worth consideration.

During the early 1920s, neither the Spanish nor the French had fully consolidated control over their respective portions of Morocco. The French controlled the major towns of the plains and the coastal areas and continued to "pacify" the mountainous

---

[16] See Khoury (1987), chapter 4, for a discussion of early resistance in Syria.

regions until 1934. But the areas under French control were quiet and stable during the interwar years, and even in the areas where French conquest was ongoing, opposition did not involve organized nationalist movements. In the Spanish protectorate, the Spanish controlled little beyond the coastal towns of Melilla, Ceuta, and Larache (Ayache 1996, 8). At the close of the war, the Spanish moved to increase their authority and attempted to set up outposts in the rough terrain of the Rif Mountains. The attempt to establish control in the Rif met with fierce nationalist resistance, organized by Mohammed ben Abd el-Krim.

Abd el-Krim's father was an important authority figure in his region of the Rif. Abd el-Krim himself initially worked for the Spanish administration, serving first as an editor of the Arabic supplement to the official Spanish newspaper in Melilla, and then as a secretary in the Bureau of Native Affairs. He returned to the Rif in 1914 when he was appointed chief *cadi* by the Spanish, a position given to those who represented the Spanish in zones outside their control. Although Abd el-Krim worked with the Spanish in his early years, he turned hostile when they began to move toward establishing control in the Rif. He reportedly feared that the Spanish would find and benefit from mineral resources (Woolman 1968, 77). His father, an opponent of the Spanish, was poisoned by them in 1920 for criticizing the protectorate, an event that added further fuel to the fire (Woolman 1968, 79; Singer and Langdon 2004, 211).

In the summer of 1921, Abd el-Krim began his revolt against Spain with an army of between 3,000 and 6,000 (Singer and Langdon 2004, 211). Over the next several years, a succession of victories against the Spanish allowed him to consolidate control in the Rif. The number of recruits swelled; French army reports estimate that he had 75,000 partisans at his peak (Essakali 1983, 182). Abd el-Krim brought together chiefs from the area, created a government with an assembly, and on February 1, 1922, declared the founding of an independent Republic of the Rif (Lugan 2000). He then applied to the League of Nations for recognition of the Rif as an independent state.

The successes of the Rif rebellion just a few kilometers from their protectorate alarmed the French. In December 1924,

French Resident General Lyautey concluded that "[n]othing would be so bad for our regime as the installation near Fes of an independent Muslim state, modernized and supported by the most warlike tribes, with a spirit exalted by success against Spain."[17] Abd el-Krim asserted that he sought no war with France, but the French provoked him into fighting in the French zone and entered into war with his army in April 1924. Although the French were also defeated on several occasions by the Rif army, eventually, Abd el-Krim, now fighting two European powers, was forced to surrender. He went into exile in May 1926.

The events in the Rif have been characterized in two ways. Nationalists retroactively claimed Abd el-Krim as the first Moroccan nationalist, and some historians have accepted this view.[18] For others, the Rif War does not qualify as nationalist but as a tribal war against conquest.[19] Both of these views are problematic. Abd el-Krim never articulated a commitment to the Moroccan nation; he spoke solely on behalf of the Rif and sought its independence. Further, Moroccan leaders in Fes did not make common cause with him at the time; the *ulema* and notables opposed Abd el-Krim (Pennell 2003, 147). The dismissal of his movement as "tribal," however, makes little sense either. The Rif leaders made claims on behalf of a nation, they used a nationalist vocabulary, and they sought the trappings of statehood. As historians Ayache (1996) and Pennell (1986) suggest, Abd el-Krim's movement ought to count as Rifian nationalism. The leaders of the rebellion invoked a nationalist discourse to defend and promote their aims, but it was not a Moroccan nation they sought.

The Rif War began in the complete absence of imperial authority. It was not prompted by a disruption of already-existing imperial control, but constituted a response to the extension of imperial rule to a previously uncontrolled area. The Rif War more closely resembles wars of resistance to conquest than

---

[17] Quoted in Hoisington (1984, 18–19).
[18] See al-Fasi (1970); Essakali (1983); Lugan (2000); Woolman (1968).
[19] See Damis (1970); Habron (1956); Halstead (1969a).

nationalist mobilization against established colonial rule,[20] but unlike most other instances of resistance to French conquest, the leaders of the Rif used the now universally available language of nationalism, making nationalist claims on behalf of their besieged region.

In the interwar years, stable imperial authority characterized most of the French empire, and there was little nationalist activity. Political organizing during the interwar years largely took the form of demands to reform French rule, not to overthrow it. Nationalist mobilization occurred only where imperial authority had been disrupted (Syria and Lebanon) or where imperial authority was entirely absent (the Moroccan Rif). French imperial rule was not destined to be stable forever, however. During World War II, French rule was disrupted in a number of colonies and territories.

The Empire at War: Nationalist Mobilization during World War II

World War II has been recognized as perhaps the key event prompting both nationalist mobilization and decolonization.[21] Although many scholars have focused on France's loss of prestige after its defeat in 1940, this argument cannot make sense of variation in nationalist activity across the empire. If the loss of French prestige prompted nationalist mobilization, we would expect to see nationalist responses throughout the empire. But World War II did not trigger nationalist mobilization in every colony; the effects of the war varied across the empire. It was not France's overall weakness that led to nationalist protest, but the state of French rule in each colony. During the war, nationalist

---

[20] For a categorization of the differences between wars of conquests and nationalist movements, see Coleman (1954).

[21] Abernethy (2000) describes the war as a catalyst for independence, not an uncommon formulation. War has been linked more generally to anti-colonial opposition, including in the Spanish Americas. See Klooster (2009).

TABLE 4.1. *Nationalist Mobilization by World War II Occupation*

Post-Invasion Mobilization?	Invaded or Occupied during World War II?	
	Yes	No
Yes	9 (82%)	0 (0%)
No	2 (18%)	21 (100%)

mobilization occurred in the territories that were invaded and occupied by foreign forces.

Table 4.1 shows the relationship between occupation during the war and nationalist mobilization. To code the dependent variable, I asked whether or not there was nationalist activity during the war through 1946. To code invasion or occupation, I looked at whether or not troops from a country other than France entered the territory and remained there for at least a few months. None of the twenty-one places that remained under French control throughout the period saw nationalist mobilization during the war or in its immediate aftermath.[22] Nine out of the eleven places that were occupied by foreign forces experienced popular mobilization in favor of national independence between the beginning of the occupation and 1946.

Table 4.2 lists the territories that were invaded and occupied during the war. Nationalist mobilization did not occur in New Caledonia, but it would be surprising if it had, as New Caledonians had not been denied political rights. As the argument in previous chapters has suggested, territories that were on a path toward equitable reform are not expected to suddenly turn nationalist; the disruptions argument predicts nationalist mobilization where calls for political equality have failed. The ethnically divided Djibouti

---

[22] The twenty-one territories with no occupation and no nationalist mobilization are: Martinique, French Guiana, Guadeloupe, Mauritania, Cameroon, Senegal, Chad, Guinea, Gabon, Ivory Coast, Middle Congo (PRC), Dahomey (Benin), Ubanghi-Shari (CAR), French Sudan (Mali), Reunion, Upper Volta, French Polynesia, Niger, Togo, Wallis and Futuna, St. Pierre & Miquelon.

TABLE 4.2. *Territories Invaded/Occupied in World War II*

Territory	Occupying State	Date of Occupation	Post-Invasion Nationalist Mobilization?
Vietnam	Japan	August 1940 in Tonkin; July 1941 in South	Yes
Cambodia	Thailand	May 1941	Yes
Laos	Thailand	May 1941	Yes
Djibouti	Britain	December 1942	No
Madagascar	Britain	May 1942 initial landing; September 1942 in Tananarive	Yes
Syria	British and Free French	June 1941	Yes
Lebanon	British and Free French	June 1941	Yes
Morocco	United States	November 1942	Yes
Tunisia	Axis/Allied Forces	November 1942	Yes
Algeria	United States & Britain	November 1942	Yes
New Caledonia	Australia and United States	March 1942	No

had neither nationalist mobilization after the war nor calls for reform before it. Following the invasion by British and Free French forces, its population did not mobilize for independence.[23]

The level of mobilization in the territories that were invaded and occupied was not uniform. Although nine of the eleven saw some degree of nationalist mobilization, its intensity and duration varied. In Syria and Lebanon, nationalist movements already existed. The invasion of British forces intensified national mobilization rather than starting it. In Syria, the British presence led

[23] There are very few sources on Djibouti's history, but its lack of mobilization may be due to ethnic competition between the Afar ethnic group, Arabs, French settlers, and Somalis. Djibouti would elect to remain in the French empire longer than any other African colony, becoming independent only in 1977.

nationalists to believe that independence was at hand; historian Martin Thomas (1998, 108) states: "One feature common to the Syrian nationalist groups and their external Arab backers was their expectation that the other powers might be enlisted to hasten the process of French withdrawal." The head of the Free French forces in the Levant, General Georges Catroux, further encouraged nationalist organizations when he announced right after the invasion that Syria and Lebanon would henceforth be "sovereign, independent peoples."[24] In response, mobilization increased rapidly.

In Algeria, the invasion of Allied forces in November 1942 prompted those who had previously advocated reform to begin speaking of independence. Ferhat Abbas, the longtime advocate of rights for Algerian Muslims, called for the creation of an independent Algerian state. He founded an organization, the Amis du Manifest de la Liberté, in March 1944 and began attracting support. The followers of nationalist leader Messali al-Hadj likewise amplified their calls for an independent state (Yacono 1971, 59). On May 8, 1945, as France celebrated victory, nationalist mobilization broke out in the Algerian town of Sétif. People marched in the streets, shouting slogans such as, "For the Liberation of the People! Long Live Free and Independent Algeria!" The demonstration turned violent, settlers were massacred, and the French retaliation in the days and weeks following the uprising was brutal.[25]

In Madagascar, nationalist mobilization erupted after the British invasion (Manning 1988, 141). Britain recognized the supremacy of Free France in Madagascar, but took over the

---

[24] Quoted in Betts (1991, 62). Nationalists in Syria and Lebanon were correct in their estimation that they could gain British support for independence. Despite Catroux's announcement, the Free French authorities subsequently did all they could to break Lebanese and Syrian opposition to French rule. British pressure led to elections in Lebanon and Syria, which nationalist leaders won. When the newly-elected Lebanese government unilaterally abolished the French mandate, the French responded by arresting the entire cabinet. The British intervened, forcing the French to release the members of parliament. France agreed to end its rule in Lebanon and Syria shortly thereafter. See Thomas (1998, 113–125) and (2000) for more on the end of colonial rule in the Levant.

[25] For more on the events in Sétif, see Jauffret (1990).

colony's defense. The instability caused by the occupation, as one historian put it, "allowed the independence movement to take on a magnitude it lacked at the beginning of the war" (Tronchon 1974, 23). The Malagasy National Socialist Party denounced French rule, and secret nationalist societies began to spring up in various regions with the aim of mobilization. In April 1945, the leaders of the party addressed a letter to the French government reclaiming autonomy for Madagascar (Tronchon 1974, 25). Nationalist leaders thought the likelihood of independence was high until the British evacuated in 1946 and the Fourth Republic was established in France (Tronchon, 30). Also in 1946, nationalists founded the Democratic Movement for Malagasy Renewal, a party with a mass following. They sought recognition of Madagascar as a nation within the French Union during the constitutional debates in France.[26] In 1947, a violent nationalist rebellion broke out.[27]

Elsewhere, in Tunisia, Cambodia, and Laos, nationalist mobilization during the war was less violent and involved fewer participants. In Tunisia, Allied and Axis forces battled for control starting in November 1942; the wartime disruption was followed by a demand for internal autonomy by the Tunisian Front, and the number of nationalist associations multiplied (Yacono 1971, 58).[28] In Laos and Cambodia, nationalists declared independence from France in 1945, after the Japanese in Indochina had arrested Vichy leaders and publicly executed French military and police officers (Clayton 1994, 20).

Although its type and character varied, nationalist mobilization occurred in nearly all of the territories where imperial control was disrupted. World War II was indeed a catalyst for nationalist movements, but in a very specific sense. It was not the general atmosphere of war or the overall weakness of France that

---

[26] Tronchon (1974, 29) estimates that the party had 300,000 members by the time of the 1947 revolt.
[27] For more on the 1947 rebellion in Madagascar, see Tronchon (1974) and Cole (2001).
[28] For more on mobilization in Tunisia during the war, see Government of Tunisia (1989); Perkins (2004).

explains the location of nationalist activity. World War II was more disruptive in the empire than World War I or other events because of the military operations that took place in France's colonies (Young 1994, 184). These disruptions triggered nationalist demonstrations in favor of independence.

Grievances and Nationalist Mobilization: Vichy Rule in the French Empire

There is another potential explanation for the observed variation in nationalist mobilization during World War II. The French not only competed with foreign invaders for control over colonial territories during the war, they also competed with other Frenchmen. Some colonial territories declared their allegiance to de Gaulle and fell under the authority of Free France, whereas others spent much of the period under Vichy rule. An alternative hypothesis is that nationalist mobilization was a function of this division. Specifically, territories that fell under Vichy rule for an extended period of time may have been more likely to mobilize for independence for two reasons. First, the Vichy administration was notoriously cruel and authoritarian in the colonies (Person 1982, 143). In French West Africa, French-educated Africans were scorned and the Africans of Senegal's Four Communes were stripped of their citizenship (Chafer 2002, 40). The installation of Vichy rule is thus a way to evaluate arguments about the proximate effects of injustice and inequality on mobilization.

Second, the alternation of rule between Vichy and the Free French may have created enough instability to provide an opening for mobilization. In his history of the French empire at war, Martin Thomas (1998) focuses particularly on the contest between Vichy forces and the Free French, and he suggests that these contests were highly disruptive to politics in some territories, although he largely focuses on the consequences for colonial administrators and French settlers.[29]

---

[29] Young (1994, 184) likewise points to the importance of the cleavage dividing Vichy supporters and supporters of de Gaulle.

TABLE 4.3. *Nationalist Mobilization in Predominantly Vichy-Ruled Territories*

	Vichy-Ruled through Nov. 1942 or after		Liberated by Nov. 1942	
Nationalist Mobilization	30%	Vietnam Cambodia Laos Morocco Algeria Tunisia	25%	Syria Lebanon Madagascar
No Nationalist Mobilization	70%	French Guiana Mauretania Senegal Guinea Ivory Coast Dahomey French Sudan Upper Volta Niger Togo Martinique Guadeloupe Djibouti Réunion	75%	St Pierre & Miquelon Cameroon Chad Gabon Middle Congo Ubanghi-Shari Polynesia New Caledonia Wallis and Futuna

Table 4.3 examines the relationship between Vichy rule and nationalist mobilization. The table divides the empire into two categories: territories that spent a significant amount of time under Vichy rule, and those that were administered for most of the period by Free French forces.[30]

Most Vichy territories (and most Free French territories) did not have nationalist mobilization. Thirty percent of Vichy territories and 25 percent of those under Free French control

[30] I split the sample in November 1942, when Operation Torch liberated North Africa from Vichy rule. Those territories that were under Vichy rule up until Operation Torch were under Vichy rule for more than two years. I treat territories that were under Free French rule prior to the invasion of North Africa as largely under Free French rule during the war.

saw nationalist demonstrations, a fairly small difference that is not statistically significant. The comparative evidence does not suggest an association between Vichy rule and nationalist mobilization. Indeed, in French West Africa, the changes of regime may have made little difference to the indigenous population, as it produced minimal disruptions in day-to-day governance; in most cases Africans faced the same colonial officials and policies (Chafer 2002, 55). Shifts between one French administration and another may have meant little to local populations; the French were still in control. The argument that occupation by foreign forces led to mobilization appears to better differentiate places that had nationalist mobilization from places that did not.

This section has used a broad brush to depict nationalist mobilization across the empire during the war. The disruption of imperial authority by foreign forces accounts for why some places experienced nationalist mobilization during the war or soon thereafter and others did not. Arguments that rely on the overall prestige of France in the eyes of colonized subjects cannot explain variation within the empire. The hardship of imperial rule under the Vichy regime is likewise a poor candidate for explaining nationalism. To look more closely at the relationship between imperial authority and nationalist mobilization, I turn to a discussion of two cases.

Nationalist Mobilization in Vietnam and French West Africa

Vietnam: The Disintegration of Imperial Authority

In Vietnam, nationalist movements got their start in the interwar years. Moderate nationalists founded the Viêt Nam Quôc Dân Dang (VNQDD) in 1927, although membership was limited. In 1930, the VNQDD staged an armed uprising in Yen Bay, which was crushed by the French, who arrested and executed VNQDD leaders (Clayton 1994, 18). The uprising challenged a prevalent view that the Indochinese were model colonial subjects (N. Cooper 2001, 95). The VNQDD did not have a large membership, and when Nguyen Ai Quoic (later known as Ho Chi Minh) established the Indochinese Communist Party (ICP) in 1930, it became the dominant nationalist force in Vietnam, favoring the overthrow of the colonial system (Tucker 1999, 39). The 1930s also saw the growth of two religious groups – the Cao Dai and Hoa Hao – which later attracted nationalist support. But during the interwar years, few groups expressed the desire to see the colonial system overthrown; most questioned the injustices of the colonial system rather than the system itself (N. Cooper 2001, 91). The ICP was severely repressed, and Ho Chi Minh spent the years from 1933 to 1941 in Moscow and China. Nationalist mobilization in Indochina occurred on a small scale before World War I.

With the German defeat of France in 1940, Japan quickly assumed effective indirect control of the colonial administration in Indochina (Betts 1991, 56). The Japanese allowed the French to retain formal sovereignty of the territory, but in September 1940 General Catroux, at this time the French governor in Indochina, was forced to permit Japan to garrison the northern port of Haiphong and use the Tonkin-Yunnan railway to transport military supplies (Thomas 1998, 47). In the north, a Japanese general attacked the French at Lang Son, killing more than 800 French soldiers (Clayton 1994, 19). In July 1941, Japan expanded its presence, moving into Southern Vietnam (Tucker 1999, 41).

Japan had become the master of the region (Betts 1991, 57).[31] The French struggled to maintain authority. Then, in March 1945, after learning that de Gaulle planned to attack them in Indochina, the Japanese arrested the French governor general, publicly executed French military and political officers, and massacred French garrisons – only one unit managed to escape into China (Clayton 1994, 20). French authority in Vietnam was effectively destroyed.

The Japanese occupation accelerated nationalist mobilization in Vietnam. Chiang Kai-shek released Ho Chi Minh from a prison in Northern China to organize the resistance movement against the Japanese and Vichy administration (Springhall 2001,

---

[31] Yacono (1971, 60) described the regime as "Franco-Japanese."

38). In May 1941, Ho Chi Minh founded the League for the Independence of Vietnam, better known as the Viêt Minh, with Chinese and American support (Yacono 1971, 60–61). The Viêt Minh set up bases along the Chinese border with Tonkin; then Viêt Minh leader Võ Nguyên Giáp moved into Tonkin and established numerous bases. In 1943, the French began to view the Viêt Minh as a serious threat to colonial rule (Tucker 1999). By September 1944, they had an army of 5,000 and controlled three provinces in Northern Vietnam (Springhall 2001, 39).

Ho Chi Minh himself understood that a collapse in imperial authority was crucial for nationalist mobilization. In a circular on August 4, 1944, he announced:

> The armed uprising of our people should break out in the last phase of the world war: when England, America and China are trying to take possession of Indochina; when Gaullists are opposing French fascists in Indochina; when the French and Japanese are slaughtering each other and the Franco-Japanese fascists come into conflict with the Democrats.... All incapable and weak puppet regimes will then fall. Indochina will fall into anarchy. *"We will not need to seize power then, because there will no longer be any power"* (quoted in Ansprenger 1989, italics added).

In August 1945, the destruction of authority that Ho Chi Minh had hoped for came to pass. Immediately after the attacks on Hiroshima and Nagasaki and Japan's subsequent capitulation, the Viêt Minh called for a general insurrection (Yacono 1971, 61). In Low's (1982, 15) terms, the Japanese defeat created a "vortex" that prompted a massive uprising. The Viêt Minh elected a provisional government, headed by Ho Chi Minh. On September 2, 1945, Ho Chi Minh, quoting from the American Declaration of Independence (the text of which had been provided by the Office of Strategic Services), proclaimed the birth of the independent Democratic Republic of Vietnam in Hanoi (Springhall 2001, 39).

The French in Indochina not only had to share authority with another power, their authority was ultimately destroyed. Nationalist mobilization accelerated following the collapse of France's authority, with increased numbers of recruits joining the Viêt Minh. Following the Japanese surrender, participation in nationalist demonstrations soared, with 500,000 people gathering to hear Ho Chi Minh declare independence. Vietnam is thus one of the clearest examples of how disruptions in authority can facilitate nationalist action. The Japanese occupation and the subsequent defeat of Japan provided an opening that Ho Chi Minh recognized and seized. In the turbulence and uncertainty that followed the departure of the French and the defeat of Japan, he rallied the Vietnamese for independence.

When the French decided to retain Vietnam, they effectively had to reconquer the entire territory. With British assistance, they managed to regain control of the South. But France would fight a long and costly war against the Viêt Minh before relinquishing Vietnam in 1954.

French West Africa: Continuity and Imperial Authority

The eight territories that made up French West Africa – Mauritania, Senegal, French Sudan, Dahomey, Guinea, Côte d'Ivoire, Niger, and Upper Volta – experienced stable colonial authority in the pre-war period, during World War II, and in the decade following the war. During this time period, there was little to no nationalist mobilization.

Yet the people of French West Africa were not politically inactive. Mobilization occurred during the war, but it was primarily non-nationalist. One incident occurred during demobilization. The first group of liberated African POWs arrived in Dakar in November 1944. They had endured years in German prisons and were then sent to camps in France to await embarkation. They were treated differently from French POWs, who received better food rations and housing, plus their pay arrears. African POWs were promised that their pay arrears and demobilization allowances would be given to them when they arrived in Dakar, but upon arrival they were taken to a camp to wait for their money. When the payments had still not been made after some time, the soldiers feared that they would not be paid at all, and organized a protest on December 1. During the demonstration, French troops opened fire, killing thirty-five soldiers and injuring thirty-five others. The governor general made immediate arrangements to settle back pay. Despite this event, war veterans largely continued to support French rule in Africa. One group, however, called the Mouvement Nationaliste Africaine, was started by veterans just after the war. It had no mass following, however, and ceased activity after two years.[32] The majority of incidents during the war involved no nationalist discourses at all; protests were centered on immediate economic problems and the lack of political rights.

In the decade following the war, African politicians continued to seek increased rights and services as members of the new French Union. Political parties sprang up once African territories could send representatives to the French National Assembly. One of the most important parties was the Rassemblement Démocratique Africain, launched in Bamako in October 1946. It was not a secessionist party, but sought instead a genuine French Union with rights and freedoms for the citizens of the overseas territories (Chafer 2002, 72). Political parties were not the only forms of political mobilization. Trade union associations and student organizations also mobilized participants (Adamolekun 1969, 69). These organizations operated within the framework provided by the institutions and laws of the French Union, but they pushed for greater rights and representation.[33]

France's policy in Africa changed in June 1956, with the passage of the Loi-cadre (enabling law), granting internal autonomy to the eight territories in the federation. African territories were henceforth to be ruled by parliamentary assemblies elected through universal suffrage. The law thus extended the franchise: electoral rolls jumped from 117,700 for all of French West Africa to more than 10 million (Ansprenger 1989, 246–247). The law also shifted politics away from Paris to the individual territories of the union. Territorial assemblies gained ministerial powers over the governments in each colony (Manning 1988, 148). The French government retained responsibility for defense, the customs service, some police forces, the financial and monetary regime, the media, and higher education, but all other public services became

---

[32] This account comes from Chafer (2002, 46–47). See also Manning (1988, 140).
[33] See Chapter 3.

the responsibility of local authorities.[34] Each territory would set its own budget and administer its own domestic affairs.

Granting internal autonomy produced two effects relevant to the arguments made here. First, it devolved authority away from imperial administration to the territory itself, effectively establishing two sources of authority (Young 1994, 207). France remained powerful, but elected African politicians also controlled important policy areas. This hand off was a departure from the previous policy of more centralized control. The Loi-cadre thus bears a resemblance to the wartime disruptions in other territories – the French created alternative power holders, albeit voluntarily, when they turned over responsibilities to local leaders. It was not the abrupt disruption that occurred via invasion, but it did divide authority between the French and African politicians by giving the latter greater power within the territory.

Second, the Loi-cadre was also a response to the African quest for political equality. Instead of increasing the participation and representation of Africans in Paris, it made the colonial territory the main political unit. It was a step away from incorporation, although not an outright refusal because Africans remained citizens as they had been since 1946. But the devolution of authority was an answer to those claiming that Africans merited rights equivalent to French citizens in France. Henceforth, Africans were to be set apart within their own territories.

Thus, for French Africa, unlike Morocco or Algeria, a change in political authority and a response to mobilization for equality occurred simultaneously.[35] Neither was a dramatic departure, but the theory here would suggest that both ought to be consequential for subsequent organizing. We ought to observe movement toward nationalist mobilization after the 1956 decision to grant autonomy.

---

[34] For a longer discussion of the Loi-cadre and its effects, see Chafer (2002, 165–172).

[35] Because they occurred simultaneously, it is not possible, for these cases, to know whether it is the increase in the power of local authorities or the decrease in the likelihood of full incorporation that better accounts for subsequent changes in mobilization.

The evidence suggests that nationalist mobilization did start to occur with greater frequency and intensity after 1956, although it did not replace other forms of mobilization. One historian contends that "the movement toward independence for francophone Africa began imperceptibly in the early 1950s, then accelerated rapidly from 1956" (Manning 1988, 146). Chafer (2002, 18) notes the emergence of nationalism in French West Africa at the "11th hour."[36] Young (1994, 237) suggests that the weakening will and authority of the colonial state prompted nationalist mobilization.

After 1956, nationalist demands began to play an important role in mobilization. Nationalist movements were not as dramatic or violent as elsewhere in the empire, but they involved popular participation in and support for parties seeking either independence for individual territories or on behalf of a broader African identity. African leaders engaged in mass electoral mobilization in order to demonstrate their mandate to succeed the colonial rulers (Young 1994, 239).

Not every political figure or organization began advocating independence in 1956. Cooper (2005, 22) writes: "Political activists in the colonies, until well into the 1950s, were not all intent upon asserting the right to national independence; many sought political voice within the institutions of the French Empire while claiming the same wages, social services, and standard of living as other French people." Debates centered on the possibility of an African federation within the French Union or an independent African federation with continued linkages to France. The future was still open to multiple possibilities.

In 1958, the structure of colonial rule in West Africa changed again under the new constitution of the Fifth Republic of France. The French Union became the French Community. The idea was to link France to autonomous republics in a voluntary community. Community members would have their own

---

[36] See also Wallerstein (1961), who links the granting of autonomy to nationalism, as well as Adamolekun (1969, 66) who writes that the word "independence" was unheard of in the public vocabulary of leading African politicians until after WWII, and in French West Africa was not heard until as late as 1958 in some places.

national assemblies and increased autonomy. In September 1958, a referendum was held throughout the French Union and voters were asked to decide whether or not to join the new French Community. De Gaulle himself campaigned in person for yes votes. There was extensive pressure to vote yes, and thus the vote cannot be seen as a reliable measure of what West Africans wanted. All of the territories of French West Africa elected to become community members, with the exception of Guinea. Voters in Guinea chose immediate independence, and were punished for doing so by the French, who departed immediately, withdrawing development aid and refusing to participate in the transition process. Most African political parties campaigned in favor of the referendum to avoid this kind of abrupt, unfriendly rupture with France.

Only one colony showed ongoing mobilization for incorporation. Voters in Gabon asked to become a French department, an option that was at least hypothetically extended to those who had voted to stay in the French Community. In his memoir, Louis Sanmarco (1983, 211), governor of Gabon at the time, describes his reception when he flew to Paris after the decision to become a department: "I was received like a dog in a bowling alley. The minister, Bernard Cornut-Gentile, was even rude: 'Sanmarco, have you fallen on your head? ... We don't have enough Antilles? Go on, independence like everyone else.'" France was no longer sincerely offering incorporation.

The French Community was short-lived. In 1960, it collapsed, and French West Africa became fully independent. Although the Mali Federation, created at independence, was an attempt at establishing a wider African federation, the territories of French Africa ultimately became independent as individual units (Foltz 1965).

Nationalist goals were not widespread in French West Africa until the post-1956 period.[37] Nationalist mobilization, in these cases, was endogenous to the prospect of independence itself; it

[37] African nationalism was expressed before 1956 by students studying in Paris. But after completing their studies and returning to Africa "they revealed themselves as far less radical than they had been at Paris, some reversed their positions in the most spectacular fashion" (Person 1982, 158). Rather than

began only after France voluntarily reduced its responsibilities in Africa. As France began to withdraw from its empire, calls for independence became more common.

Conclusion

Nationalist movements are often treated as an important cause of decolonization. This chapter showed that nationalist action was endogenous to imperial crises and thus called the direction of causality into question. Nationalist mobilization was less a trigger of decolonization and more an "on rush of opposing forces into the political vacuum" (Betts 1991, 3). The crisis was not, however, a grave loss of prestige following the French defeat in 1940, as many have claimed. Nationalist mobilization across the empire was far more variable than the prestige argument suggests it should be. Changes in the exercise of French power at the level of the individual colonial territory better explains variation in outbursts of nationalist activity, accounting for the unevenness of nationalist action over time and place.

The evidence also suggests that nationalist mobilization did not occur in places that experienced the worst colonial injustices. Nationalist mobilization during the post–World War I era and during World War II sprang up where French authority had collapsed, not where its rule was most direct or cruel.[38] A focus on grievances might lead us to expect nationalist mobilization in the territories of French Africa, where the population experienced serious hardships such as forced labor, famine, and racism. But, with the exception of Madagascar, the African colonies did not mobilize for independence early on. Further, nationalist mobilization was not more likely to occur under the notoriously racist Vichy regime than it was under Free French rule.

pointing to hypocrisy, which Person seems to imply, the change in students' attitudes upon their return to the colonies suggests instead that imperial authority was indeed important for restricting political opposition and foreclosing active nationalist mobilization in the territories.

[38] On direct rule as a cause of nationalism, see Hechter (2000).

This account also differs from approaches in the literature that see nationalism as a slow-growing, gradual phenomenon; I have shown that nationalist mobilization erupted swiftly in the French empire, following a rupture in state control. Nationalist mobilization was then path dependent; once an organizational structure and membership base had emerged, it became easier to mobilize the population in later periods.

Chapter 5 takes a closer look at the dynamics of nationalist organizing over time. It examines the relationship between disruptions in imperial authority and nationalist mobilization in the north and south of Morocco over the entire colonial period. The macro analysis here has used a broad brush to depict the consequences of ruptures in imperial control. Chapter 5 studies the impact of these ruptures on organizations and individuals seeking to mount a nationalist challenge.

5

Nationalist Mobilization in Colonial Morocco

Considering that Morocco has always constituted a free, sovereign state ...

Considering that the regime was supposed to provide Morocco with a set of administrative, financial, and military reforms without affecting the traditional sovereignty of the Moroccan people under the protection of the King;

Considering that the Protectorate authorities have instead substituted a system of direct administration and acted to benefit the French colony ...

Considering that through this system, the French colony was able to capture power and become master of the country's vital resources to the detriment of the indigenous people;

Considering that the regime, using various means, has tried to shatter the unity of the Moroccan people, prevented them from participating effectively in the government of their country, and deprived them of all individual civil liberties ...

It is decided to demand the independence of Morocco.

– Excerpted from the *Manifeste de l'Indépendance*,
January 11, 1943

"In the streets, clashes between the French and natives are multiplying. The 'Young Turk' will tolerate no sign of disrespect; the native woman will no longer put up with a French woman addressing her in the familiar '*tu*' or taking her seat on the bus.... They act against all that is foreign."

– Commandement en chef, Inspection des Affaires Militaires Musulmanes, *Note sur l'Évolution de l'Opinion Musulmane de l'Afrique du Nord de 1920 à Nos Jours, Juin 1943.*

In 1943, nationalist mobilization began in French Morocco: leaders of the newly formed Hizb al-Istiqlal issued a call for independence, and people across the protectorate began to demonstrate publicly against the French and in favor of national independence. This chapter takes a closer look at how nationalist mobilization began and progressed through independence in 1956. It examines the relationship between disruptions in imperial authority and nationalist mobilization using subnational data, and it considers alternative explanations.

The analysis takes advantage of both cross-sectional and temporal variation, subjecting the argument outlined in Chapter 4 to two lines of evidence. The first is a comparison between two separately governed zones of the country: Spanish and French Morocco. The division of Morocco in 1912 produced variation on the independent variable: imperial authority varied across the two zones, with disruptions occurring at different moments in time. The first part of this chapter evaluates how well the argument about disruptions in imperial authority explains divergent patterns of nationalist mobilization onset in French and Spanish Morocco.

The second part focuses on nationalist mobilization in the French zone, studying variation over time. Using data from French reports, I demonstrate that a collapse in imperial authority in Morocco coincided with the start of mobilization for independence. I also draw out the implications of the argument for patterns of nationalist mobilization beyond its initial outbreak. The argument in Chapter 4 spoke primarily to the question of onset; disruptions helped initiate nationalist protest or prompted participation at far greater levels than had been seen before. But thinking through the impact of disruptions points to hypotheses concerning other ways that mobilization should vary. The state of French authority not only affected onset, it also affected the type, location, and timing of social movement events. The chapter thus develops and tests predictions for different but related dependent variables. It looks at how mobilization unfolded during moments of disruption, and how it changed when authority was reestablished.

A subnational analysis provides the opportunity to consider other factors that affect nationalist mobilization. The first part assesses whether different levels of education, development, and colonial penetration explain divergent mobilization patterns in French and Spanish Morocco. The third part uses data on French Morocco to investigate how international events and the use of repression affected nationalist protest.

Imperial Authority and Nationalist Mobilization in Spanish and French Morocco

Although Morocco was considered a sovereign state at the turn of the twentieth century, it was divided and occupied by two imperial powers.[1] Spanish Morocco extended primarily along the Mediterranean coast, occupying approximately 8,000 square miles, a tiny fraction of the size of the French protectorate (Landau 1956, 163).[2] It included the territory between Ceuta and Mellila on the Mediterranean coast and the small town of Larache on the Atlantic coast. The official head of state was the Moroccan *Khalifa*, who was appointed by the sultan as his representative in the Spanish zone. The Khalifa worked with the Spanish high commissioner much as the sultan worked with the French resident general, and was likewise subordinate to colonial authority throughout the protectorate period. Nationalist mobilization in Morocco occurred first in the Spanish zone: in the 1920s in the Rif, as Chapter 4 discussed; and in the 1930s in the capital of Tetouan. The next

---

[1] See Porch (1982) on the run-up to the establishment of the French and Spanish protectorates and international competition over Morocco more generally. The city of Tangier was not included in either zone; it was designated an international city in 1912. It was incorporated into Spanish Morocco during World War II, but reverted to international status at the war's conclusion.

[2] The population of the Spanish zone in 1936 was 795,202; the population of the French zone was 6,296,012. "Note succinct sur l'organisation générale de la Zone Espagnole," *Situation Politique et Economique 16–31 Août 1936*; *Bulletin Official du Protectorat du Maroc, Mai 29, 1936*. SHAT 3H1413. Spain also occupied the Western Sahara until 1975.

section describes how the nationalist mobilization centered in Tetouan began.

Spanish Morocco and Nationalist Mobilization Onset in Tetouan

By the close of the Rif War, Spain had consolidated control over its assigned portion of Morocco. Opposition to Spanish rule now came from Moroccan elites living in the capital city of Tetouan.[3] Like their counterparts in French Morocco, these elites initially challenged Spanish rule by asking for democratic reforms. The first to do so was `Abd as-Salam Bennouna. He implemented a number of important changes, founding the first Arabic newspaper in Morocco, *Al Islah* (Reform); starting a school for notables in 1923; and reforming the *khalifien* administration (Wolf 1994, 149–152; Rézette 1955, 84). He and historian Mohammed Daoud formed a group called al Muslihun (the Reformers) in 1926. In 1930, Bennouna founded the Kutlat al-Wataniya (National Bloc) with other elites, including `Abd al-Khaleq Torrès, a future leader of the nationalist movement. This bloc did not issue nationalist demands, but called on the Spanish to reform colonial rule.

The fall of Alphonso XIII and the establishment of the Spanish Republic in 1931 raised the hopes of reformists and accelerated political activity (Rézette 1955, 85). In April, Moroccans in Tetouan participated in public celebrations of the change. On May 4, under the leadership of the reformists, workers participated in the first mass demonstration ever to occur in Morocco (Wolf 1994, 178). Bennouna presented a one-page list of requested reforms to the Spanish administration signed by 800 petitioners (Zade 2001). Their demands included elected municipal councils,

---

[3] Unlike the Rifian nationalists, nationalists in Tetouan mobilized in favor of independence for the entire Spanish zone (and sometimes the entire country). Although these nationalists drew inspiration from Abd el Krim's rebellion, they were themselves not involved in the Rif War. In fact, the Tetouan leaders who would later lead the nationalist movement opposed the Rif rebellion and feared invasion from the tribes of the Rif (Rézette 1955, 83). The Spanish zone had two mobilization onset periods among different populations: the Berbers of the Rif and the Andalusian population in the towns.

a general council, a free press, freedom of association, better education for Moroccans, education in Arabic, access to administrative posts, and measures against rural poverty (Wolf 1994,
177; Rézette 1955, 85). The high commissioner agreed to hold
elections for municipal councils in 1931, and Bennouna's group
won a majority of seats (Wolf 1994, 181).

After some initial enthusiasm, the reform plan was ignored
(Halstead 1969a, 201). The Spanish, like the French, did not
implement far-reaching democratic reforms, and reformers'
aspirations for a greater degree of equality were denied. The
Spanish did, however, use less repression than the French, and
granted some liberties. They were more tolerant toward opposition groups and newspapers than the French were, and they
allowed Moroccans to meet with Arab nationalists such as
Chakib Arslan.[4] In part, this leniency stemmed from Spanish
competitiveness with the French protectorate; these liberties
irritated French officials (Pennell 2000, 233).[5] The Spanish high
commissioner actively encouraged Tetouan's elites to direct
their criticism toward the French. Moroccan newspapers in the
Spanish zone published virulent attacks against French policies
(Pennell 2000, 235; Halstead 1969a, 202).[6] In return for relative
freedoms, leading elites contrasted the Spanish administration
favorably to French rule.

After Bennouna's death in 1935, Torrès became the primary
leader of the reform movement. In June 1936, the Popular
Front, a coalition of left-wing parties, came to power in Spain.

---

[4] Arslan, a well-known figure, did not advocate separation from Spain at this
time. In a letter to Torrès, he suggested that Spanish rule could prove beneficial
to Northern Morocco, giving as a model the example of Catalonia (quoted in
Wolf 1994, 179).

[5] Competition between Spain and France over the acquisition and governance of
colonies was long-standing; in the mid-nineteenth century, Juan Donoso Cortés
lyrically wrote, "We will encircle Africa with our arms, that daughter caressed
by the sun, who is the slave of the Frenchman and should be our wife" (in
Balfour 2002).

[6] When France fell in 1940, Moroccans in the French zone proclaimed their support for France, and the sultan reportedly wept (Rivet 1999, 382). But in the
Spanish zone, Torrès and his supporters carried a coffin draped in a French flag
through the city streets, then burned it (Pennell 2000, 257).

Torrès, like his colleagues in the French zone, saw an opportunity for change. He transformed the Kutlat into a political party, Hizb al-Islah al-Watani (Party of National Reform), and founded party branches in the towns of Larache, Azilah, and Acarzarquivier (Pennell 2000, 247–248). The purpose of these branches was not mass recruitment but negotiation with the administration (Halstead 1969a, 237).

But the Popular Front had only just taken power in Madrid when civil war broke out. On July 19, 1936, General Francisco Franco led the Spanish army into rebellion against the Popular Front. Subsequently, Torrès and his followers changed their platform and began asking for independence (Benjelloun 1986, 7). The disorder of war made it difficult to determine to whom this demand should be directed; the future was uncertain (Benjelloun 1983, 315). Torrès turned first to the republican government in Madrid, offering to aid President Azaña against Franco in return for independence for the Spanish zone. Fearing that Spanish concessions would lead to an independent state in Northern Morocco, French Prime Minister Léon Blum counseled Azaña to refuse (Halstead 1969a, 238; Pennell 2000, 248).

Franco seized upon Azaña's refusal and made vague promises of independence to Torrès in return for his support.[7] Franco's immediate concern was to recruit Moroccan soldiers.[8] In October 1936, General Queipo de Llano, speaking from Radio Tangier on behalf of Franco, said that the rebel government was drafting a law that would grant the Spanish zone the independence denied it by the Republic (Halstead 1969a, 238). Moroccan elites then threw their allegiance behind the Spanish nationalists. Not everyone agreed; some opposed helping Franco, arguing that

[7] Torrès first had to be released from prison, where he had been locked up by rebels at the start of the civil war for his relationship with Spanish leftists (Halstead 1969a, 238).
[8] The sultan issued a *dahir* in the French zone forbidding Moroccans from fighting in the Spanish Civil War, but Moroccans from both zones joined Franco's force (Hoisington 1984, 138). Estimates suggest that more than 60,000 Moroccans fought for Franco in the Spanish Civil War (Hoisington 1984, 147; Pennell 2000, 249). On recruitment, see Benjelloun (1994) and Balfour (2002, 272).

supporting a fascist autocracy went against Islamic principles. Mohammed Bennouna, son of the reformist leader, answered this argument by stating that independence had to be the first and foremost goal (Rézette 1955, 117–118).

The Spanish Civil War affected imperial authority in the zone in three ways. First, the initial outbreak of hostilities produced uncertainty about who was in control. The authority of the republican government in the Spanish zone had been violently contested by Spanish nationalists, who began their rebellion right in Spanish Morocco. Moroccans did not initially know whether the republicans or the rebels were in charge, nor did they know which party would emerge victorious. The future of the protectorate was in doubt. Some worried that France would take advantage of the disorder and invade the Spanish zone (Benjelloun 1994, 225). Second, although the rebels quickly established territorial control in Spanish Morocco, their position remained precarious. They needed manpower for the war and could not expend resources policing the population and monitoring nationalist activities. Moroccans thus had more latitude to organize. Third, imperial authority was further undermined by the promise of independence, a promise made precisely because of the tenuous hold on authority. The Spanish high commissioner in Morocco, Colonel Juan Beigbeder, not only promised independence, but actually gave Moroccan leaders greater autonomy than they had ever had before. The French reported a "frightening" increase in the power of native leaders (Hoisington 1984, 147).[9]

The ongoing contest between two warring parties and the prospect of independence had multiple consequences for political organizing. The first was a switch from seeking reform to advocating independence. Before the Spanish Civil War, Torrès and his colleagues had sought to cooperate with Spanish authorities, gain reforms, and gradually increase Moroccan participation in government. They failed to achieve these aims, and when the

---

[9] French administrators often complained that Spanish policy seemed to invite "native agitation" (Montagne 1943, 49).

war started, independence became the goal.[10] This switch does not imply that leaders were insincere in their quest for reform. In 1934, Torrès had written in the newspaper *Al Hayat* that although he considered Moroccan nationalism to be part of a natural evolution and understood the protectorate to be temporary (as the protectorate treaty stated), he and his colleagues did not seek separation from Spain (Wolf 1994, 187). In the context of stable Spanish rule, reforms were a reasonable way to increase their role in government, particularly after the fall of the king and the victory of the left. But they had not made any progress toward achieving these goals when the Spanish state fractured and was no longer capable of delivering reforms.

Demands for independence were at least in part endogenous to the offer of independence. Independence seemed much more likely, given fractured authority and the promise of independence. A November 1936 French intelligence report stated that the nationalists in the Spanish zone "believe they will be called upon to manage the destiny of their own country shortly."[11]

The collapse of authority also provided opportunities for leaders to mobilize. By the end of 1936, the Hizb al-Islah al-Watani had gained 9,000 members (Pennell 2000, 248). Party members participated in protest activities (Rézette 1955, 119). Torrès also created a youth wing, which marched through the streets in green shirts (Pennell 2000, 248).

The switch in mobilization platforms also produced a rupture between the nationalists in the Spanish zone and their counterparts in French Morocco (Halstead 1969a, 239; al-Fasi 1970, 154). Prior to the civil war, reformists in both zones cooperated periodically, traveling between Tetouan and Fes to hold meetings during the early 1930s (Rézette 1955, 86–87, 99). But the onset of nationalist mobilization in the Spanish zone put an end to cooperation. At the 1936 North African Muslim Student Association

[10] The Spanish Popular Front did bring up the issue of independence or autonomy, but nothing was done to bring it about by either the government or Torrès before the war began (Rézette 1955, 113).

[11] *Bulletin de Renseignements Politiques*, November 1936. Political Affairs Bureau, French Residency in Morocco, SHAT 3H1413.

Congress in Tetouan, Torrès openly advocated independence. Reformists from the French zone boycotted, fearing that attending a congress sponsored by advocates of independence would compromise their ability to negotiate with the Popular Front in France in favor of reforms.[12] The CAM criticized Franco's policies in the hope of pleasing the French Popular Front (Rézette 1955, 100). For their part, the Moroccan nationalists in the Spanish zone contrasted the freedom that Franco had brought to French oppression, praising fascist strength and denouncing French weakness (Hoisington 1984, 41). Cooperation between elites in the French and Spanish zone became difficult when they developed divergent agendas and confronted different kinds of regimes.

Franco's government ultimately failed to follow through on promises of independence. During the war, Beigbeder had made some concessions, permitting publication of the nationalist newspaper *El Hurriya* (Liberty) and providing funding to nationalist groups. But he also tried to foster divisions within the nationalist movement, encouraging Mekki Naciri, a rival of Torrès, to found a separate party, which he did in March 1937, creating the Hizb al-Wahda al Maghribiya (the Party of Moroccan Unity).[13] Beigbeder further tried to direct nationalist sentiment against the French. Nationalists were happy to attack the French regime, but by the end of the war, they had also become more critical of the Spanish administration. When the war ended, Beigbeder announced a general amnesty for political prisoners, loans for public works and education, and autonomy for the Islamic justice system, but said nothing about the earlier promise of independence (Halstead 1969a, 258). Franco declared that he wished the Spanish zone to be "the most flourishing province of the Moroccan Empire."[14] Despite this refusal, after 1936 the dominant goal of Moroccan

---

[12] *Bulletin de Renseignements Politiques*, October 1936, Political Affairs Bureau, French Residency in Morocco, SHAT 3H1413. See also Rézette (1955, 101); Halstead (1969a, 238–239).

[13] Both Naciri and Torrès sought independence during the Spanish Civil War, but each had a different idea of what independence would mean. Naciri was committed to independence for all of Morocco, whereas Torrès could envision a separate state in the Spanish zone and sought independence only for that zone during the war.

[14] Quoted in Rézette (1955, 115).

political organizers in the Spanish zone was national independence. The Spanish would reluctantly concede in 1956, when the French protectorate came to an end.

French Morocco and Nationalist Mobilization Onset
In November 1942, as Allied forces began their invasion of North Africa, administrators in French Morocco saw few signs that Moroccans would shortly begin publicly mobilizing in favor of national independence. Since 1937, when the French rejected appeals for meaningful reform of the protectorate structure, jailing reformists and crushing hopes that reforms could be achieved, there had been little public opposition, although reformists had begun speaking privately of the need for independence. At the beginning of World War II, Moroccan leaders pledged their support for France.[15] Even when France fell in 1940, Moroccan city streets saw no mobilization against French rule. The French worried about the loss of prestige following the armistice; but in their reports they note that even their adversaries were cooperating fully with the protectorate.[16]

---

[15] In September 1939, this speech by the sultan was announced in mosques and newspapers:

> Since the Protectorate Treaty, peace has been assured in your homes, in your towns, in the country, and your honor and religion have likewise been safeguarded. Today, France takes up arms to defend her land, her honor, her dignity, her future and ours; we are ourselves faithful to the principles of the honor of our race, history and religion. It is our most absolute duty to demonstrate to the government of France our recognition of all that she has done for us, and the first who fails to fulfill this elementary duty will be excluded from our history and will disobey the orders of the Being who has imposed this duty upon us. From today, and until the standard of France and the Allies are crowned with glory, we must face the test without reserve, without withholding any of our resources, and without recoiling from any sacrifice. We have been tied to her in the era of peace and wealth, it is just that we remain at her side through the ordeal that she undergoes now, and from which she will emerge, we are convinced, grand and glorious (quoted in Levisse-Touze 1994, 211).

[16] As with other cases, some scholars have suggested that the loss of prestige in 1940 helped produce nationalist mobilization, but mobilization did not begin until after the Allied invasion. See, for example, Bernard (1968, 16); Damis (1970, 83); Knapp (1977, 277); Zisenwine (2010, 17). The French later attributed the onset of nationalist mobilization to France's defeat, stating in reports that it tarnished France's image; they explained the three-year gap

Nationalist mobilization in Morocco began after the Allied invasion in November 1942. French reporting records a marked shift from compliance with French rule to agitation to end it.[17] By the time the war ended, nationalist mobilization for independence was widespread: Moroccans had taken to the streets in all major towns to demand national liberation.

The rise in nationalist activity following the Allied invasion has been noted, but few have theorized the effects of the invasion on protest activity.[18] The Allied invasion meant that the French were no longer the sole authority in the territory. The presence of American forces created uncertainty about the future, made France's hold over Morocco seem tenuous, and led Moroccans, French settlers, and the government to believe that the likelihood that the French would lose the protectorate had risen. Further, the inability of French forces to prevent nationalist groups from organizing and mobilizing sympathizers increased the general sense of French vulnerability. Although Resident General Nogues hoped that France's authority would be respected despite the invasion, he admitted, "In truth, this is a real occupation against which we are powerless."[19] De Gaulle himself worried about the state of French authority in North Africa, writing in 1944, "We must prevent North Africa from slipping between our fingers while we are liberating France."[20]

The disruption of French authority had a number of consequences for political organizing among Moroccans. The first

before mobilization erupted by stating that time was needed to organize. *Note sur l'Evolution de l'Opinion Musulmane de l'Afrique du Nord de 1920 a nos jours, Commandement en chef, Inspection des Affaires Militaires Musulmanes, juin 1943.* SHAT.

[17] *Rapport Mensuel sur la Situation Politique en Milieux Indigènes*, February 1944. *Commandement Superieur des Troupes du Maroc*, SHAT 3H249.

[18] Damis (1970, 83); Halstead (1969a, 261); Rivet (2002, 338). Sarmany and Roucaud (2000) note the importance of the Allied landing; Damis conceives of it as a further sign of French weakness. Zisenwine (2010, 25) sees the Allied landing as marking the end of the war in the region, and in contrast with the account here, suggests it strengthened Moroccans' sense of political stability.

[19] Quoted in Hoisington 1984, 236.

[20] Quoted in Martel 1994, 248.

was its effect on regime intermediaries, those who worked for the French administration.[21] After the invasion, longtime regime allies began to worry that French rule was coming to an end. Some intermediaries – including the sultan, the primary collaborator of the French administration in Morocco until this point – switched sides and began advocating independence. In January 1943, the sultan met with Roosevelt, who reportedly promised American support for Moroccan independence (Sangmauh 1992, 131; Pervillé 1991, 96).[22] Subsequently, the sultan contacted Moroccan nationalists to indicate his support. A July 1943 French protectorate report cited a rumor circulating that said the sultan had simply to conclude a treaty with the United States and the French would leave.

The report noted that other regime allies were worried; notables in Fes demanded that the French retake the reins of command. The report decried the protectorate policy of "weakness and abandon."[23] Other *pashas* and *caids* developed contacts with leaders of the budding nationalist movement during the war, alarming the French.[24] Even al Glaoui, the pasha of the South and longtime collaborator of the French, briefly changed sides and supported the nationalists, until he heard they did not actually have substantial American support (Bernard 1968, 21). Wavering support among regime intermediaries increased people's sense of the fragility of French rule. Rumors that the sultan

---

[21] For more on the structure of government and the role of Moroccan intermediaries, see Belseur (1995).

[22] In Elliot Roosevelt's 1946 biography of his father, *As He Saw It*, he reported that Franklin Roosevelt said, "Why does Morocco, inhabited by Moroccans belong to France? ... Anything must be better than to live under French colonial rule! ... When we've won the war, I will work with all my might and main to see to it that the US is not wheedled into the position of accepting any plan that will further France's imperialistic ambitions" (quoted in Landau 1956, 213). Roosevelt also sent two letters to the sultan after their meeting; the contents are unknown.

[23] *Politique Musulman au Maroc*, 1943. MAE DI341.

[24] *Situation Politique du Maroc*, 1 Dec. 1944. MAE DI341. To deter further defections, four intermediaries were fired during the war, including the pasha of Rabat.

and other notables now supported national liberation fueled participation in nationalist activities.[25]

Another consequence of the disruption was that the former leaders of the reform movement were able to engage in outreach efforts to mobilize the urban public. In February 1943, following the sultan's meeting with Roosevelt, a group of fifty Moroccan leaders met in Rabat. Throughout the rest of the year, meetings were held in Rabat, Sale, Fes, Casablanca, and Marrakech. Moroccan leaders opened new centers in the towns of Mogador, Oujda, Safi, and Sefrou. In August of 1943, they organized a demonstration in Casablanca on the occasion of the sultan's visit to the city; demonstrators cried, "Vive la liberté!" and "Vive l'ancien Maghreb!"[26]

The planning, outreach, and recruitment conducted during 1943 prepared the way for widespread popular mobilization. In January 1944, former members of the CAM founded the Hizb al-Istiqlal.[27] On January 11, the party submitted the manifesto for independence, quoted at the start of this chapter, to the sultan, the French authorities, and the commander of the Allied forces in Morocco (Julien 1972, 514). The January 1944 French intelligence report noted solemnly, "The word independence has been openly pronounced for the first time in the history of the Protectorate." Tracts and graffiti went up on town walls to publicize the manifesto and the party.

Before they submitted the manifesto, party leaders had asked the sultan to do what he could to prevent repression, and the

---

[25] In May 1945, the French wrote: "Certain notables whose loyalty has always been unquestionable feel torn between the growing hostility of a sovereign who may represent the future and the passive weakness of the protectorate authority, which seems to them already diminished." *Note sur la situation politique en milieu musulman au Maroc Français*, May 1945. SHAT 3H249. A large number of notables failed to show up to the annual Bastille Day festivities in 1945, an event they typically attended, prompting further concern that regime intermediaries were switching sides. *Note sur la situation politique en milieu musulman au Maroc Français (suite)*, July 1945. SHAT 3H249

[26] These meetings and demonstrations are documented in the 1943 issues of the *Bulletin de Renseignements Politiques*, a report of the Political Affairs Bureau, French Residency in Morocco. SHAT 3H1414.

[27] *Bulletin de Renseignements Politiques*, January 1944. SHAT 3H1414.

sultan had obtained the agreement of the residency to allow its submission. But after it was distributed, Philippe Boniface, director of the interior, announced that leading signatories had been collaborating with Germany, and ordered their arrest (Julien 1972, 516; Bernard 1968, 23).[28]

The arrests triggered what French reports describe as a "wave of madness" as Moroccans demonstrated in favor of the Hizb al-Istiqlal.[29] Protests broke out in Rabat, Casablanca, Oujda, Sale, and Fes, with demonstrators insisting on the liberation of the leaders. The French responded with force. In Rabat, on the morning after the arrest of nationalist leader Belafrej, stores in the Moroccan *medina* closed in protest and 400–500 demonstrators went to the sultan's residence, shouting, "Belafrej or death!" By midday, the number of demonstrators exceeded 1,000. The sultan appeared, but unable to calm the crowd, he rushed away from what he called "a scene of savagery." Nationalist leader Lyazidi, who had been interrogated and released, arrived to speak to the demonstrators and turned them away from the residence. The crowd marched to the medina, which was then occupied by Moroccan *spahis* forces, who shut the gates, trapping the demonstrators.[30] Likewise, in the neighboring town of Sale, the army pushed demonstrators into the medina and arrests were carried out. In Fes, unrest lasted for more than a week. Moroccan stores closed in protest, students at the Qariouiyne Mosque went on strike, and demonstrators took to the streets. Senegalese troops were sent to the Fes medina, where nationalists had taken

---

[28] Note the irony of the accusation, as the protectorate administration was allied with Vichy and collaborating with Germany until the Allied landing (Pennell 2000, 266). The accusation was based on knowledge of some direct links between Germany and Moroccan leaders during the Vichy period; Ahmed Belafrej in particular spent time in Berlin (Zisenwine 2010, 18).

[29] *Le Nationalism Marocain*, 1952. SHAT 3H1417.

[30] The geography of Moroccan medinas poses problems for both protestors and police. On the one hand, the small streets with many tiny dwellings provide numerous places for protestors to hide, and the streets are unsuited to tanks or armed vehicles. On the other hand, medinas are surrounded by walls, which allows police to trap protestors and prevent their movement. The Moroccan spahis were mounted cavalry, and thus able to move into the medina to quell protests.

refuge inside mosques.[31] Repression was widespread and brutal. Hundreds of arrests were carried out across the country's towns.[32] In response to the repression, the sultan disavowed the party, saying, "The word *Istiqlal* must disappear from mouths and minds" (in Ageron 1991b, 59).

Nationalist demonstrations continued until the end of the war despite repression. In April 1944, the administration began releasing some of those who had been imprisoned during the January and February demonstrations, hoping that this would reduce mobilization. Nationalists spread rumors that these measures of clemency were caused by American intervention (Bernard 1968, 25). The release of detainees did little to stop mobilization, and in June 1944 the French chief in Fes wrote, "Five months have passed since the nationalist events, and no solution has been found for the principal actors. In 1937, everything was settled in one month.... They [the Istiqlal nationalists] sense perfectly our actual weakness and exploit it to the maximum."[33]

Nationalists continued to plan demonstrations and plot international strategy. Tracts and graffiti were posted, reassuring the public that independence was indeed on its way.[34] The sultan himself told demonstrators in February 1945 that the coming days would produce "great events, particularly happy for Islam and especially Morocco." The situation was so dire that settlers began selling their property and talking about moving to France.[35]

---

[31] Descriptions of these events came from a Jan.–Feb. report by the Direction des Affaires Politiques, SHAT 3H1417; January 1944 issues of the *Bulletin de Renseignements Politiques*, SHAT 3H1414; and *Note sur la situation politique en milieu musulman au Maroc Français*, May 1945, SHAT 3H249. See also Bernard (1968, 24).

[32] The French reported in February 1944 that arrests of nationalists in January and February totaled 1,803; of which 743 were released and 1,060 given prison sentences that ranged from one month to two years.

[33] *Note sur la situation politique en milieu musulman au Maroc Français*, May 1945. SHAT 3H249.

[34] Nationalisme, Tracts 1930–1947. MAE DI360.

[35] *Note sur la situation politique en milieu musulman au Maroc Français*, May 1945. SHAT 3H249; *Bulletin de Renseignements Politiques*, August 1944. SHAT 3H1414.

The Allied presence during the war years constituted an alternative power holder to which Moroccans could appeal. Local notables and leaders met with Americans directly; dinners and social events brought together young Moroccans and American officers. In one report, the French complained about the effects the American presence had on perceptions of the French, stating, "We are poor and weak vis-à-vis the opulence and power of the Americans."[36] They worried that the strength of the Americans would undermine French authority. Indeed, General George Patton, noting the warm welcome of Moroccan crowds, declared, "I feel that if the worst comes, I shall run for sultan."[37] It is important, however, not to overstate the hopes the nationalists placed in American support. Nationalists thought the Americans were sympathetic to their cause and sought their support, both during the occupation and in the postwar era. However, by 1944 the Istiqlal knew not to count on the Americans, who had decided upon a policy of nonintervention in Moroccan affairs. The understanding that diplomacy alone would not produce independence made popular mobilization essential.[38]

The Allied invasion marked a sharp division between an era in which political opponents did not publically mobilize in favor nationalist goals and collaboration was the dominant response to French rule, and a period of nationalist organizing in favor of independence. The disruption of French authority during the occupation and the uncertainty it produced empowered nationalist actors. Moroccans and the French both estimated that the probability of independence had risen sharply.[39] The occupation also meant that the French were less able to prevent mobilization, although they retained the capacity to repress in response to it. Political organizers had more freedom to organize than they had ever had before. The result was the beginning of a vibrant

---

[36] Note *sur la situation politique en milieu musulman au Maroc Français*, May 1945. SHAT 3H249.

[37] Quoted in Hoisington (1984, 239).

[38] See Abun-Nasr (1975, 373) and Halstead (1969a, 261).

[39] Julien (1972, 508) likewise describes a perception that independence was more likely during the occupation.

nationalist movement. As the war ended, the French were left
with the difficult task of reasserting their authority over a mobilized population demanding national independence.

French and Spanish Morocco Compared

The Spanish Civil War in 1936 and the Allied invasion in 1942
mark the onset of nationalist mobilization in the Spanish and
French zones in Morocco. These cases suggest a relationship
between disruptions in imperial authority and nationalist mobilization, but a two-case comparison suffers from indeterminacy;
with only two cases, it is impossible to control for other factors
that might explain divergent outcomes. This comparison, however, should give us greater confidence than typical small-N comparisons for two reasons. First, comparisons across countries
often introduce numerous confounding variables, but because
the two cases here are subnational, they share many characteristics. The populations of the two zones were similar: both zones
contained Arabs and Berbers who were overwhelmingly Sunni
Muslim, with small Jewish and European minorities. The majority worked in agriculture. Political activity was likewise similar:
in both zones, there were reform movements that sought political equality during the 1930s. Given these shared characteristics,
there is no ex ante reason to expect these populations to engage
in different political behavior. The main differences between
the two zones stem from the fact that they were occupied by
two different imperial powers, not from differences among their
populations.

A second reason to have confidence in this comparison is that
differences between the two cases that might explain the outcome point in the opposite direction of what we would expect,
given the existing literature on nationalism. Table 5.1 summarizes some of the main similarities and differences between the
two zones.

Several predictions that can be drawn from the literature fail
to explain why French Morocco's nationalist mobilization came
later than Spanish Morocco's. First, because of both colonial
policies and geographic conditions, French Morocco was more

TABLE 5.1. *Spanish and French Morocco, Compared*

	French Zone	Spanish Zone
Population	Majority Arab-Berber	Majority Arab-Berber
Occupation	Agricultural/Rural	Agricultural/Rural
Imperial Rule	More direct	More indirect
Development	More modernized	Underdeveloped
Policies	Repressive	More permissive
Inequality	Privileged settlers	Poor settlers

modern than Spanish Morocco. The French actively worked to modernize agriculture, build the transportation system, and develop some industrial sectors, albeit primarily to the benefit of French investors and settlers (Balfour 2002, 245).[40] The French zone also experienced rapid urbanization, whereas the Spanish zone consisted mainly of rural villages.[41] Moroccans in the French zone were better educated and wealthier than those in the Spanish zone. The Spanish zone did not undergo the kind of economic transformation that the French zone experienced (Abun-Nasr 1975, 362).[42] The Spanish took less interest in administering and developing their protectorate than the French did; Spanish investments in their zone were minimal. One observer colorfully stated that the Spanish treated their territory as a combination battlefield, brothel, and tavern (Woolman 1968, 57). Disease and poverty were characteristic of the Spanish zone; in the French zone at least a portion of the population had an adequate standard of living (Landau 1956, 168–170).

[40] See Stewart (1964) on the economic policies of the French and the consequences of those policies for Moroccans. French expenditures in the protectorate led one economist to report in 1937 that the French colonial empire was an "expensive national luxury during the depression period" (in Hoisington 1984, 132).

[41] For figures on urbanization in the French zone after World War I, see Awad (1964).

[42] There were few export goods in Spanish Morocco – mainly cork, iron ore, and small quantities of lead. In 1929, Spanish Morocco accounted for 7 percent of all of the exports from Morocco (Landau 1956, 168; Pennell 2000, 197).

If modernization is associated with nationalist mobilization, the French zone should have been more conducive to nationalist organizing than the Spanish zone.[43] The French zone was far more modernized. But modernization may account for the magnitude of mobilization, rather than mobilization onset. Moroccans in the French zone participated in mobilization events in far greater numbers than Moroccans in the Spanish zone, but they did so later on.

Another set of explanations focuses on the conditions of injustice and exploitation that accompanied colonial rule and may produce nationalist mobilization. But again, this hypothesis would predict nationalist mobilization in French Morocco, rather than Spanish Morocco. The French ruled more directly than the Spanish did; Spanish administrators were scarcer throughout the zone than their counterparts in French Morocco. If direct rule leads to nationalism, French rule would have been more likely to incite nationalist mobilization than Spanish rule.[44] Further, Moroccans enjoyed more liberties in the Spanish zone than in the French zone: newspapers were censored less often, meetings were allowed, and political organizations were sometimes subsidized by the Spanish. Leaders in both zones agreed that the Spanish zone provided more political freedoms.[45] But these freedoms seemed to have fostered mobilization, rather than assuaged the need for it.

In addition, whereas the Spanish zone was poorer overall than the French zone, levels of inequality between settlers and

[43] Waterbury (1970, 43) suggests particularly that social and economic change initiated under the French protectorate prompted the emergence of a nationalist movement. This hypothesis follows from Huntington's (1968) theory that rapidly changing societies are susceptible to political disorder. The rapid changes in French Morocco might have facilitated nationalist unrest, but Spanish Morocco experienced nationalist mobilization without similar rates of change.

[44] See Hechter (2000).

[45] Al-Ouazzani, a leader in the French zone, pointed out that in the Spanish zone of Morocco, freedom of the press, speech, and right to assemble were respected: "It is truly regrettable that we are reduced to such a level of inferiority in comparison to other protectorates and colonies that we envy the situation of our brothers of the Rif under a military dictatorship in a time of war" (quoted in Hoisington 1984, 42).

Moroccans were lower in the Spanish zone, where both Spaniards and Moroccans tended to be poor. In the French zone, settlers had a better quality of life than most Moroccans and occupied the best land. Marked differences between settlers and the population might be expected to create grievances that foster nationalist resistance, but the Spanish zone turned to nationalism first.[46]

Another potential reason Spanish Morocco saw nationalist mobilization first is economic hardship. It is possible that the timing of mobilization corresponds to particular periods of economic hardship that just happened to correspond with periods of disrupted rule. This may explain why a poorer, less-developed region experienced nationalist mobilization first. This argument is, however, unsatisfactory because it does not explain the observed pattern over time. Harvests were poor in both zones from 1935 to 1937, during the period of civil war and nationalist protest in the Spanish zone, but there was no nationalist mobilization in the French zone.[47] Economic hardship in the Spanish zone during the civil war was also offset in part by lucrative opportunities to serve in the Spanish army, and many chose to join up with the Spanish rather than mobilize against Spain. Economic hardship may thus provide incentives to support the regime, not oppose it.

Economic hardship due to shortages and high prices during World War II might explain the outbreak of nationalist mobilization in the French zone, but these years were even worse in the Rif mountains of the Spanish zone, where drought caused widespread famine (Hart 1976, 417). Yet nationalist mobilization was not as common during World War II in the Spanish

---

[46] The role of settlers in Morocco and how it differs from elsewhere in the empire remains a largely unexplored subject worthy of investigation. As in Algeria, settlers in Morocco blocked attempts at equitable reform and can therefore be seen as contributing to the failure of the reform movement. For a discussion of their possible role in triggering violent nationalist resistance, see Lawrence (2010a).

[47] See SHAT 3H1413 and Benjelloun (1994, 229). There was, however, mobilization in the French zone at this time in favor of reform. Economic hardship may thus facilitate mobilization, but not specifically *nationalist* mobilization.

zone (and was entirely absent in the Rif at this time) as it was in the French zone. An overview of economic conditions thus suggests that economic hardship does not account for the difference in onset of these two cases.

The existing literature on nationalism suggests that nationalist mobilization was more likely to occur in French Morocco than in Spanish Morocco. Instead, mobilization for independence occurred *first* in Spanish Morocco, years before political leaders in the French zone began articulating nationalist goals. The onset of nationalist mobilization – in the Rif in the 1920s and then in Tetouan in the 1930s – presents a puzzle for existing theories of nationalism. Although a comparison of two cases cannot rule out the possibility that other uncontrolled factors explain the outcome, the contrast between French Morocco and Spanish Morocco is suggestive of the importance of disruptions in imperial authority for nationalist mobilization. The medium-N analysis in Chapter 4 provides another stream of evidence.

The contrast between these two regions is provocative because it suggests that it is the state of the regime that matters for nationalist organizing, not the level of evolution of the population. Both nationalism and political mobilization more generally are associated with modern, sophisticated populations. In Morocco, it was the underdeveloped North that saw nationalist mobilization first, not the more modern South. It may be that it is the opportunity to mobilize that produces sophisticated political actors, rather than the other way around.

Nationalist Mobilization in the French Protectorate

This section examines temporal variation in mobilization in the French zone, using a dataset of mobilization events from the end of the conquest in 1934 through independence in March 1956. I begin by describing the data. Next, I describe the general pattern of mobilization over time, and I demonstrate the relationship between disruptions in imperial authority and nationalist mobilization. Then, I look at the implications of the argument for periods when imperial authority was robust and the French were in full control.

Data on Moroccan Mobilization, 1934–1956

I compiled data from *bulletins de renseignement* (information reports) issued by the political bureau of the French Residency in Morocco on a monthly, biweekly, or weekly basis for the entire colonial period, with more frequent reports issued during times of intense political activity. They summarize the main events in the protectorate for the specified time period and include information sent to the Residency from civil controllers in the administrative regions. The reports follow a similar format throughout the period: they summarize political activity among the European, Muslim, and Jewish communities; they include the main activities of the protectorate government and the sultan; and they discuss relevant international events.

The reports document a wide variety of nationalist activities. The French recorded the activities of the major opposition groups starting with the reform-oriented CAM in the 1930s and including the nationalist Istiqlal Party, as well as the smaller and less popular Parti Démocratique de l'Indépendance and Parti Communiste Marocain. The reports describe 526 mobilization events for the period, categorized into demonstrations, strikes, store closings, meetings, petitions, and elections (see Table 5.2).[48] Of these events, 383 were explicitly nationalist, meaning that participants sought independence on behalf of the nation. In contrast, 143 events were organized to demand changes within the structure of French rule, asking for alterations to the existing system rather than its overthrow.

The events are organized into a time-series dataset in which the observation is the month.[49] Table 5.3 summarizes the main characteristics of the data.

The dataset focuses on events that visibly challenged French rule: they were public and participatory, involving Moroccans who often came from diverse backgrounds. I included any event

[48] Contact the author for more detailed information about the data, including descriptions of each type of event.
[49] The main obstacle in creating a panel dataset, which would compare across regions or municipalities, is the absence of monthly cross-sectional data to use as independent variables.

TABLE 5.2. *Mobilization Events in Morocco, 1934–1956*

	Demonstration	Strike	Store Closing	Large Meeting	Petition	Election	Total Events	Avg. # Per Month
1934	1	0	4	2	0	0	7	0.88
1935	1	0	0	3	1	0	5	0.42
1936	13	4	0	8	0	0	25	2.08
1937	13	2	4	4	0	0	23	1.92
1938	1	3	0	0	0	0	4	0.33
1939	0	0	0	0	0	0	0	0.00
1940	1	0	0	0	0	0	1	0.08
1941	0	1	0	0	0	0	1	0.08
1942	0	2	0	0	0	0	2	0.17
1943	3	1	0	5	0	0	9	0.75
1944	36	4	2	10	3	0	55	4.58
1945	16	2	0	8	1	0	27	2.25
1946	11	0	0	11	0	0	22	1.83
1947	12	2	4	11	0	5	34	2.83
1948	1	6	0	7	0	0	14	1.17
1949	3	4	0	5	0	1	13	1.08
1950	15	7	0	3	0	0	25	2.08
1951	12	7	34	1	0	7	61	5.08
1952	30	5	12	0	0	0	47	3.92
1953	9	0	0	0	1	0	10	0.83
1954	5	11	14	3	0	0	33	2.75
1955	47	5	27	1	0	0	80	6.67
1956 (Jan.–Mar.)	17	6	3	2	0	0	28	9.33
TOTAL	247	72	104	84	6	13	526	2.00

TABLE 5.3. *Morocco Mobilization Summary Statistics*

Observation:	
Number of months:	263
Total number of events:	526
Average # of events per month:	2
Total number of nationalist events:	383
Number of months with at least 1 nationalist event:	92
Total number of reform events:	143
Number of months with at least 1 reform event:	80

with approximately fifty or more participants. Demonstrations, defined as protests in public spaces such as the street, town square, or outside public buildings, constituted the largest category of mobilization events. The second-largest category was store closings. The Istiqlal Party would issue an order, typically through tracts, graffiti, or word of mouth, that Moroccans should close their shops on particular days as a sign of protest. Mobilization also took the form of strikes by workers and students, and large meetings. These meetings involved outreach efforts by Moroccan parties, who made speeches and recruited new members. They were a less dramatic form of protest than demonstrations or strikes. The final two types of mobilization were petitions and elections. Petitions were included if they were widely disseminated and included at least fifty signatories. The French administration held elections that Moroccans could participate in during 1947 and 1951. These elections showed the level of support for the nationalist party, but they differ from the other forms of mobilization because they were permissible activities, not contentious action.

The French administration's efforts to collect information on Moroccan political activity were extensive, and not all activities described in the reports are included in the dataset. The French tracked the actions of nationalist elites, making note of leaders' meetings, their travels to and from various towns and abroad, their contacts with foreigners, and internal rivalries. The reports describe the diplomatic strategies of the parties and their attempts

to call international attention to their cause. My focus on public mobilization events represents a departure from studies that
concentrate on these kinds of elite political maneuvers. The over-
whelming majority of the historical literature on the Moroccan
nationalist movement has focused on elite activities rather than
popular mobilization.[50] Gelvin (1998, 8–9) has criticized this
inattention to popular politics in his study of Syrian nationalism, calling the attempt to locate nationalism solely among the
elites ill-conceived. He points out that popular politics is not a
straightforward reflection of elite designs; elite messages had to
resonate with other elements of the population to produce mobilization. The ubiquity of elite-centered approaches is due largely
to two considerations: the availability of information about
elite activity in contrast with the relative scarcity of information
about mass activities; and most scholars' concern with decolonization, a process that explicitly involved elite-level negotiations.
But popular mobilization is also important: it affects elite activity and the stability of the state itself.

There are several potential sources of bias to consider when
using reports written by a colonial power. Underreporting is one
plausible source of bias, if administrators left mobilization events
out of their reports in order to minimize the threat they posed
and emphasize the colonial state's capacity to maintain control.
But there are multiple reasons to believe that the French did not
underreport nationalist activities. First, the primary reason the
French kept these reports was to monitor political activity in
order to better police it. Underreporting would have undermined
the purpose of the reports. Second, the reports were classified;
they were not for public circulation. Administrators were thus
unlikely to use the reports as propaganda because readership
was limited; they had other means to publicize the achievements
of the protectorate. Third, the level of detail in the reports shows

---

[50] Burke (2000, 23) notes that nationalist historiography on North Africa has
   privileged the urban elite and neglected other participants. For excellent
   examples of histories of the Moroccan nationalist movement that focus on the
   parties and elites, see Rézette (1955) and Bernard (1963).

that the authors sought to be as inclusive as possible. The reports provide far more than a description of major events – they include minor activities such as small meetings, samples of handwritten tracts, and notes about rumors conveyed by officials' servants. The thoroughness of the French intelligence effort is at times astonishing; one protectorate file included pictures of graffiti collected in the bathroom of the Qaraouyine Mosque in Fes, carefully numbered by stall, with an accompanying translation.[51]

Although French reporting was extensive, they may still have missed some mobilization events or miscoded some kinds of unrest as apolitical when they were in fact political, or vice versa. The French saw the countryside in particular as a place without politics or nationalism. They relied on Moroccan notables to administer rural areas, and these notables may have downplayed local opposition. It is therefore likely that political activity was not tracked as accurately in rural areas as it was in towns. To guard against potential biases that stem from relying on French reporting, I checked the data against a number of secondary sources, as well as a publication approved by the Moroccan government that described nationalist mobilization events during the colonial period.[52]

It is plausible that the French could underreport their repressive responses to mobilization, but surprisingly, the reports do not reflect a reluctance to discuss repression. Some reports betray a certain pride in the skillful use of repression; one report described repression as "swift and just."[53] Each report with a mobilization event describes the response of the administration, detailing the actions of the police and the number of arrests, if

---

[51] In June 1939, for example, stall number six in the men's room read: "Long live the North African People! Down with Italy!" *Nationalisme*, Tracts 1930–1947, DI 360 MAE.

[52] Secondary sources include Rézette (1955); Bernard (1968); Halstead (1969a); Bidwell (1973); Hoisington (1984); Ghallaab (2000). Essakali (1984; 1985) is the official Moroccan source. Better reporting in urban areas may be a problem for all of these sources, but I expect that the data are fairly reliable largely because protest activities are typically an urban phenomenon.

[53] *Bulletin de Renseignements Politiques et Economiques*, November 1936. SHAT 3H1413.

repression occurred. If there were casualties, the reports typically list any available figures. I coded whether or not the French employed repression for each month of the period. Specifically, I coded repression as occurring in months where the French carried out political arrests or engaged in violence against those leading or participating in mobilization events.

The body of French reports provides a unique look at decision making in an authoritarian setting. This kind of information is typically difficult to come by; most authoritarian regimes do not provide information on how they choose to respond to popular demands. This information is only available because the colonial period has ended and the documents have been declassified. These reports provide an unusual opportunity to systematically consider the effects of repression on popular mobilization.[54]

The main source of bias is the attempt to gauge popular sentiment. The reports mistake compliance for loyalty: they code public opinion on the basis of whether or not there was any popular mobilization, without considering the constraints the regime placed on mobilization. Moreover, when there was mobilization, administrators claimed either that it reflected the discontent of only a minority group of rabble-rousers, or that it was caused by grievances that were temporary and circumstantial. The reports betray a significant amount of wishful thinking. For example, reports in early 1951 claimed that 100,000 rural chiefs continued to feel loyal to France and wanted the sultan to condemn the Istiqlal Party.[55] There is no way that they could know the opinion of such a large number of chiefs, nor could they know if such sentiments were genuine. To take another example, the French failed to anticipate the public outcry after they sent the sultan into exile in 1953; the administration had underestimated his popularity and overestimated the power of the pasha of the South, Thami al Glaoui, who helped orchestrate

---

[54] On the importance of repression for revolutions, see Goodwin (2001).
[55] *Bulletin de Renseignements Politiques,* February and March 1951. SHAT 3H1416.

the deposition.[56] The French lacked reliable information about public opinion among Moroccans; they had to rely on the word of regime allies.[57] The reports therefore cannot be used to gain a sense of popular sentiment.

Disruptions in Imperial Authority and Nationalist Mobilization over Time

In Morocco, the nationalist mobilization that began in 1943 did not cease when Allied forces departed. Although repression limited protest in the postwar era, the nationalists had an established organizational structure and membership. The collapse in imperial authority provided the initial conditions for mobilization; in the postwar period, the nationalist movement continued to organize protest activities. Figure 5.1 shows the pattern of nationalist mobilization in Morocco from 1934 to 1956.

Disruptions in imperial rule are important not only for onset, but also for the magnitude of mobilization. Given the authoritarian nature of colonial rule, it ought to be easier to organize protest activities when authority is contested than when the imperial power has full authority over the territory. We should expect to see *more* mobilization when imperial rule is unstable, not only in the initial period of imperial instability but also in any subsequent periods in which colonial rule is disrupted. If this logic is correct, disruptions in imperial rule should be associated with more nationalist mobilization events. Figure 5.1 shows two time periods during which French authority was compromised. The first coincides with the Allied invasion, discussed previously.

The second occurred at the end of the colonial era, when French authority was affected by the decision to decolonize.

---

[56] Resident General Grandval (1956) recounts the missteps in French policy in his memoir. For more on Thami el Glaoui, see Maxwell (2000) as well as his son's biography (Glaoui 2004).

[57] The French in Morocco faced what Wintrobe (1998) has described as the "dictator's dilemma." A dictator cannot reliably know the level of public support he enjoys because as an authoritarian ruler he cannot know if his subjects' claims to support him stem from loyalty or fear of repression.

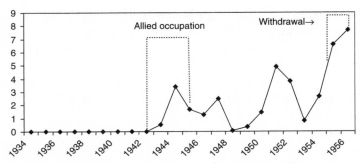

FIGURE 5.1. Average number of nationalist events per month in colonial Morocco, 1934–1956.

After the war ended, the French sought to dampen nationalist opposition and retain control over Morocco, but despite policing efforts, the movement remained active. In December 1952, French officials moved to severely repress nationalist activities. French police and tanks confronted demonstrators in the city of Casablanca, killing hundreds. The police then arrested the leaders of the Istiqlal Party, Moroccan trade union, and smaller Moroccan Communist Party, decapitating the nationalist movement. Eight months later, the French decided to remove the sultan, sending him into exile in August 1953 and replacing him with a pretender to the throne. These actions, designed to eliminate the nationalist threat and ensure stable French rule, backfired.[58] In the wake of the removal of the nationalist leadership and sultan, the nationalist movement fragmented. Protests continued in the cities, a violent insurgency began in the countryside, and small violent organizations began carrying out terrorist attacks in Moroccan towns (Lawrence 2010b).

[58] Speaking before the French parliament on June 10, 1954, Pierre Mendès-France noted that leadership repression had prompted nationalist violence in Morocco, saying, "The force which was designed to prevent or delay events has in fact accelerated them. It is, among the most advanced, transforming demands into open revolt, and, among the hitherto indifferent masses, it is creating the concept of a national conflict and driving them to take arms against us" (quoted in Bernard 1963, 216).

In 1955, the French began to withdraw from Morocco. The administration's decapitation strategy had failed, and led only to violence. France had already granted autonomy to Tunisia, and French attention was focused on the growing conflict in Algeria. In June, Gilbert Grandval was appointed resident general and assigned to end "the Moroccan problem" (Grandval 1956). He convened leading nationalists upon his arrival, and official negotiations began in August. In September 1955, General Catroux met with the sultan to discuss his return. At the United Nations on September 29, France announced that Morocco was to be independent. In November, the sultan returned in triumph and announced Morocco's independence to cheering crowds. The treaty of independence was concluded in March 1956.

The period from June 1955 to March 1956 was one of flux, as power began to shift from the French administration to Moroccan actors. France was no longer the sole authority; it had inaugurated a period of transition. The period of decolonization, much like the Allied occupation, was an interval of disrupted French rule. I hypothesized that the number of nationalist events would be higher during these two time periods than at other times, when the French had full authority.

The data are supportive of the hypothesis. During the entire period, there were 41 months of unstable imperial authority out of the total 263-month period. During these periods of imperial instability, the average number of nationalist events per month was 3.4. When imperial authority was stable, the monthly average was 1.1. Table 5.4 shows the relationship between imperial authority and nationalist mobilization.

The dependent variable is coded 1 if the month had one or more nationalist mobilization event, 0 otherwise. The frequency of months with nationalist events was significantly greater when imperial authority was disrupted than when authority was stable. Nationalist events occurred in 71 percent of the months of imperial instability, whereas during periods of uncontested authority only 29 percent of months saw nationalist activity.

TABLE 5.4. *Nationalist Mobilization by Imperial Authority*

	Months with Stable Imperial Authority	Months with Imperial Authority Disrupted	Total
No nationalist event	158	12	170
	71%	29%	65%
Nationalist event	64	29	93
	29%	71%	35%
Total	222	41	263
	100%	100%	100%

Chi-squared = 26.6, p < .01.

The magnitude of mobilization was much higher when imperial authority was disrupted, as the argument predicts.[59]

Mobilization Activities under Stable Imperial Rule

Disruptions in imperial authority were important for a number of reasons: independence seemed more likely; the imperial power was less able to police and prevent mobilization; and regime intermediaries were more likely to defect and begin cooperating with nationalist organizations. But how are we to understand nationalist mobilization during the periods in between, when imperial authority was stable? We might expect that if a disruption in imperial authority caused the onset of nationalist mobilization, then the reassertion of authority after World War II would have put an end to it. But this prediction does not conform to the intuition that mobilization is path dependent; once people have publicly demonstrated for a cause, it is easier to organize subsequent protest activities. Political organizers are able to draw on a base of supporters and benefit from previous periods of organization and recruitment. Initial mobilization is particularly

[59] For this contingency table, I coded the period of decolonization as June 1955 to March 1956. Because it is difficult to precisely date the beginning of decolonization, I recoded the start date as November 1955, when France ended the protectorate in the declaration of La Celle-Saint Cloud and the sultan returned from exile. This alternate coding did not change the results.

difficult to achieve. Figure 5.1 shows nationalist activity between the end of World War II and the decision to decolonize in 1955, with spikes of activity in 1947 and 1951. This section considers how stable imperial authority affected the type, location, and timing of mobilization.

When the war ended, the French reestablished their authority. In June 1945, the administration sent the sultan on a trip to Paris, where he was applauded and decorated for his dedication to France during the war. The purpose of the trip was to cast doubt on his nationalist commitments by demonstrating that he was still an official ally and beneficiary of French rule.[60] Leading nationalists, starting from July 1945, conceded that independence was not imminent and started speaking of it as a long-term goal. Nationalist speeches and articles began to take a different tone than they had during the war, discussing gradual, evolutionary progress, rather than immediate separation. The immediate postwar years saw a decline in mobilization, which we might expect.[61]

The postwar years also saw a change in the kind of mobilization activities that occurred. I hypothesized that the state of imperial authority would affect how nationalists organized protest. Under robust imperial authority, it was more difficult to organize dramatic and costly forms of protest such as street demonstrations and strikes, which were illegal, because the administration could more effectively police and prevent large-scale mobilization. As the French wrote in 1946, "The nationalists

[60] *Note sur la situation politique en milieu musulman au Maroc Français (suite)*, June 1945. SHAT 3H249. A report the following month suggested that nationalists began worrying that the sultan had abandoned his support for their movement. The sultan's support for independence became clearer, however, as the postwar years went on. In 1946, when Morocco was included as an associated state in the French Union, the sultan declined to participate in the French Union's assemblies, sending no representatives. Tunisia likewise did not participate.

[61] The December 1945 *Bulletins de Renseignements Politiques* attributed this decline to internal rivalry and indecision among nationalists, rather than the changed climate in the protectorate, but this interpretation seems to stem more from wishful thinking than evidence of internal problems. In reality, the Istiqlal expanded in the postwar years.

TABLE 5.5. *Average Number of Protest Activities per Month by Imperial Authority*

	Divided Imperial Authority	Stable Imperial Authority
Demonstrations	2.8	0.6
Strikes	0.4	0.2
Store closings	0.3	0.4
Large meetings	0.5	0.3

know that France has decided to maintain order; they do not want to risk arrests and searches that would potentially undermine their movement with ill-timed demonstrations."[62] Less visible forms of opposition, such as store closings and meetings, should be more common under these conditions.

The data suggest that the state of imperial authority did affect the type of protest. Although nationalist mobilization in general happened with greater frequency when imperial authority was disrupted, the frequency of different types of protests varied (see Table 5.5).

Demonstrations were nearly five times more likely to occur when imperial authority was disrupted than when it was stable. Strikes also occurred twice as often when imperial authority was divided. In contrast, store closings, the most passive form of resistance in the dataset, happened more often when imperial authority was stable.[63] Large meetings and rallies took place with greater frequency under divided imperial authority, although the difference is not very large.

Nationalist mobilization was also expressed through elections. Elections provided nationalist parties with the opportunity to mobilize followers and demonstrate public support. Unlike

---

[62] *Bulletin de Renseignements Politiques*, December 1947. SHAT 3H1415.

[63] Petitions are also a passive form of mobilization, but there are only five cases in the dataset because I excluded elite-only petitions. Boycotts are another category of mobilization that we might expect to see more often under periods when the regime is limiting political mobilization, but compliance with a boycott is difficult to observe.

the other protest activities in the dataset, however, elections were organized by the administration and thus were permitted forms of mobilization. The French held elections twice, both at times when imperial authority was stable, as might be expected. Figure 5.1 shows a spike in nationalist mobilization in both of these years; the elections account in part for the observed peaks, as each major town's election counted as an event.

The first elections were held in December 1947, when Istiqlal Party members competed for seats in the consultative chambers – advisory bodies with both French and Moroccan members – in Rabat, Fes, Meknes, Casablanca, and Port Lyautey. Before 1947, the Moroccan representatives had been appointed, but in 1947 the French decided that they would be elected by limited suffrage. The Istiqlal achieved considerable success and won fifteen of the twenty-one seats designated for Moroccans on the General Council.[64] These representatives served on the council until December of 1950, when a delegate from the Istiqlal presented a number of criticisms of protectorate administration during a council session. French Resident General Juin responded by dismissing the offending delegate, saying, "In every assembly, there must be a limit to insolence and provocation" (in Julien 1972, 559). Eleven of his colleagues followed him out of the assembly, and the party's representation in the council came to an end.[65]

On October 17, 1951, the resident general announced that new elections would be held on November 1. He also expanded the franchise, according 220,000 Moroccans the right to vote.

[64] Only Moroccan évolués could vote in these elections; 3,000 were qualified to vote for the chamber of agriculture and 8,000 qualified to vote for the chamber of commerce and industry. Rézette (1955, 45) has argued that the limited franchise in the 1947 elections favored the Istiqlal Party, because their main supporters came from the commercial and industrial elite. Members of the general council were drawn from the consultative chambers. The general council was also an advisory board; its task was to review the annual budget and make recommendations to the resident general, who was not bound to follow them. French settlers were overrepresented on the council (Julien 1972, 546). For more on the political system and the functioning of parties in Morocco during the protectorate, see Rézette (1955).

[65] *Le Nationalisme Marocain*, 1952. SHAT 3H1417.

The Istiqlal Party protested that the resident general had allowed no time for campaigning, and asked that the election not be held on a workday. The intention of the government was undoubtedly to limit the ability of the party to campaign effectively among the mass of new voters and show that the party lacked broad support. The strategy backfired when the Istiqlal organized a successful boycott of the election in all the major towns (Rézette 1955, 45–48).[66]

In the postwar period, nationalists organized other activities that are not captured in the dataset because they were purposely less public or overtly nationalist. The Istiqlal Party worked on expanding their membership; they organized Muslim scouts in different towns, sponsored soccer teams and sporting events, created study groups, and started a woman's organization (al-Fasi 1970, 395; Landau 1956, 250). The party also devoted resources to the free schools, where nationalist sympathizers served as teachers.[67] These activities exemplify the types of mobilization that are easier to organize under an authoritarian regime with full control of the state.

Sites of Nationalist Mobilization

The state of imperial authority was also important for the location of nationalist mobilization. During periods of fragmented authority, mobilization took place on the street. When imperial authority was stable, nationalist activity was more likely to occur in places outside the direct control of the colonial

[66] I included this boycott in the dataset because compliance with it was measurable, and the absence of voters at the polls was a visible sign of support for the party. Rézette (1955, 48) reports that out of eligible voters, the percentage abstaining was: 96 percent in Casablanca; 97 percent in Safi; 95 percent in Agadir; 93 percent in Port Lyautey; 93 percent in Sale; 98 percent in Petit-Jean; and 83 percent in Khemisset. Some of the abstentions were likely due to the expansion of the franchise and the decision to announce the elections with very little notice, but these extremely high rates of abstention suggest that the boycott was fairly effective in major towns.

[67] The free schools were initially set up by the religious reformists of the 1930s, as an alternative to French education (Pennell 2000, 255), and new ones continued to be established in the postwar era with the approval of the French, as these schools served to meet some of the educational needs of the population.

power. In fact, nationalist mobilization occurred first outside the protectorate entirely, in Paris.[68] Anti-French activity also took place in the Spanish zone.[69]

Even within its borders, no authoritarian regime has full control everywhere, and the protectorate was no exception. Regime opponents made use of sites where public gatherings were permissible. Mosques were privileged places where police could not enter and they became prime sites of mobilization. Many demonstrations began at the mosque; after prayer, a group would gather and march through the streets. Mosques also provided meeting places and places of refuge during waves of repression.[70]

The importance of the mosque to the nationalist movement can be linked to two factors: its position as a permissible gathering spot and the role of religion in the movement. Moroccan leaders at the outset of the colonial period were part of a *salafiyya* movement that advocated a return to more orthodox religious practices. Subsequent political organizing retained religious elements. In speeches, leaders attempted to link religious obligations with obligations to the nation. Thus, Friday store closings, for example, had both a religious and nationalist purpose: they demonstrated the ability of the nationalists to organize; flew in the face of French orders; and emphasized the holy nature of

---

[68] The French began worrying about the effects of "radical" North Africans in Paris in the mid 1930s, with the creation of the nationalist Étoile Nord Africaine. Students and workers in Paris were the first to call for independence. *Situation Politique et Economique, Periode du 1 au 15 Octobre 1934, Direction des Affaires Indigènes*. SHAT 3H1413. Indeed, students home for the summer claimed that nationalist politics in Paris was far more active and interesting than in the protectorate. *Bulletin de Renseignements Politiques,* August 1950. SHAT 3H1416.

[69] During the mid-1950s, Moroccans engaged in violent resistance took refuge in the Spanish zone. On the use of violence during the nationalist movement, see Lawrence (2010a; 2010b).

[70] Despite the prohibition on entering mosques, the French were still able to exercise some control over what happened in them. They placed informers in the congregations to identify people who were disseminating political messages. Using the mosques for political purposes was punishable by arrests and fines (Rézette 1955, 10).

the day. Nationalists invoked Islam and religious obligations to recruit followers, and some have suggested that members understood the party as a type of religious brotherhood (Rivet 1999, 369–371; Halstead 1969a, 252).

This marriage between politics and religion did not occur without resistance. In May 1934, one reformist tried to make a speech at the Grand Mosque in Taza. The congregation refused to hear him, summoning the police (Rézette 1955, 8). That same year, the *ulema* of the Qarawiyne stripped an `alim of his title when he claimed to love his nation, saying that the nation is an idol and only God can be loved in this way (Rivet 1999, 393). The nation was considered a potential obstacle to the unity of the Muslim community. Between 1934 and World War II, Muslim scholars engaged in debates about the nation and religion. Reformists such as Rachid Rida put forth the idea that love of the nation is a part of belief (*hub al watan min al imân*), but such claims were contested. As late as 1951, the sultan received petitions from people who protested the invocation of Islam by the Istiqlal (Rivet 1999, 393). Nationalists continued to invoke religion, but their appropriation of Islam was sometimes contested.

The palace was another site of mobilization during the years of stable imperial rule. Traditionally, Moroccans appealed to the sultan to redress any grievances. During the nationalist movement, demonstrators often headed to the seat of the sultan's government to express their opposition. The sultan's role was ambivalent: on the one hand, he was the official head of government and was supposed to hear complaints; on the other hand, he was also a symbol of the sovereignty of the nation. In the postwar period, the French increasingly sought to limit contact between the sultan and the nationalists, particularly as they began to see the sultan as an enemy. In 1947, the sultan gave an unauthorized speech in Tangier that branded him an unreliable ally in the eyes of the French. The palace continued to serve as a site of mobilization.

Nationalists also took advantage of a number of other sites where assembly was permitted. They used occasions such as weddings and funerals to make speeches and plan strategy. They gave speeches and held rallies to celebrate the opening of new free schools, and they used these occasions to increase their visibility. The French monitored this activity closely, but they could not close off all sites of mobilization. When the Istiqlal began holding night classes in 1950 with the stated aim of decreasing illiteracy, for instance, the French explained the difficulty: the night classes "place the administration in an embarrassing position. It would be very easy [for the party] to benefit from a ban on these night courses by claiming to the masses that the Protectorate Government is hostile to any improvements in the Moroccan level of intellect."[71] They recognized that the party benefited from such activities. By transforming sites of apolitical activity into sites where nationalists could disseminate their message, the nationalist party effectively undermined some of the restrictions on political activity.[72]

The Timing of Mobilization under Stable Imperial Rule

Just as particular sites served as gathering places for the nationalists, certain dates also provided opportunities for mobilization. Three Muslim holidays have traditionally been times of celebration in Morocco: Aïd as-Seghir, Aïd al-Kebir, and Aïd Mouloud.[73] To this, two other secular holidays were added during the protectorate era: the Fête du Thrône, celebrating the accession of the sultan to the throne; and Labor Day, a French holiday that often saw strike activity.[74] On these holidays, the administration allowed and expected public gatherings. The Fête du Thrône was accompanied by parades and demonstrations. On religious

---

[71] *Bulletin de Renseignements Politiques,* June 1950. SHAT 3H1416.

[72] The transformation of everyday settings into places of nationalist mobilization makes it likely that some nationalist mobilization was not tracked in French reports. Moroccan nationalists deliberately tried to disguise their activities, and they succeeded at times in blurring the line between the political and the apolitical.

[73] Aïd es-Seghir marks the end of Ramadan; Aïd al-Kebir celebrates Abraham's willingness to sacrifice Isaac; Aïd Mouloud is the birthday of the Prophet.

[74] The Fête du Thrône was an initiative of the reformists, who created the holiday with protectorate support in 1933 (Waterbury 1970, 48). In the postwar years, the Istiqlal organized nationalist demonstrations as part of the holiday.

TABLE 5.6. *Nationalist Events by Holiday, Stable Imperial Authority (Partial table)*

	Months with no Holiday	Months with an Approved Holiday	Total
No nationalist event	106	52	158
	76%	63%	71%
Nationalist event	34	30	64
	24%	37%	29%
Total	140	82	222
	100%	100%	100%

Chi-squared = 3.8, p < 0.05.

TABLE 5.7. *Nationalist Events by Holiday, Disrupted Imperial Authority (Partial table)*

	Months with no Holiday	Months with an Approved Holiday	Total
No nationalist event	8	4	12
	33%	24%	29%
Nationalist event	16	13	29
	67%	76%	71%
Total	24	17	41
	100%	100%	100%

Chi-squared = .46, p = .5.

holidays, notables traveled to see the sultan and present gifts; these days thus involved a lot of travel and activity in the streets. I hypothesized that holidays would be particularly important days of nationalist mobilization when imperial authority was stable. Tables 5.6 and 5.7 show the relationship between holidays and nationalist mobilization when imperial authority is disrupted and when it is stable.

As expected, holidays appear to be more important for nationalist organizing during months of stable imperial rule. When imperial authority was stable, 37 percent of months with one of the French-approved holidays saw nationalist events, as opposed to 24 percent of months with no holiday, and the difference is statistically significant. When imperial authority was disrupted, more holiday months saw nationalist events than non-holiday months, but the difference is smaller and not statistically significant. Nationalist organizers strategically chose existing holidays to promote nationalist aims. Writing in February 1953, the French lamented that "no event of any importance can take place in Morocco today entirely free of political incidents."[75]

In February 1948, the French wrote that "if the international climate remains favorable, and if we signal our firm intention not to allow disorder in this country, the nationalists will give up the fight."[76] From 1945 to 1955, the French did indeed show their commitment to ruling Morocco, but the nationalists did not concede. Nationalist mobilization changed, however, under stable French authority. Facing a powerful authoritarian regime, nationalists chose different times and places to mobilize than they had during the Allied occupation and they favored less visible forms of protest.

A comparison between two years illustrates the point. During the years of stable imperial rule, the greatest number of nationalist events took place in 1951, with fifty-nine nationalist events. The majority was passive or permitted: there were thirty-four store closings, one large meeting, and seven elections. Of the remaining seventeen events (demonstrations or strikes), thirteen took place in a holiday month. Unions marched on Labor Day and nationalist demonstrators followed the sultan to the mosque on the Prophet's birthday. There were two other demonstrations, both centered on the palace. One was a protest at the Palace of Justice, where four nationalist leaders were on trial. The second was a demonstration to greet the sultan as he went to pray; demonstrators shouted nationalist slogans. Two student strikes also occurred to protest the dismissal of nationalist teachers.

In 1944, during the Allied invasion, there were forty-one nationalist events. Only seven out of the forty-one events took the form of store closing or meetings, meaning that thirty-four

[75] *Bulletin de Renseignements Politiques*, February 1953. SHAT 3H1416.
[76] *Bulletin de Renseignements Politiques*, February 1948. SHAT 3H1415.

were events that challenged public order. There were twenty-seven street demonstrations in 1944, as opposed to ten in 1951. Fifteen out of the forty-one events took place on a holiday. Contentious nationalist protests were more common in the year of disruption.

The contrast between the two months highlights the creativity of political organizers in colonial Morocco, who found solutions to the problems of organizing under a stable authoritarian regime. When imperial authority began to disintegrate for the second time, in June 1955, nationalist mobilization escalated, benefiting from the collapse of the colonial order. But this escalation might not have been possible without the work of nationalist organizers during the postwar years of stable colonial rule.

Other Explanations

Two other factors may contribute to an explanation of temporal variation in nationalist activity: international events and repression. These factors are not alternatives, but they may operate in conjunction with my argument about disruptions.

International Events

Mobilization may diffuse from successful cases to other places; events outside Morocco may have affected mobilization within Morocco. To evaluate the impact of international events on nationalist mobilization, I constructed a variable that included three categories of events: the onset of violent and nonviolent nationalist mobilization in other parts of the French empire; international conferences condemning imperial rule in general; and decolonization or the granting of autonomy in other parts of the empire or the region.[77] The hypothesis was that these

---

[77] I also tested this proposition with a variable that indicated whether decolonization had occurred elsewhere in the French empire or the larger Arab or Muslim world (not shown), but I found no statistically significant relationship between decolonization elsewhere and nationalist events in Morocco, likely because there were only eleven such decolonization events during the protectorate era.

TABLE 5.8. *Nationalist Events by International Events*

	Months with no International Event	Months with International Events	Total
No nationalist event	163	7	170
	67%	39%	65%
Nationalist event	82	11	93
	33%	61%	35%
Total	245	18	263
	100%	100%	100%

Chi-squared = 5.6, p < 0.05.

events may have affected mobilization in Morocco because they indicated the vulnerability of France's imperial authority in general.

Table 5.8 provides a cross-tabulation of nationalist events by instability in imperial rule at the international level. Sixty percent of months with an international event undermining imperial rule also had nationalist mobilization events in Morocco, whereas in 33 percent of months without international events, mobilization still occurred in Morocco. There was indeed an association between international events and nationalist activity in Morocco.

The meaning of this association is not entirely clear. On the one hand, international events may have provided an occasion for protests, which could be carried out in solidarity with events happening elsewhere. For instance, when Tunisia gained autonomy in April 1955, Moroccans might have used the event to indicate their support or to show that they, too, merited concessions. Alternatively, nationalists may have calculated that mobilization occurring while France was facing challenges elsewhere would be more effective at convincing the French to leave. On the other hand, correlation does not imply causation. It is not evident how or whether international events could cause events in Morocco that happen in the same month; events elsewhere could take a longer period of time to alter mobilization. This variable also

TABLE 5.9. *Nationalist Events by Imperial Authority, without International Events (Partial table)*

	Months with Stable Imperial Authority	Months with Imperial Authority Disrupted	Total
No nationalist event	151	12	163
	73%	32%	67%
Nationalist event	56	26	82
	27%	68%	33%
Total	207	38	245
	100%	100%	100%

Chi-squared = 24.7, p < 0.01.

TABLE 5.10. *Nationalist Events by Imperial Authority, with International Events (Partial table)*

	Months with Stable Imperial Authority	Months with Imperial Authority Disrupted	Total
No nationalist event	7	0	7
	47%	0%	39%
Nationalist event	8	3	11
	53%	100%	61%
Total	15	3	18
	100%	100%	100%

does not measure the cumulative effect of events around the world. The relationship is suggestive, but it does not point to a compelling account of how international events affected local events, because this kind of analysis does not capture the dynamic process that occurs as nationalist protest evolves over time.

For my argument, the key question is whether international events explain the variation. Tables 5.9 and 5.10 provide a three-way cross-tabulation that controls for international events. It shows that disruptions in authority still matter.

Table 5.9 shows that in months with no international events, disruptions in imperial authority were highly associated with nationalist mobilization: 68 percent of months with divided imperial authority had nationalist events, as opposed to 27 percent of months with stable imperial authority, and the difference is statistically significant. In months where there were international events (Table 5.10), the results are inconclusive due to low cell counts. Although the number is too small for a chi-squared test to be appropriate, the expected pattern holds; all of the months with disrupted imperial authority saw nationalist mobilization, whereas only 53 percent of the months with stable imperial authority had nationalist events.

Repression

For each month, I coded whether or not the French used repression in response to Moroccan mobilization. Out of the 263 months in the dataset, the French repressed Moroccan political activists during 71 months, nearly a third of the period. Repression most often took the form of political arrests, but sometimes the French used violence against demonstrators.

Despite the existence of good data, evaluating the impact of repression on nationalist mobilization presents an extremely thorny problem. Repression and mobilization raises the chicken-and-egg question: does repression affect mobilization, is repression a reaction to mobilization, or both? The effects of repression have been difficult to disentangle in studies of authoritarian rule.[78] The French reports reveal their own confusion over the effects of repression and leniency. Residents general and other administrators varied in their attitude toward the effectiveness of repression. Sometimes they felt that taking "a strong line" was the only way to show resolve and stop mobilization, whereas at other times repression was seen as counterproductive. A report in February 1945 claimed that the release of political prisoners helped quell "the resentment that stemmed from repression,"

---

[78] Elsewhere, I have studied the effects of repression on nationalist organizing by disaggregating repression and focusing on leadership repression, which is easier to sequence. I show that leadership repression preceded violent nationalist mobilization, and I delineate the logic that connects the two (Lawrence 2010b).

suggesting that repression was counterproductive because it provoked anger. But another report in May 1945 suggested that leniency was incomprehensible to the population and implied that repression was all Moroccans could understand.[79] One report stated in frustration that the nationalists abided by the Moroccan proverb, "If you act like a lion, I will act like a sheep, if you act like a sheep, I will eat you." In other words, there was no winning policy because the nationalists could benefit from both repression and leniency.[80]

The relationship between repression and mobilization cannot be disentangled using contingency tables. It is clear from the data that the use of repression is associated with the occurrence of mobilization: months with mobilization events were far more likely to see repression than months without events, but this is unsurprising and says nothing about the direction of causality. Using lagged variables likewise does not solve the problem, because just as prior repression may be associated with current mobilization, prior mobilization is also associated with current repression. Moreover, autocorrelation poses a further obstacle: repression in one month is not independent of repression in the following month.

The relationship between repression and mobilization does not diminish the importance of imperial discontinuities for nationalist mobilization. Tables 5.11 and 5.12 present a three-way contingency table that controls for repression.[81] Regardless of whether the French used repression, there continued to be a substantial difference between months with stable imperial authority and those with disrupted imperial authority.

Conclusion

This chapter has demonstrated the importance of the state of imperial authority for nationalist organizing in Morocco. A close

---

[79] *Bulletin de Renseignments Politiques*, February 1945, SHAT 3H1415. *Note sur la situation politique en milieu musulman au Maroc Français*, May 1945. SHAT 3H249.

[80] *Bulletin de Renseignments Politiques*, December 1950. SHAT 3H1416.

[81] Repression is lagged one month. Using current repression produced similar results.

TABLE 5.11. *Nationalist Events by Imperial Authority, without Prior Repression (Partial table)*

	Months with Stable Imperial Authority	Months with Imperial Authority Disrupted	Total
No nationalist event	125	11	136
	77%	39%	71%
Nationalist event	38	17	55
	23%	61%	29%
Total	163	28	191
	100%	100%	100%

Chi-squared = 16.3, p < 0.01.

TABLE 5.12. *Nationalist Events by Imperial Authority, with Prior Repression (Partial table)*

	Months with Stable Imperial Authority	Month with Imperial Authority Disrupted	Total
No nationalist event	32	1	33
	55%	8%	46%
Nationalist event	26	12	38
	45%	92%	54%
Total	58	13	71
	100%	100%	100%

Chi-squared = 9.6, p< = 0.01.

examination of one case raises three issues pertinent to ongoing scholarly debates. First, the argument casts doubt on claims that nationalism is a population characteristic, present if the population is sufficiently advanced. Nationalism is thought to require a degree of political sophistication: the ability to imagine oneself as a part of a community that extends beyond local ethnic or kinship groups, literacy, and contact with Europe have all been tied to nationalism. More modern populations are expected to become nationalists; urbanization, economic development, and education have also been tied to nationalism. But the history of

Spanish and French Morocco suggests that the authority of the state may be more important for nationalist organizing than the level of progress among the population. The onset of nationalist mobilization in the towns of the Spanish zone rather than the towns of the French zone in the 1930s is puzzling if we consider the level of economic development in both places. The relative advantages of the French zone suggest that, net of other factors, we should expect nationalism to have emerged there first, rather than in the Spanish zone.

Neither zone, however, could be accurately described as fully modern in the colonial era. Mass education and industrialization lay in the future; Morocco today continues to have high rates of illiteracy and a majority rural population. The presence of nationalist movements in both zones, as well as in other parts of the French empire, thus suggests that modernization is not a necessary precondition for the formation of nationalist movements after all.

Second, this argument inverts the claim that nationalist mobilization causes crises in imperial authority. The conventional understanding of nationalist mobilization is that it produces instability by challenging the authority of the state. Hence, nationalist mobilization has been linked to colonial withdrawal. In Morocco, a crisis in imperial authority *preceded* nationalist mobilization. During the colonial period, France underwent two crises that affected its ability to control the territory: one during World War II, when Morocco was invaded by Allied forces, and a second when France decided to cede power. The initial crisis prompted the onset of nationalist mobilization. Ongoing mobilization then affected the decision to grant independence. This decision was followed by an upsurge in nationalist activity. The evidence suggests that nationalist mobilization is endogenous to crises in imperial authority; the causal arrow does not solely run from nationalist activity to colonial collapse, but involves a process during which the French and their opponents acted and reacted to one another.

The third contribution comes from the discussion of nationalist mobilization during times when imperial authority was stable. Mobilization against authoritarian regimes continues to be mystifying; we know little about how repression works or how mobilization is organized given the constraints of operating in restrictive contexts. There is a temptation to focus entirely on periods of crisis, when mobilization makes more sense. But although stable imperial authority limited the options available to nationalists, it did not foreclose mobilization. Authoritarian rulers can very rarely close off all avenues of opposition; at the very least, the population retains "weapons of the weak" with which they can resist (Scott 1987). I developed implications for how mobilization worked even when the imperial power had reasserted its authority, and I considered the effects of stable and unstable imperial authority on multiple dependent variables. When the imperial power's authority was disrupted, mobilization was highly visible and contentious. When it was stable, the nationalist movement took advantage of important dates and sites with apolitical significance, mobilizing in less dramatic ways. By disseminating nationalist goals at weddings or appropriating religious holidays or asking shopkeepers to close their shops, nationalists managed to continue mobilizing even when the conditions for opposition were less than ideal. By studying how Moroccans organized to challenge the French, this chapter points toward some of the general mechanisms of mobilization in authoritarian contexts.

6

Conclusion

Looking back at the end of the era of European colonialism, it is easy to tell a story in which nationalist protest appears unavoidable, the utmost and final "stage" of anti-colonialism. But an interpretation that privileges nationalist modes of opposition fails to makes sense of how challenges to colonial rule varied. The history of nationalist movements in the colonial world is uneven: opponents of imperialism employed multiple anti-colonial discourses other than nationalism, and they were restricted by a colonial state that sought to shut down contestation. This book has argued that nationalism was not bound to triumph in French empire for two reasons: political equality offered an alternative remedy for the injustices of imperial rule; and nationalist protest required opportunities that were not easy to come by under authoritarian governments.

The anti-colonial theorist Frantz Fanon (1963, 148) acknowledges that responses to colonial rule varied, writing: "History teaches us clearly that the battle against colonialism does not run straight away along the lines of nationalism." He persists, however, in telling a teleological story in which nationalist responses must prevail: "For a very long time the native devotes his energies to ending certain definite abuses: forced labor, corporal punishment, inequality of salaries, limitation of political rights, etc. This fight for democracy against the oppression of mankind will slowly leave the confusion of neo-liberal universalism to emerge, sometimes laboriously, as a claim to nationhood" (ibid.). Fanon sees "neo-liberal universalism" as fatally flawed, a misguided form of anti-colonialism destined to give way to nationalism. In contrast, in the first half of this book, I advocated taking aspirations for political equality seriously. In Chapter 2, I asserted that demands for equality were not embryonic forms of nationalism. I drew a stark distinction between calls for a higher degree of equality and nationalist claims because of the tendency to overlook the former and portray the latter as the pervasive form of anti-colonialism. These demands are conceptually different; calls for equality are not reducible to nationalism, although activists sometimes drew on both discourses, proposing arrangements such as federalism that reflected concerns for both equality and the recognition of national distinctiveness.

In Chapter 2 I also maintained that demands for political equality were genuine, arguing that advocates saw reform as a way to redress the injustices of the colonial system, in which the interests of colonial subjects were subordinated to those of French citizens. Reformists spoke about universal rights and made reference to the democratic principles of the French Revolution. Although Fanon thought that "neo-liberal universalism" was shrouded in confusion, advocates proposed concrete reforms designed to improve the economic and political status of colonial subjects. Not all political actors in the colonies agreed with these proposals; in some places, nationalist parties existed alongside reform-oriented groups and vehemently opposed their programs. These disputes are themselves evidence against the dominant nationalist narrative, for they show that one's nationality did not dictate one's politics. Moroccans, Algerians, and other Africans disagreed among themselves about how to combat imperialism. Anti-colonial politics was more diverse than nationalist discourses allow.

I drew heavily on the history of colonial Morocco to make these arguments, even though it is a hard case to use to illustrate the importance of political equality. Morocco had a long history of statehood before it became a protectorate in 1912. Morocco's current king is a member of the Alawite Dynasty, which has ruled since the seventeenth century. Neither the French nor Moroccans proposed that Moroccans be assimilated as French citizens because Moroccans already had their own nationality and a history of independent statehood. Although we might not expect alternatives to nationalism to resonate where a sense of nationality already exists, during the 1930s the effort to reform French rule and make it fairer and more equitable was the dominant mode of opposition. The very existence of this reform movement is surprising, given the literature's claims about the incompatibility of national identity and foreign rule. A sense of national identity is supposed to lead nations to reject outsiders and insist on independence, not seek accommodation with them. Although Moroccans had a nationality from the start of the period, however, their politics were not always particularly nationalistic. Scholars of North Africa have attempted to explain this fact away by questioning the sincerity of reform advocates, but it is implausible that these reformists would eschew nationalist discourses, already present elsewhere in the Middle East and in the Rif mountains of Morocco, and instead engage in a decade-long effort to gain reforms that they did not actually want.

That calls for equitable reforms were heard even in Morocco points to the general appeal of discourses about political equality. Calls to reform colonial rule in an egalitarian direction were common in the French empire. Taking them seriously helps resolve a number of puzzling questions about opposition in the colonial world: why, for instance, nationalist opposition came to Algeria so late despite widespread colonial abuses; why some colonies failed to see nationalist opposition at all; and why critics of colonial rule so often stressed universal rights and denied nationalist aspirations.

Chapter 3 showed that demands for reform do not lead inexorably to nationalist claims. Looking at political activism in the cases that were granted French citizenship – the four communes of Senegal, Martinique, Guadeloupe, New Caledonia, and the rest of the DOM-TOMs – it is clear that movements for political equality were not all superseded by nationalist movements. Nationalist mobilization followed exclusion; inclusion produced demands for further rights and recognition. The extension of French citizenship was not a panacea for the political and social problems of the colonial period; it neither erased a sense of cultural distinctiveness on the part of indigenous populations nor did it eliminate the racism of the French when they interacted with their former subjects. But it did forestall a move toward nationalist organizing. Mobilization emphasizing national distinctiveness depended upon what happened to prior political movements; nationalist mobilization was the outcome of politics, not the endpoint of a trajectory that all colonial territories would follow.

By focusing on cases that did achieve political equality, Chapter 3 also showed that attempts to reform colonial rule were not destined to fail. The achievement of political equality in the DOM-TOMS and Senegal made egalitarian reforms appear possible elsewhere. Further, the 1946 extension of citizenship under the new French Union expanded the rights of erstwhile colonial subjects and went some way toward meeting their demands for equality. It was a significant step, and it could have led to greater incorporation; the failure of the French Union and the move to decolonize was no more inevitable than nationalism. African and French politicians proposed and considered a variety of arrangements to address political inequality, including various federal arrangements that would combine local autonomy with French citizenship rights. These proposals addressed the problem of economic inequality, offering a response to concerns that incorporation would entail massive redistribution to the colonies. There was no reason why a federal arrangement had to fail; if the French Union or the French Community had forged lasting federal institutions, the outcome would have been different.[1] Only in hindsight does France's refusal to incorporate colonial subjects on a large scale appear unsurprising.

---

[1] A French state that included an African federation is not easy to imagine today, decades after decolonization, but changes in sovereignty are typically difficult to envision before they happen. In the early or mid-twentieth century, the creation of a European Union that included states with widely varying degrees of economic development would likewise have seemed impossible, but the European Union found ways to establish a degree of political equality among member states without solving the problem of economic inequality.

That political equality seemed feasible at the time is important, regardless of the ultimate outcome, because it allows us to observe how people from different ethnic, racial, and religious groups responded to the prospect of equality. Contrary to many postcolonial narratives, colonial subjects were willing to entertain incorporation on fair and equal terms and were not committed to the sole objective of independent nation-statehood. This point is missed in a literature that portrays nationalism as the primary anti-colonial ideology. I cannot stress this point enough: the willingness of colonial subjects to end imperialism via equality is remarkable because it undercuts the claim that nationalism is the primary, even natural, response to rule by foreigners. This finding is important irrespective of the number of cases that ultimately actually achieve political equality. French colonial subjects turned to nationalism not because it was the superior, stronger form of opposition, but because other alternatives were foreclosed.

In Chapters 4 and 5, I addressed how nationalist protest got underway in the places that were denied political equality. Organizing protest activity was difficult where political equality had been denied and authoritarianism persisted. Mobilizing participants to engage in contentious activity is nearly always difficult, as the literature on social movements has shown. Restrictions on the political activity of colonial subjects made it even harder. Hence, long periods passed without visible protest, leading French administrators to complacently assume that their rule had been accepted. But it is not necessarily the case that nationalist aspirations were absent; it is more likely that they could not be openly expressed.

I argued that disruptions in the colonial power's control of its territory were crucial for triggering mass protest. Periods in which French authority was undermined by the presence of other powerful actors suggested that imperial rule was temporary and precarious. Populations that had seemed compliant mobilized rapidly. The effects of fractured authority then lasted, making mobilization easier even when imperial rule was reestablished. These chapters help account for the sudden emergence of nationalist protest in the French empire. Nationalist mobilization was not a gradual phenomenon; it often erupted unpredictably.

This book has thus argued that nationalist mobilization was contingent upon the continued exclusion of colonial subjects and disruptions in the political order that allowed nationalist action to happen. Neither of these conditions was bound to occur; they varied across the empire. This variation invites the consideration of counterfactuals. What if the French had implemented democratic reforms more widely? What if they had extended the franchise to many of their colonies, instead of only a few? What if they had chosen not to repress indigenous leaders in places such as Algeria and Morocco, but had instead encouraged local leaders to participate in governing? Alternatively, what if the French had been able to maintain a firm grip over their colonies, even during wartime? What if they had invested more heavily in maintaining imperial authority following World War II? In raising these questions, I have sought to unsettle conventional understandings of politics in the colonial world, in which nationalism is presumed to be the obvious organizing idiom for colonized populations. If any of these hypothetical scenarios had occurred, the history of nationalist mobilization in the colonial world would have been dramatically different.

In the remainder of this conclusion, I first discuss how my two arguments fit together. Next, I describe the implications of each argument for general understandings of nationalism and protest, and I consider how my arguments speak to other cases. Finally, I suggest that an examination of the history of anti-colonial opposition in the empire helps make sense of political life in the postcolonial era.

Putting the Pieces Together: Political Equality and Empire Disrupted

The arguments of this book are complementary, addressing both the motive and the opportunity for nationalist action. The first argument, about the consequences of rejecting appeals for political equality, helps make sense of the paradigm shift from reformist to nationalist mobilization. The second provides an explanation for the timing of nationalist protest. For the French empire, these two conditions were jointly sufficient to produce nationalist mobilization: where we observe both a denial of political equality and a disruption in imperial control, we also see active mobilization for nationalist ends; where both factors are absent, there is no nationalist mobilization.

It is possible that one of these conditions matters more than the other. The subnational evidence points to the possibility that disruptions may be sufficient on their own to trigger nationalist mobilization. In Spanish Morocco, the disruption of the Spanish Civil War brought about a shift to nationalist organizing, although reforms had not been definitively rejected by the Spanish administration before the war began. In Madagascar, reforms were likewise not entirely off the table when nationalist protest began following the British invasion during World War II. In both of these cases, reforms had neither succeeded nor failed, and it is important to keep in mind that it is difficult to precisely date the refusal of reform or track changes in how feasible reform seemed to elites at any given time.

If nationalist mobilization followed disruptions in imperial authority in places where reform movements had in fact succeeded, this evidence would contradict my argument about the importance of political equality and support the claim that disruptions alone are sufficient. In the French empire, the majority of places that gained political equality also had stable imperial rule at the time, making it impossible to know how their populations would have reacted to a disruption. Only New Caledonia was subjected to a disruption during World War II; as the theory predicts, there was no nationalist mobilization.[2]

---

[2] Additionally, Bora Bora in French Polynesia was a military supply base for the United States during the war and was occupied by American troops. No nationalist movement erupted, but Bora Bora is only one piece of French Polynesia. Disruptions in the DOM-TOMS have occurred later in the twentieth century, when France devolved some authority to them, but nationalist movements have had only limited support in most places.

Theoretically, however, it makes little sense to posit that territories with political equality needed a disruption to begin nationalist organizing. Disruptions are important precisely because of the restrictive nature of authoritarian rule. French citizens do not need disruptions to oppose the government, because France protects the right to protest and create opposition parties. Mobilization was easier and less risky for French citizens than it was for colonial subjects. French citizens in Martinique, Guadeloupe, or the other DOM-TOMs could have made nationalist claims without a disruption of authority, but they did not.

For the majority of the French empire, reform efforts had failed prior to the onset of mobilization. In French Morocco, for instance, both factors mattered. Elites there began advocating independence following the failure of the reform movement at the end of 1937, but mass mobilization began only after the Allied invasion during World War II. The Moroccan nationalist al-Fasi pointed to the importance of both factors, although he gives greater causal weight to the denial of reform:

It had become obvious since 1937 that an irrevocable divorce had occurred between the people on the one hand and the protectorate regime on the other. … It is futile to deny the impact of the war … [but] it must be said that the real driving force behind the new approach had been the bitter experiences of the nationalist movement [in failing to achieve reform] (quoted in Halstead 1969a, 256).

Moreover, it is difficult to base an explanation for nationalist mobilization on disruptions alone. State crises and wartime occupations have been associated with a wide variety of outcomes: they have prompted riots, looting, revolutions, civil wars, and socialist and communist opposition, to name a few. Theoretically, it is hard to see why disruptions in imperial authority alone would produce *nationalist* mobilization in particular, as opposed to mobilization for other goals. Disruptions may help stimulate contentious action oriented toward varied objectives.

Attention to the struggle for political equality helps explain why disruptions in the French empire prompted mobilization that was nationalist in character. The prior work of appealing for equitable reform served to structure the terms of the conflict that began during the revolutionary moment, when imperial rule was disrupted and vulnerable. The failure of activists to budge the French in the direction of reform, despite the political openings that had made equitable reforms appear possible, shaped their perceptions of what France would offer to the colonies. It dashed the hopes raised by the promises of the French left and the steps taken to extend equality in other parts of the empire. It strengthened the boundaries between the French and their subjects. The rejection of an appeal to universal values rendered the nation more salient, as a community set apart from the imperial core and defined in part by a lack of rights.

Both arguments presented here suggest a set of diverse microfoundations for participation. In the literature on national and ethnic conflict, motivations are often described in binary terms: are political actors aggrieved or greedy? Are they idealistic or hungry for power? Are they influenced by structure and opportunity or by ideology? In formulating the two central arguments of this book, I suggest that this is a false set of choices. Political actors may simultaneously seek positions of power and be committed to principles of equality or national pride. They may be both aggrieved and greedy. They may be affected both by ideology and by opportunities to act. They may be influenced by past failure and by their estimations of future success. My arguments point to the importance of studying mobilization as a process that unfolds over time, during which both motivations and structures can change in ways that are consequential for contentious action.[3]

Theoretical and Empirical Implications

This section considers the contribution the arguments of this book make to ongoing debates about the causes of nationalist mobilization and social protest more generally. It also takes a look at the potential applicability of these arguments beyond the

---

[3] Wood (2003) provides an exemplary approach to studying processes in and motivations for collective action in her study of mobilization by rural people in El Salvador.

French empire. My arguments reflect the French colonial context; the colonial state itself shaped opposition by affecting the kinds of demands colonized populations made, and how and when they made them. The arguments cannot be directly transplanted to other places with nationalist conflicts, but these cases share characteristics with others, and some of the mechanisms we observe in the French empire can be seen elsewhere.

Disruptions in Authority

The argument that disruptions in imperial authority produced mobilization in favor of independence offers three contributions to the literatures on empire and contentious action. First, it counters studies that see state or regime collapse as a consequence of nationalist mobilization. For the colonial empires, nationalist mobilization is often thought of as a destabilizing force that produced decolonization. The evidence here shows that mobilization can be endogenous to a collapse of authority rather than a cause of it. In the French empire, disruptions in state authority *preceded* widespread participation in nationalist movements. Mass protest then further challenged state authority. This analysis points to the importance of considering the direction of causality. Nationalist mobilization is not an exogenous force affecting the state; it is shaped by the state of the state itself.

This insight matters for studies of conflict outside the colonial milieu. Political scientists have published a number of studies that treat nationalism as an independent variable determining various outcomes: imperial collapse, foreign occupation, terrorism, and nationalist conflict.[4] These studies treat nationalism as exogenous – a stable characteristic of modern populations that may be harnessed for political action when the nation is under threat. Instead, nationalist action may be endogenous to the very processes that it is supposed to explain. It may, for instance, be triggered by a climate of civil or international conflict that heightens national or ethnic affinities that were previously politically

---

[4] See, for example, Doyle (1986); Edelstein (2010); Lustick (1993); Pape (2005); Spruyt (2005).

unimportant (Bulutgil 2010). Or, a foreign occupation may itself create the conditions for nationalist mobilization by triggering competition among local actors.[5] Studies that rely on preexisting nationalism as an explanatory variable need to defend treating it as exogenous and consider the conditions that affect the expression of nationalist commitments.

Second, the argument offers an innovative approach to understanding the relationship between state crises and popular revolt. In the literature on revolutions, state crises have been associated with revolt, state collapse, and the replacement of the regime. The outcome in these studies is typically binary: revolution or no revolution. But these are not the only possible outcomes; states can weather crises and persevere; political opposition can appear but fail to topple the state. My analysis disaggregates the outcome, focusing on mobilization itself rather than the success or failure of a movement in achieving independence, an outcome with a number of determinants. The revolutions literature has little to say about mobilization that fails to topple the state. My analysis calls attention to mobilization that is not immediately successful, as well as mobilization that occurs outside periods of crisis. The subnational analysis examines variation over time, looking at how opposition functions before, during, and after crises of authority.

Third, the argument theorizes political opportunities in a deductive way, facilitating measurement and testing. The social movement literature has emphasized the importance of political opportunities for mobilization, but identifying what counts as a political opportunity has been an ongoing challenge. Some have focused on state weakness as the key variable facilitating challenges to the state, but weakness can be difficult to evaluate and measure. The focus on serious disruptions to state authority, narrowly defined, makes the argument observable and verifiable.

Scholarly work on other regions of the world supports the claim that disruptions such as the ones discussed here prompt

---

[5] To take another example, a campaign of suicide bombing may trigger nationalist sentiment, rather than resulting from preexisting nationalism.

mobilization against states and empires. In the Spanish Americas, mobilization for independence was affected by the Napoleonic Wars in Europe (Klooster 2009, 2). In the Austro-Hungarian and Ottoman empires, ethnic and nationalist conflict erupted during and immediately after World War I in a context of intense interstate competition (Bulutgil 2010). In Southeast Asia, mobilization was triggered when imperial authority was disrupted during World War II. In Malaya and the Philippines, the Japanese occupation sparked conflict between communist and anticommunist forces. Mobilization in the Dutch Indies and Burma resembled wartime mobilization in Vietnam; following Japan's surrender, both declared independence and nationalist agitation began (Slater 2010, 75–107). Beissinger (1996, 106) argues that mass nationalist mobilization in the Soviet Union was triggered by political opportunities created by instability. Disruptions are not only important in imperial contexts, but also in other types of authoritarian regimes. Revolutions, as discussed, have been widely associated with periods of state crisis (Goldstone 1991; Skocpol 1979).

Sewell (1996, 843) has emphasized the importance of events for producing "moments of accelerated change." Disruptions to the state's authority are among the events that can change political activity rapidly and prompt people to take to the streets. It can be very difficult to theorize the effects of events. Political scientists therefore sometimes treat them as exogenous shocks and control for them statistically, or leave them out of macro models entirely, rather than seeing them as critical components of a causal account. Specifying a class of similar events provides a way to consider their impact systematically.

Political Equality

This book also argued that political equality reduced the demand for independence, while the failure of reform movements to produce meaningful change led elites to begin articulating nationalist goals. This argument points to a criticism of collective action approaches that treat preferences as exogenous and fixed. Studies of collective action often assume that actors have stable goals at the outset. By looking at the shift from discourses about equality to discourses of nationhood, this book suggests that preferences may be endogenous to political mobilization, and that their content ought not to be assumed ex ante. Political activists alter their goals in the course of interacting with the state; in the French empire, the actions of the French government delimited what could be achieved. The change in goals in this context points to a more general lesson: the need to consider political mobilization as a process – one that involves bargaining, negotiation, reevaluation of goals, and change. The objectives of actors cannot be assumed to remain stable over the course of a conflict.[6]

The finding that nationalist mobilization did not occur when colonial subjects were treated as political equals provides an insight into the nature of nationalist conflict: it is not a straightforward consequence of the presence of different national groups. Conflict databases continue to use measures of diversity as predictors of ethnic and nationalist conflict, relying on data about the number of groups or the degree of ethnolinguistic fragmentation. But the number of groups, or the cultural distance between them, may matter less than the way those groups behave toward one another. Horowitz (1985) has argued that ethnic groups that are "ranked," that exist in a hierarchy, are more likely to come into conflict with one another.[7] Similarly, I have suggested that institutionalized political equality dampens nationalist conflict, even when there are ethnic, racial, and linguistic differences. Political inequality, in contrast, motivates nationalist organizing; independence becomes a different route to equality (Wallerstein 1961, 50). The French were not initially despised for being alien; they came to be framed as alien in part because of their refusal to recognize colonial subjects as equals. Political equality can,

---

[6] This insight has implications for cross-national work on violent and nonviolent conflict that seeks to code mobilization as a success or failure. When asking whether a particular tactic worked or did not, researchers are forced to identify a set of goals and may fail to note changes in movement goals over time. See Chenoweth and Stephan (2011) and Pape (2005) for work that codes movement objectives.

[7] See also Hechter (2009), on how the fairness and efficiency of foreign rulers affect the responses to foreign rule.

in some contexts, go a long way toward defusing antagonisms between groups. Political equality may even be a minimum requirement for avoiding contentious challenges over the long term within ethnically diverse states.

Other cases lend credence to this view. In the American colonies, future revolutionaries first praised the British constitution while criticizing British colonial policy (Klooster 2009, 26). Their call for "no taxation without representation" shows their concerns with unequal status. American leaders were divided over whether to seek separation from England; some expressed allegiance with the throne and advocated continuing to press the British for reform. Later in American history, African Americans sought political equality during the Civil Rights Movement. When that goal seemed unfeasible, separatism was a powerful alternative doctrine (McAdam 1999, 107–108). In South Africa, Nelson Mandela and the African National Congress drew on the history of the American Civil Rights Movement, also seeking to end institutionalized inequality and promote a nonracial democracy. Israel provides yet another case that this argument illuminates; Israeli Arabs have formal political equality (although informal discrimination persists), and they have been far less contentious than Palestinian Arabs, who lack both political rights within Israel and a state of their own.

In other twentieth-century empires, calls for reform differed from those heard in the French empire. The British did not have an assimilation policy, and colonial subjects in the British empire did not seek citizenship. But like the French, the British did have a reform-oriented liberal imperial ideology – their "civilizing mission" to install modern Western social and political forms in British colonies. This ideology began to shift in the mid nineteenth century, when British thinkers articulated a need to preserve traditional native "culture" through indirect rule.[8] British colonial subjects like their counterparts in the French empire, called upon the British to live up to their promises of reform throughout the colonial era. In Britain's African colonies, postwar reform

---

[8] For an account of this shift in British imperial ideology, see Mantena (2010).

advocates sought greater participation of Africans in local legislatures, whereas in the French empire reformists sought to participate in French legislatures (Wallerstein 1961, 71). Elsewhere,
British subjects debated the merits of joining the commonwealth
and considered other federal arrangements. In the former Soviet
Republics, calls for reform likewise preceded nationalist mobilization. In Armenia, for instance, initial demands were for the
redrawing of internal boundaries rather than independence
(Beissinger 2002).

This brief discussion of cases outside the French empire points
to the potential applicability of these arguments elsewhere and
suggests future avenues of research. The empirics in this book
are based on subnational studies and a medium-N analysis. This
approach has its advantages, particularly for investigating cases
and time periods that have been overlooked in contemporary
political science. Subnational data collection allows for comparisons across units and over time. A medium-N approach is
complementary because it can indicate whether or not subnational patterns are found in other states, but it is still manageable
enough that researchers can carry out thorough data collection
and avoid measurement error. The disadvantage of a combined
subnational and medium-N research design is that it sacrifices
generalizability in favor of a more thorough understanding of
the central cases. But addressing mobilization in one context is
an important task in its own right, and the French empire in particular spanned a large portion of the globe.

Explaining mobilization in one empire is itself a worthy
achievement, but the arguments here also have the potential to
be more widely applicable. Aspirations for equality, articulated
in diverse ways and through varied institutional arrangements,
have been professed by social movements confronting states
around the world. State crises are associated with protest onset
in a variety of settings. More generally, the analysis here has
emphasized the importance of studying the interplay between
regimes and their opponents to better understand how regimes
may shape opposition by making and breaking promises to rule
in a better and more just way. Further research and testing is

required to show how the determinants of nationalist mobilization in the French empire contribute to understanding nationalist conflicts elsewhere.

Independence and the Postcolonial Era

Indigenous leaders in the French colonies followed a remarkable trajectory: they went from requesting reform to seeking independence to leading new nations, often in one generation (Betts 1991, 134). This book's central outcome of interest has been the quest for independence, not its attainment or the establishment of new states. But an examination of the nationalist movements and how they got underway may help explain some of the troubling characteristics of postcolonial states. By way of conclusion, this section takes a brief look at the postcolonial era and considers the long-term consequences of mobilization during the colonial period. The discussion is necessarily speculative, as the relationship between anti-colonial mobilization and postcolonial outcomes merits its own investigation.[9] My purpose is to propose some possible linkages between the two periods for further research. I begin in Morocco and conclude with some general trends in postcolonial states.

In Morocco, the regime that replaced the French protectorate was a disappointment to many of those who mobilized for both reform and independence. The interviews I conducted with former participants in the nationalist movement reflected a profound dissatisfaction with the postcolonial order. Every single respondent told me that the monarchy was "no better than the French."[10] They focused particularly on the regime of Hassan II, who ruled from 1962 until his death in 1999. One respondent stated that Hassan II had learned the skills of repression and social control from the French.

---

[9] See Slater (2010), whose book specifically looks at the formation of postcolonial states in Southeast Asia. Mobilization at the end of the colonial era plays a key role in his analysis.

[10] Interviews in Rabat and Oued Zem, January–May 2006.

The monarchy did not immediately emerge as the primary power holder. The transition to independence included a period of instability. *Time Magazine* described the situation when the king, who had been exiled by the French, returned to take control: "Mohammed V stepped from a life of luxurious discontent into a chaos caused by the abdication of the French and a vying among the Moroccans themselves, some to retain their feudal fiefs, others to spread violence born of ignorance, a few to seek a difficult adjustment between ancient ways, present misery and future progress."[11] The new king confronted a number of independent actors: a rural insurgent army; small bands of urban and rural terrorists; notables who had backed the protectorate; and the nationalist party, all of whom were maneuvering for control of the administrative apparatus (Waterbury 1970, 54–55). As one historian noted, the political fragmentation in Morocco in the mid-1950s meant that the sultan's sovereignty was "arguable and fragile" (Lahbabi 1975, 67). The monarchy moved to consolidate control and limit the role of the Istiqlal and other nationalist actors in the government, although rural rebellions continued to break out periodically during the first decade after independence.[12]

The monarchy succeeded in its quest for control, consolidating an authoritarian regime that has lasted to the current day. Lahbabi (1975, 7; 182) blames the French for backing the monarchy during the transition to independence; he argues that their decision to support authoritarian rule was the final evidence of the failure of their mission to bring modern government to Morocco. French responsibility may run even deeper than he suggests. By repressing the reform movement in the mid-1930s, the French undermined the democratic orientation of Moroccan elites and lost an opportunity to introduce democratic institutions. When nationalist mobilization began during World War II, it had a decidedly more authoritarian bent. Dissidents, who had previously had a more ambivalent relationship with the sultan,

---

[11] "Return of the Distant Ones," *Time*, November 28, 1955.
[12] On the establishment of order in the postcolonial period, see Hart (2000); Moore (1970); Zartman (1964).

made common cause with him to gain his support for independence. According to one former nationalist, the sultan would never have been able to seize power without the Istiqlal Party's support during the struggle for independence. The French and nationalists contributed to making the sultan a powerful leader; in the postcolonial period he would weaken his opponents and constrain opposition. In Morocco today, openly criticizing the king is a punishable offense, and there is no single political party or group that has the support the Istiqlal enjoyed during the immediate aftermath of World War II.

In other parts of the empire, the regimes that replaced the French were often similarly disappointing. Wherever possible, the French turned over the reins of government to rulers who would, above all else, cooperate with France. The French supported strongmen over democratic leaders. As in Morocco, the failure of movements for political equality was also consequential. In Africa, the collapse of the French Community and the subsequent creation of small African states following the boundaries of the former French territories resulted in an Africa that looked much different from the one envisioned by leaders such as Senghor. If the French Community or an African federation had survived, the degree of economic inequality between French Africa and the wealthier states of the world might have been less dramatic. An Africa broken into small territories was, as Senghor and others lamented, weaker and less able to thrive in the global economy. Continued dependency on France, but without the forms of layered sovereignty proposed during the last years of colonial rule, left leaders with little bargaining power and the temptation to serve as gatekeepers between their national economies and the outside world.[13]

Additionally, where democratically oriented elites were sidelined during the colonial period, those with more authoritarian inclinations were sometimes able to gain the upper hand. Algeria exemplifies this trajectory; the FLN eliminated their rivals during

[13] My thanks to an anonymous reviewer for this point.

the struggle for independence and established authoritarian rule. The Algerian case also points to another consequence of the nationalist struggle; in places where it took a war to attain independence, moderate leaders were often imprisoned, exiled, or murdered in the course of the struggle. The experience of violence created a terrible legacy for postcolonial states to overcome and increased the likelihood of postcolonial violence.[14]

Some have suggested that the nationalist movements bear some responsibility for postcolonial ills because they articulated a "shallow" ideology. Nationalists took a strong anti-colonial position without always formulating a positive plan for what would happen after independence. Further, nationalist ideology was compatible with authoritarianism and could be appropriated by rulers in the postcolonial era. Leaders invoked nationalist discourses to construct a unified identity, but in so doing they privileged some identities over others and fostered social hierarchies (Pratt 2007, 34).

Nationalism is hence arguably not a firm basis for state building; it is a flexible ideology, but also an empty one – it defines the borders of the political community without specifying its purpose or type. For Africa, Young (2004, 1) observes: "Although anti-colonial nationalism as a mobilizing doctrine was clearly visible, much less evident was its possible naturalization as state ideology of territorial solidarity." He recognizes that Africans had come to have some sense that the territories defined by the colonial boundaries now enclosed nations, but that sense of nationhood was a weak one (ibid., 3). Fanon (1963, 148), too, bemoaned the fact that "nationalist consciousness, instead of being the all-embracing crystallization of the innermost hopes of the whole people, instead of being the immediate and most obvious result of the mobilization of the people, will be in any case, only an empty shell, a crude and fragile travesty of what it might have been." Nationalist projects failed because the new nations were too young or state borders did not fit the nations or there were too many nations.[15]

---

[14] See Lawrence (2010b). For the finding that prior violence raises the probability of future violence, see Fearon and Laitin (2003a), among others.

[15] See the discussion in McDougall (2003).

But it is unfair to attribute postcolonial outcomes entirely to either the nationalists or the depth of national attachment among postcolonial populations. Structural impediments and continued relations of dependency also caused underdevelopment, weak regimes, and authoritarianism.[16] The leaders of the new states had many obstacles to overcome (Owen 2000, 21).

The period of anti-colonial mobilization affected politics in postcolonial societies in other, more positive ways. The demands made on the French shaped people's perceptions of the kinds of duties that governments should fulfill. Thompson (2000b, 11) argues that the civic order in Syria and Lebanon changed during the French mandate, as colonial subjects began to make welfare demands upon the French. She writes (ibid., 6): "Paternalistic social aid once bestowed by France through its collaborating intermediaries was gradually transformed into social rights claimed directly upon the state itself." The idea that the state should protect individual rights and provide social benefits continues to resonate with citizens who oppose the authoritarianism of the regimes that replaced the French. In Morocco, for instance, citizens continue to ask for jobs, positions of power in the state, and a meaningful say in their own governance.

The quest for self-determination and political equality did not end with independence; it is ongoing in many of the former colonies of the French empire. The experience of mobilizing, whether for reform or independence, provided a model for people organizing opposition in the postcolonial world. That model continues to resonate among opposition groups engaged in making claims on the postcolonial state. It is a legacy that points to the promises and limitations of challenging regimes through contentious action.

---

[16] For examples of work on these outcomes in postcolonial settings, see Anderson (1986); Herbst (2000); Slater (2010); Wallerstein (1961).

Bibliography

Archives Consulted

Centre des Hautes Études sur l'Afrique et l'Asie Modernes, Paris (cited as CHEAM).
Ministère des Affaires Étrangères, Centre des Archives Diplomatiques de Nantes (cited as MAE).
Service Historique de l'Armée de Terre, Vincennes (cited as SHAT).
Centre des Archives d'Outre-mer, Aix-en-Provence (cited as CAOM).
Biblothèque Nationale du Maroc, Archives Coloniales (cited as BNM).

Secondary Works Cited

Abbas, Ferhat. 1931. *De La Colonie Vers La Province. Le Jeune Algérien*. Paris: Julliard.
Abernethy, David B. 2000. *The Dynamics of Global Dominance: European Overseas Empires, 1415–1980*. New Haven: Yale University Press.
Abu-Lughod, Janet. 1980. *Rabat: Urban Apartheid in Morocco*. Princeton: Princeton University Press.
Abun-Nasr, Jamil M. 1975. *A History of the Maghrib*. Cambridge: Cambridge University Press.
Acemoglu, Daron, Simon Johnson, and James A. Robinson. 2001. "The Colonial Origins of Comparative Development: An Empirical Investigation." *American Economic Review* 91 (5): 1369–1401.
Acemoglu, Daron, and James A. Robinson. 2006. *Economic Origins of Dictatorship and Democracy*. Cambridge: Cambridge University Press.

Adamolekun, Ladipo. 1969. "The Road to Independence in French Tropical Africa." *Tarikh* 2: 72–85.

Ageron, Charles-Robert. 1968. *Les Algériens Musulmans et La France (1871–1919)*. Paris: Presses Universitaires de France.

1986a. *Les Chemins de la Décolonisation de l'Empire Colonial Français*. Paris: Éditions du Centre National de la Recherche Scientifique.

1986b. "L'opinion Publique Face aux Problèmes de l'Union Française." In *Les Chemins de la Décolonisation de l'Empire Colonial Français*, 33–48. Paris: Éditions du Centre National de la Recherche Scientifique.

1991a. *Modern Algeria: A History from 1830 to the Present*. Trans. Michael Brett. London: Hurst.

1991b. *La Décolonisation Française*. Paris: Armand Colin.

Aldrich, Robert, and John Connell. 2006. *France's Overseas Frontier: Départements et Territoires d'Outre-mer*. Cambridge: Cambridge University Press.

Anderson, Benedict. 1983. *Imagined Communities: Reflections on the Origin and Spread of Nationalism*. London: Verso.

Anderson, Lisa. 1986. *The State and Social Transformation in Tunisia and Libya, 1830–1980*. Princeton: Princeton University Press.

Ansprenger, Franz. 1989. *The Dissolution of the Colonial Empires*. London: Routledge.

Appianus. 1996. *The Civil Wars*. London: Penguin Books.

Awad, Hassan. 1964. "Morocco's Expanding Towns." *The Geographical Journal* 130 (1): 49–64.

Ayache, Germain. 1996. *La Guerre du Rif*. Paris: L'Harmattan.

Balfour, Sebastian. 2002. *Deadly Embrace: Morocco and the Road to the Spanish Civil War*. Oxford: Oxford University Press.

Beissinger, Mark R. 1996. "How Nationalisms Spread: Eastern Europe Adrift the Tides and Cycles of Nationalist Contention." *Social Research* 63 (1): 97–146.

2002. *Nationalist Mobilization and the Collapse of the Soviet State*. Cambridge: Cambridge University Press.

Belseur, Philippe. 1995. *Étude Institutionnelle et Archivistique du Protectorat Français au Maroc*. Angers: Université de Belle-Beille.

Benjelloun, Abdelmajid. 1983. "Contribution à l'Étude du Mouvement Nationaliste Marocain dans l'Ancienne Zone Nord du Maroc." Casablanca: Université Hassan II.

1986. "La Part Prise par le Mouvement Nationaliste Marocaine de la Zone d'Influence Espagnole dans le Processus de Libération du Maroc." *Revue d'Histoire Maghrebine* (43–44): 5–42.

1994. "Reevaluation des Causes de l'Enrolement de Marocains dans les Rangs Franquistes, 1936–39." *Revue Maroc-Europe* (7): 219–234.

Benoist, Joseph-Roger de. 1982. *L'Afrique Occidentale Française de la Conférence de Brazzaville (1944) à l'Indépendance (1960)*. Dakar: Nouvelles Éditions Africaines.

Bernard, Stéphane. 1963. *Le Conflit Franco-Marocain 1943–1956*. Brussels: Editions de l'Institut de Sociologie de l'Université Libre de Bruxelles.

1968. *The Franco-Moroccan Conflict, 1943–1956*. New Haven: Yale University Press.

Berque, Jacques. 1962. *Le Magrib entre Deux Guerres*. Paris: Editions du Seuil.

Betts, Raymond F. 1991. *France and Decolonisation 1900–1960*. London: Palgrave Macmillan.

Bidwell, Robin. 1973. *Morocco under Colonial Rule: French Administration of Tribal Areas 1912–1956*. London: Frank Cass.

Blérald, Alain Philippe. 1988. *La Question Nationale en Guadeloupe et en Martinique. Essai sur l'Histoire Politique*. Paris: L'Harmattan.

Boix, Carles. 2003. *Democracy and Redistribution*. Cambridge: Cambridge University Press.

Boix, Carles, and Susan Carol Stokes. 2003. "Endogenous Democratization." *World Politics* 55 (4): 517–549.

Bourdieu, Pierre. 1991. *Language and Symbolic Power*. Trans. Gino Raymond and Matthew Adamson. Cambridge, MA: Harvard University Press.

Brady, Henry E., and David Collier. 2010. *Rethinking Social Inquiry: Diverse Tools, Shared Standards*. Second ed. Lanham: Rowman & Littlefield Publishers.

Brubaker, Rogers. 1996. *Nationalism Reframed: Nationhood and the National Question in the New Europe*. Cambridge: Cambridge University Press.

Bruné, Paulin. 1996. *Mon Dieu, Que Vous Êtes Français ... Essai sur la Décolonisation par Assimilation Martinique, Guadeloupe, Guyane, Réunion*. Paris: Editions France-Empire.

Brunschwig, Henri. 1986. "De l'Assimilation à la Décolonisation." In *Les Chemins de la Décolonisation de l'Empire Colonial Français*, eds. Charles-Robert Ageron, 49–53. Paris: Éditions du Centre National de la Recherche Scientifique.

Bulutgil, H. Zeynep. 2010. "War, Collaboration, and Endogenous Ethnic Polarization: The Path to Ethnic Cleansing." In *Rethinking Violence: States and Non-State Actors in Conflict*, eds. Erica Chenoweth and Adria Lawrence, 143–172. Cambridge, MA: MIT Press.

Bunce, Valerie. 1999. *Subversive Institutions: The Design and the Destruction of Socialism and the State*. New York: Cambridge University Press.

Burbank, Jane, and Frederick Cooper. 2010. *Empires in World History: Power and the Politics of Difference*. Princeton: Princeton University Press.

Burke, Edmund III. 1976. *Prelude to Protectorate in Morocco: Pre-Colonial Protest and Resistance, 1860–1912*. Chicago: University of Chicago Press.

2000. "Theorizing the Histories of Colonialism and Nationalism in the Arab Maghrib." In *Beyond Colonialism and Nationalism in the Maghrib: History, Culture, and Politics*, ed. Ali Abdullatif Ahmida, 17–36. London: Palgrave Macmillan.

Burton, Antoinette M. 2003. "Introduction: On the Inadequacy and the Indispensability of the Nation." In *After the Imperial Turn: Thinking with and Through the Nation*, ed. Antoinette M. Burton, 1–25. Durham: Duke University Press.

Césaire, Aimé. 1955. *Discours sur le Colonialisme*. Paris: Textuel.

Chafer, Tony. 2002. *The End of Empire in French West Africa: France's Successful Decolonization?* Oxford: Berg.

Chamberlain, M.E. 1999. *Decolonization: The Fall of the European Empires*. Oxford: Blackwell Publishers.

Chandra, Kanchan. 2007. *Why Ethnic Parties Succeed: Patronage and Ethnic Head Counts in India*. New York: Cambridge University Press.

Chatterjee, Partha. 1993a. *Nationalist Thought and the Colonial World: A Derivative Discourse*. Minneapolis: University of Minnesota Press.

1993b. *The Nation and Its Fragments: Colonial and Postcolonial Histories*. 4th ed. Princeton: Princeton University Press.

Chenoweth, Erica, and Maria J. Stephan. 2011. *Why Civil Resistance Works: The Strategic Logic of Nonviolent Conflict*. New York: Columbia University Press.

Cherif, M. 1971. "Rapport De Synthèse – Pays Arabs." In *Mouvements Nationaux d'Indépendance et Classes Populaires aux XIXe et XXe Siècles en Occident et en Orient*, Commission Internationale d'Histoire Des Mouvements Sociaux Et Des Structures Sociales, ed. A. Colin, 231–252. Paris: Librarie Armand Colin.

Clancy-Smith, Julia A. 1994. *Rebel and Saint: Muslim Notables, Populist Protest, Colonial Encounters (Algeria and Tunisia, 1800–1904)*. Berkeley: University of California Press.

Clayton, Anthony. 1994. *The Wars of French Decolonization*. London: Longman Group.

Cleveland, William L., and Martin P. Bunton. 2008. *A History of the Modern Middle East*. 4th ed. Boulder: Westview Press.

Cohen, William B. 1972. "The Colonial Policy of the Popular Front." *French Historical Studies* 7 (3): 368–393.

Cole, Jennifer. 2001. *Forget Colonialism? Sacrifice and the Art of Memory in Madagascar*. Berkeley: University of California Press.

Coleman, James S. 1954. "Nationalism in Tropical Africa." *American Political Science Review* 48 (2): 404–426.

Collier, David, Henry E. Brady, and Jason Seawright. 2010. "Outdated Views of Qualitative Methods: Time to Move On." *Political Analysis* 18: 506–512.

Collier, Paul, and Anke Hoeffler. 2004. "Greed and Grievance in Civil War." *Oxford Economic Papers* 56 (4): 563–595.

Collins, Randall. 1999. *Macrohistory: Essays in Sociology of the Long Run*. Stanford: Stanford University Press.

2008. *Violence: A Micro-Sociological Theory*. Princeton: Princeton University Press.

Comaroff, John L. 1995. "Ethnicity, Nationalism and the Politics of Difference in an Age of Revolution." In *Perspectives on Nationalism and War*. eds. John L. Comaroff and Paul C. Stern, 243–169. Amsterdam: Gordan and Breach Science Publishers.

Conklin, Alice L. 1997. *A Mission to Civilize: The Republican Idea of Empire in France and West Africa, 1895–1930*. Stanford: Stanford University Press.

Cooper, Frederick. 2002. *Africa since 1940, the Past of the Present*. Cambridge: Cambridge University Press.

2005. *Colonialism in Question. Theory, Knowledge, History*. Berkeley: University of California Press.

2009. "From Imperial Inclusion to Republican Exclusion? France's Ambiguous Postwar Trajectory." In *Frenchness and the African Diaspora: Identity and Uprising in Contemporary France*, eds. Charles Tshimanga, Didier Gondola, and Peter J. Bloom, 91–119. Bloomington: Indiana University Press.

Cooper, Nicola. 2001. *France in Indochina: Colonial Encounters*. Oxford: Berg.

Coquery-Vidrovitch, Catherine. 2001. "Nationalité et Citoyenneté en Afrique Occidentale Français: Originaires et Citoyens dans le Sénégal Colonial." *Journal of African History* 42 (2): 285–305.

Damis, John. 1970. "Developments in Morocco under the French Protectorate, 1925–1943." *Middle East Journal* 24 (1): 74–86.

Darden, Keith A. Forthcoming. *Resisting Occupation: Mass Schooling and the Creation of Durable National Loyalties*. New York: Cambridge University Press.

Derluguian, Georgi M. 2005. *Bourdieu's Secret Admirer in the Caucasus: A World-System Biography*. Chicago: University of Chicago Press.

Descamps, Henri. 1981. *La Politique aux Antilles Françaises de 1946 à Nos Jours*. Paris: Librairie générale de droit et de jurisprudence.

Deschamps, Hubert. 1954. *Peuples et Nations d'Outre Mer*. Paris: Librarie Dalloz.

Deutsch, Karl Wolfgang. 1953. *Nationalism and Social Communication: An Inquiry into the Foundations of Nationality*. Cambridge, MA: Technology Press of the Massachusetts Institute of Technology.

Dirks, Nicholas B. 2004. "Colonial and Postcolonial Histories: Comparative Reflections on the Legacies of Empire" Occasional Paper, *UNDP Human Development Report Office* (July).

Domergue-Cloarec, Danielle. 1995. *La France et l'Afrique après les Indépendances*. Paris: CDU SEDES.

Doyle, Michael W. 1986. *Empires*. Ithaca: Cornell University Press.

Duara, Prasenjit. 1996. "Historicizing National Identity, or Who Imagines What and When." In *Becoming National*, eds. Geoff Eley and Ronald Grigor Suny, 151–178. Oxford: Oxford University Press.

       1997. *Rescuing History from the Nation: Questioning Narratives of Modern China*. Chicago: University of Chicago Press.

       2004. *Decolonization: Perspectives from Now and Then*. London: Routledge.

Easton, Stewart C. 1964. *The Rise and Fall of Western Colonialism*. New York: F.A. Praeger.

Edelstein, David M. 2010. *Occupational Hazards: Success and Failure in Military Occupation*. Ithaca: Cornell University Press.

Eickelman, Dale F. 1985. *Knowledge and Power in Morocco: The Education of a Twentieth Century Notable*. Princeton: Princeton University Press.

Emerson, Rupert. 1960. *From Empire to Nation: The Rise of Self-Assertion of Asian and African Peoples*. Cambridge, MA: Harvard University Press.

       1969. "Colonialism." *Journal of Contemporary History* 4 (1): 3–16.

Entelis, John P. 1980. *Comparative Politics of North Africa: Algeria, Morocco, and Tunisia*. Syracuse: Syracuse University Press.

Entelis, John P., and Lisa J. Arone. 1995. "Democratic and Popular Republic of Algeria." In *The Government and Politics of the Middle East and North Africa*, eds. David E. Long and Bernard Reich, 394–422. Boulder: Westview Press.

Essakali, Larbi. 1983. *1906–1934: Morcellement et Résistance*. Rabat: Nord Organisation.

       1984. *1934–1953: Lutte du Roi et du Peuple*. Vol. 6. Rabat: Nord Organisation.

1985. *1953–1983: Dans le Concert des Nations.* Vol. 7. Rabat: Nord Organisation.

Fanon, Frantz. 1963. *The Wretched of the Earth.* New York: Grove Press.

al-Fasi, Allal. 1970. *The Independence Movements in Arab North Africa.* New York: Octagon Books.

Fearon, James D. 1991. "Counterfactuals and Hypothesis Testing in Political Science." *World Politics* 43: 169–195.

Fearon, James D., and David D. Laitin. 1996. "Explaining Interethnic Cooperation." *American Political Science Review* 90 (4): 715–735.

2003a. "Ethnicity, Insurgency, and Civil War." *American Political Science Review* 97 (1): 75–90.

2003b. "Sons of the Soil, Immigrants, and Civil War." *Unpublished paper* (April 25).

Foltz, William J. 1965. *From French West Africa to the Mali Federation.* New Haven: Yale University Press.

Gagnon, V.P. 1994. "Ethnic Nationalism and International Conflict: The Case of Serbia." *International Security* 19 (3): 130–166.

Gallissot, R. 1989. "La Question Nationale au Maghreb: Une Approche Comparée Maroc-Algérie-Tunisie." In *Le Monde Arabe au Regard des Sciences Sociales Vol 1,* ed. Institut de recherche sur le Maghreb contemporain, 11–27. Tunis: Centre de Documentation Tunisie-Maghreb (CDTM).

Gamson, William A., and David S. Meyer. 1996. "Framing Political Opportunity." In *Comparative Perpectives on Social Movements: Political Opportunities, Mobilizing Structures, and Cultural Framings,* eds. Doug McAdam, John D. McCarthy, and Mayer N. Zald, 275–290. Cambridge: Cambridge University Press.

de Gaulle, Charles. 1970. *Memoirs of Hope: Renewal and Endeavor.* New York: Simon and Schuster.

Gellner, Ernest. 1983. *Nations and Nationalism.* Ithaca: Cornell University Press.

Gelvin, James L. 1998. *Divided Loyalties: Nationalism and Mass Politics in Syria at the Close of Empire.* Berkeley: University of California Press.

Gershovich, Moshe. 2003. "Stories on the Road from Fez to Marrakech: Oral History on the Margins of National Identity." In *Nation, Society and Culture in North Africa,* ed. James McDougall, 42–57. London: Frank Cass.

Ghallaab, 'Abd al-Karīm. 2000. *Tārīkh al-Harakah al-Watanīyah bi al-Maghrīb.* Vol. 1 & 2. Casablanca: al-nejaah.

Gifford, Prosser, and William Roger Louis. 1982. *The Transfer of Power in Africa: Decolonization, 1940–60.* New Haven: Yale University Press.

Glaoui, Abdessadeq el-. 2004. *Le Ralliement: Le Glaoui, Mon Père.* Rabat: Marsam.

Glissant, Edouard. 1989. *Caribbean Discourse.* Trans. J. Michael Dash. Charlottesville: University Press of Virginia.

Goldstone, Jack A. 1991. *Revolution and Rebellion in the Early Modern World.* Berkeley: University of California Press.

Goodwin, Jeff. 2001. *No Other Way Out: States and Revolutionary Moments, 1945–1991.* Cambridge: Cambridge University Press.

Gorski, Philip S. 2000. "The Mosaic Moment: An Early Modernist Critique of Modernist Theories of Nationalism." *American Journal of Sociology* 105 (5): 1428–1468.

Goswami, Manu. 2004. *Producing India: From Colonial Economy to National Space.* Chicago: University of Chicago Press.

Gould, Roger V. 1991. "Multiple Networks and Mobilization in the Paris Commune, 1871." *American Sociological Review* 56: 716–729.

1995. *Insurgent Identities: Class, Community, and Protest in Paris from 1848 to the Commune.* Chicago: University of Chicago Press.

Grandhomme, Hélène. 2001. *La Politique Musulmane de la France au Sénégal de 1936 à 1964.* Dissertation. Nantes: Université de Nantes.

Grandval, Gilbert. 1956. *Ma Mission au Maroc.* Paris: Librarie Plon.

Greenfeld, Liah. 1993. *Nationalism: Five Roads to Modernity.* Cambridge, MA: Harvard University Press.

Grimal, Henri. 1985. *La Décolonisation de 1919 à nos Jours.* Bruxelles: Editions Complexe.

Gueriviere, Jean de la. 2001. *Les Fous d'Afrique: Histoire d'une Passion Francaise.* Paris: Editions du Seuil.

Guillebaud, Jean Claude. 1976. *Les Confettis de l'Empire: Martinique, Guadeloupe, Guyane Francaise, la Reunion, Nouvelle-Caledonie, Wallis-et-Futuna, Polynesie Francaise, Territoire ....* Paris: Editions du Seuil.

Gurr, Ted Robert. 1971. *Why Men Rebel.* Princeton: Princeton University Press.

Haas, Ernst B. 1993. "Nationalism: An Instrumental Social Construction." *Millennium* 22 (3): 504–545.

1997. *Nationalism, Liberalism, and Progress: The Rise and Decline of Nationalism.* Ithaca: Cornell University Press.

Habron, J.D. 1956. "Spain, Spanish Morocco and Arab Policy." *African Affairs* 55 (219): 135–143.

Hahn, Lorna. 1960. *North Africa: Nationalism to Nationhood.* Washington, DC: Public Affairs Press.

Hailey, Lord. 1943. *The Future of Colonial Peoples.* London: Oxford University Press.

Hale, Henry. 2008. *The Foundations of Ethnic Politics: Separatism of States and Nations in Eurasia and the World.* New York: Cambridge University Press

Halstead, John P. 1969a. *Rebirth of a Nation: The Origins and Rise of Moroccan Nationalism, 1912–1944.* Cambridge, MA: Harvard University Press.

1969b. "A Comparative Historical Study of Colonial Nationalism in Egypt and Morocco." *African Historical Studies* 2 (1): 85–100.

Harmand, François-Jules. 1910. *Domination et Colonisation.* Paris: Ernest Flammarion.

Hart, David M. 1976. *The Aith Waryaghar of the Moroccan Rif: An Ethnography and History.* Tucson: University of Arizona Press.

2000. *Tribe and Society in Rural Morocco.* London: Frank Cass.

Hechter, Michael. 2000. *Containing Nationalism.* Oxford: Oxford University Press.

2009. "Alien Rule and Its Discontents. " *American Behavioral Scientist* 53 (3): 289–310.

Herbst, Jeffrey Ira. 2000. *States and Power in Africa: Comparative Lessons in Authority and Control.* Princeton: Princeton University Press.

Hintjens, Helen M. 1995. *Alternatives to Independence: Explorations in Post-Colonial Relations.* Aldershot: Dartmouth Publishing Company.

Hobsbawm, E.J. 1990. *Nations and Nationalism since 1780: Programme, Myth, Reality.* Cambridge: Cambridge University Press.

Hodgkin, Thomas. 1957. *Nationalism in Colonial Africa.* New York: New York University Press.

Hoisington, William A., Jr. 1984. *The Casablanca Connection: French Colonial Policy, 1936–1943.* Chapel Hill: University of North Carolina Press.

Horne, Alistair. 1977. *A Savage War of Peace: Algeria 1954–1962.* New York: The Viking Press.

Horowitz, Donald L. 1985. *Ethnic Groups in Conflict.* Berkeley: University of California Press.

Hroch, Miroslav. 1985. *Social Preconditions of National Revival in Europe.* Cambridge: Cambridge University Press.

Hume, David. 1978. *A Treatise of Human Nature.* 2nd ed. Oxford: Oxford University Press.

Huntington, Samuel P. 1968. *Political Order in Changing Societies.* New Haven: Yale University Press.

Jauffret, Jean-Charles. 1990. *La Guerre d'Algérie par les Documents.
Tome 1: l'Avertissement 1943–1946.* Vincennes: Service Historique de l'Armée de Terre.

Joffé, E.G.H. 1985. "The Moroccan Nationalist Movement: Istiqlal, the Sultan, and the Country." *Journal of African History* 26 (4): 289–307.

Johnson, G. Wesley, Jr. 1971. *The Emergence of Black Politics in Senegal: The Struggle for Power in the Four Communes, 1900–1920.* Stanford: Stanford University Press.

Julien, Charles-André. 1972. *L'Afrique du Nord en Marche. Nationalismes Musulmans et Souveraineté Française.* Tunis: Cérès Editions.

Kaddache, Mahfoud. 1982. *Histoire du Nationalisme Algérien. Question Nationale et Politique Algérienne, 1919–1951.* Algiers: Société nationale de l'édition.

Kalyvas, Stathis N. 2006. *The Logic of Violence in Civil War.* Cambridge: Cambridge University Press.

Kelly, John D., and Martha Kaplan. 2001. *Represented Communities: Fiji and World Decolonizaiton.* Chicago: University of Chicago Press.

Keris, Georges Le Brun. 1953. *Mort Des Colonies? Colonialisme, Anticolonialisme Et Colonisation.* Paris: Le Centurion.

Khoury, Philip S. 1987. *Syria and the French Mandate: The Politics of Arab Nationalism, 1920–1945.* Princeton: Princeton University Press.

Klooster, Wim. 2009. *Revolutions in the Atlantic World: A Comparative History.* New York: New York University Press.

Knapp, W. 1977. *North West Africa: A Political and Economic Survey.* Oxford: Oxford University Press.

Kocher, Matthew Adam. 2004. *Human Ecology and Civil War.* PhD Dissertation, Department of Political Science: University of Chicago.

  2010. "State Capacity as a Conceptual Variable." *Yale Journal of International Affairs* 5 (2): 137–145.

Koulakssis, Ahmed, and Gilbert Meynier. 1987. *L'Émir Khaled: Premier Zai'm? Identité Algerienne et Colonialisme Français.* Paris: L'Harmattan.

Kuran, Timur. 1991. "Now Out of Never: The Element of Surprise in the East European Revolution of 1989." *World Politics* 44: 7–48.

Lacheraf, Mostefa. 1965. *L'Algérie: Nation et Société.* Paris: F. Maspero.

LaFuente, Gilles. 1999. *La Politique Berbère de la France et le Nationalisme Marocain.* Paris: L'Harmattan.

Lahbabi, Mohamed. 1975. *Le Gouvernement Marocain à l'Aube du Vingtième Siecle.* Rabat: Les Editions Maghrébines.

Laitin, David D. 1998. *Identity in Formation: The Russian-Speaking Populations in the Near Abroad.* Ithaca: Cornell University Press.

2001. "Secessionist Rebellion in the Former Soviet Union." *Comparative Political Studies* 34 (8): 839–861.

Lakroum, Monique. 1992. "Senegal-Soudan (Mali): Deux États pour un Empire." In *L'Afrique Occidentale au Temps des Francais*, ed. Catherine Coquery-Vidrovitch, 157–190. Paris: Editions La Decouverte.

Landau, Rom. 1956. *Moroccan Drama: 1900–1955.* San Francisco: The American Academy of Asian Studies.

Laroui, Abdellah. 1977. *Les Origines Sociales et Culturelles du Nationalisme Marocain (1830–1912).* Paris: Maspero.

Lawrance, Benjamin N. 2007. *Locality, Mobility, and "Nation": Periurban Colonialism in Togo's Eweland, 1900–1960.* Rochester: University of Rochester Press.

Lawrence, Adria. 2010a. "Driven to Arms? The Escalation to Violence in Nationalist Conflicts." In *Rethinking Violence: States and Non-State Actors in Conflict*, eds. Erica Chenoweth and Adria Lawrence, 143–172. Cambridge, MA: MIT Press.

2010b. "Triggering Nationalist Violence: Competition and Conflict in Uprisings Against Colonial Rule." *International Security* 35 (2): 88–122.

Lazraq, Selma. 2003. *La France et le Retour de Mohammed V.* Paris: L'Harmattan.

Lebow, Richard Ned. 2010. *Forbidden Fruit: Counterfactuals and International Relations.* Princeton: Princeton University Press.

Levisse-Touze, Christine. 1994. "La Contribution du Maroc pendant la Seconde Guerre Mondiale (1940–1945)." *Revue Maroc-Europe* 7: 209–217.

Lewis, Martin Deming. 1962. "One Hundred Million Frenchmen: The 'Assimilation' Theory in French Colonial Policy." *Comparative Studies in Society and History* 4 (2): 129–153.

Lewis, Mary Dewhurst. 2008. "Geographies of Power: The Tunisian Civic Order, Jurisdictional Politics, and Imperial Rivalry in the Mediterranean, 1881–1935." *The Journal of Modern History* 80 (4): 791–830.

Lomnitz, Claudio. 2001. *Deep Mexico, Silent Mexico: An Anthropology of Nationalism.* Minneapolis: University of Minnesota Press.

Lorcin, Patricia M.E. 1995. *Imperial Identities: Stereotyping, Prejudice and Race in Colonial Algeria.* New York: I.B. Tauris.

Low, D.A. 1982. "The Asian Mirror to Tropical Africa's Independence." In *The Transfer of Power in Africa: Decolonization 1940–1960*, eds. Prosser Gifford and William Roger Louis, 1–29. New Haven: Yale University Press.

1991. *Eclipse of Empire*. Cambridge: Cambridge University Press.
Lugan, Bernard. 2000. *Histoire du Maroc des Origines à Nos Jours*. Paris: Perrin.
Lustick, Ian S. 1993. *Unsettled States, Disputed Lands*. Ithaca: Cornell University Press.
Maalem, Ali. 1946. *Colonialisme, Trusteeship, Indépendance*. Paris: Défense de la France.
MacLean, Lauren M. 2010. *Informal Institutions and Citizenship in Rural Africa: Risk and Reciprocity in Ghana and Côte d'Ivoire*. New York: Cambridge University Press.
Maghraoui, Driss. 2000. "The Moroccan Colonial Soldiers: Between Selective Memory and Collective Memory." In *Beyond Colonialism and Nationalism in the Maghrib: History, Culture, and Politics*, ed. Ali Abdullatif Ahmida, 49–70 London: Palgrave Macmillan.
Mamdani, Mahmood. 1996. *Citizen and Subject: Contemporary Africa and the Legacy of Late Colonialism*. Princeton: Princeton University Press.
Manning, Patrick. 1988. *Francophone Sub-Saharan Africa, 1880–1985*. Cambridge: Cambridge University Press.
Mantena, Karuna. 2010. *Alibis of Empire: Henry Maine and the Ends of Liberal Imperialism*. Princeton: Princeton University Press.
Maran, René. 1922. *Batouala*. New York: T. Selzer.
Marshall, D. Bruce. 1973. *The French Colonial Myth and Constitution-Making in the Fourth Republic*. New Haven: Yale University Press.
Martel, André. 1994. *Histoire Militaire de la France Vol 4 – de 1940 à Nos Jours*. Paris: Presses Universitaires de France.
Maxwell, Gavin. 2000. *Lords of the Atlas*. Guilford: The Lyons Press.
McAdam, Doug. 1994. "Culture and Social Movements." In *New Social Movements: From Ideology to Identity*, eds. Joseph R. Gusfield, Hank Johnston, and Enrique Larana, 36–57. Philadelphia: Temple University Press.
1999. *Political Process and the Development of Black Insurgency, 1930–1970*. Chicago: University Of Chicago Press.
McAdam, Doug, John D. McCarthy, and Mayer N. Zald. 1996. *Comparative Perspectives on Social Movements: Political Opportunities, Mobilizing Structures, and Cultural Framings*. Cambridge: Cambridge University Press.
McAdam, Doug, and Dieter Rucht. 1993. "The Cross-National Diffusion of Movement Ideas." *The Annals of the American Academy of Political and Social Science* 528 (1): 56 –74.
McAdam, Doug, Sidney G. Tarrow, and Charles Tilly. 2001. *Dynamics of Contention*. Cambridge: Cambridge University Press.

McDougall, James, ed. 2003. *Nation, Society and Culture in North Africa*. London: Frank Cass.

McDougall, James. 2006. *History and the Culture of Nationalism in Algeria*. Cambridge: Cambridge University Press.

Mitchell, Timothy. 1991. *Colonizing Egypt*. Berkeley: University of California Press.

Montagne, R. 1943. *Six Conférences d'Initiation à la Politique Musulmane de la France en Afrique du Nord*. Paris: CHEAM.

Moore, Clement Henry. 1960. "The National Party: A Tentative Model." *Public Policy* 10: 239–267.

1970. *Politics in North Africa: Algeria, Morocco, and Tunisia*. New York: Little Brown & Company.

Moreau, Odile. 2003. "Echoes of National Liberation: Turkey Viewed from the Maghrib in the 1920s." In *Nation, Society and Culture in North Africa*, ed. James McDougall, 58–70. London: Frank Cass.

Morgenthau, Ruth Schachter. 1964. *Political Parties in French-Speaking West Africa*. Oxford Studies in African Affairs. Oxford: Clarendon Press.

Moutoussamy, Ernest. 2000. *Les DOM-TOM: Enjeu Géopolitique, Économique et Stratégique*. Paris: L'Harmattan.

Munson, Henry, Jr. 1993. *Religion and Power in Morocco*. New Haven: Yale University Press.

Mylonas, Harris. 2013. *The Politics of Nation-Building: Making Co-Nationals, Refugees, and Minorities*. New York: Cambridge University Press.

Nicolas, Armand. 1996. *Histoire de la Martinique*. Paris: L'Harmattan.

Nouschi, A. 1979. *La Naissance du Nationalisme Algérien*. Paris: Minuit.

Olson, Mancur. 1971. *The Logic of Collective Action: Public Goods and the Theory of Groups*. Cambridge, MA: Harvard University Press.

Owen, Roger. 2000. *State, Power and Politics in the Making of the Modern Middle East*. London: Routledge.

Pape, Robert A. 2005. *Dying to Win: The Strategic Logic of Suicide Terrorism*. New York: Random House.

Pennell, C.R. 1986. *A Country with a Government and a Flag: The Rif War in Morocco, 1921–1926*. Wisbeck: Menas.

2000. *Morocco since 1830: A History*. New York: New York University Press.

2003. *Morocco: From Empire to Independence*. Oxford: Oneworld.

Perkins, Kenneth. 2004. *A History of Modern Tunisia*. Cambridge: Cambridge University Press.

Person, Yves. 1982. "French West Africa and Decolonization." In *The Transfer of Power in Africa: Decolonization 1940–1960*, eds.

Prosser Gifford and William Roger Louis, 141–172. New Haven: Yale University Press.

Pervillé, Guy. 1991. *De l'Empire Français à la Décolonisation*. Paris: Hachette.

Petersen, Roger D. 1993. "A Community-Based Theory of Rebellion." *European Journal of Sociology* 34: 41–78.

2002. *Understanding Ethnic Violence: Fear, Hatred, and Resentment in Twentieth-Century Eastern Europe*. Cambridge: Cambridge University Press.

Porch, Douglas. 1982. *The Conquest of Morocco*. New York: Alfred A. Knopf.

Posner, Daniel N. 2005. *Institutions and Ethnic Politics in Africa*. Cambridge: Cambridge University Press.

Pratt, Nicola Christine. 2007. *Democracy and Authoritarianism in the Arab World*. Boulder: Lynne Rienner Publishers.

Prochaska, David. 1990. *Making Algeria French: Colonialism in Bône, 1870–1920*. Cambridge: Cambridge University Press.

Rézette, Robert. 1955. *Les Partis Politiques Marocains*. Paris: Librarie Armand Colin.

Rivet, Daniel. 1999. *Le Maroc de Lyautey à Mohammed V: le Double Visage du Protectorat*. Paris: Editions Denoel.

2002. *Le Maghreb à l'Épreuve de la Colonisation*. Paris: Hachette Litteratures.

Rivlin, B. 1955. "Context and Sources of Political Tensions in French North Africa." *Annals of the American Academy of Political and Social Science* 298: 109–116.

Roche, Christian. 2001. *Le Sénégal à la Conquête de son Indépendance (1939–1960): Chronique de la Vie Politique et Syndicale, de l'Empire Français à l'Indépendance*. Hommes et Société. Paris: Karthala.

Roeder, Philip G. 2007. *Where Nation-States Come From: Insitutional Change in the Age of Nationalism*. Princeton: Princeton University Press.

Rosenblum, Mort. 1988. *Mission to Civilize: The French Way*. New York: Doubleday.

Ruedy, John. 1992. *Modern Algeria: The Origins and Development of a Nation*. Bloomington: Indiana University Press.

Saadalla, B. 1975. *al-Harakah al-Wataniyah fi al-Jazair 1930–1945*. Cairo: Jami`at al duwwal al `arabiyya.

Sahlins, Peter. 1989. *Boundaries: The Making of France and Spain in the Pyrenees*. Berkeley: University of California Press.

Sangmauh, Egyo N. 1992. "Sultan Mohammed Ben Youssef's American Strategy and the Diplomacy of North African Liberation, 1943–61." *Journal of Contemporary History* 27 (1): 129–148.

Sanmarco, Louis. 1983. *Le Colonisateur Colonisé*. Paris: Éditions A.B.C.

Sarmany, T., and M. Roucaud. 2000. *Guide des Sources de l'Histoire du Maroc au Service Historique de l'Armée de Terre*. Paris: Château de Vincennes.

Sartori, Giovanni. 1970. "Concept Misinformation in Comparative Politics." *American Political Science Review* LXIV (4): 1033–1053.

Scott, James C. 1987. *Weapons of the Weak: Everyday Forms of Peasant Resistance*. New Haven: Yale University Press.

Searing, James F. 1985. *Accommodation and Resistance: Chiefs, Muslim Leaders, and Politicians in Colonial Senegal, 1890–1934*. Dissertation, Department of History: Princeton University.

Sewell, William H. 1996. "Historical Events as Transformations of Structures: Inventing Revolution at the Bastille." *Theory and Society* 25 (6): 841–881.

Sharkey, Heather J. 2003. *Living with Colonialism: Nationalism and Culture in Anglo-Egyptian Sudan*. Berkeley: University of California Press.

Shepard, Todd. 2006. *The Invention of Decolonization: The Algerian War and the Remaking of France*. Ithaca: Cornell University Press.

Shipway, Martin. 2008. *Decolonization and Its Impact: A Comparative Approach to the End of the Colonial Empires*. Malden: Wiley-Blackwell.

Singer, Barnett, and John Langdon. 2004. *Cultured Force: Makers and Defenders of the French Colonial Empire*. Madison: University of Wisconsin Press.

Skocpol, Theda. 1979. *States and Social Revolutions: A Comparative Analysis of France, Russia, and China*. Cambridge: Cambridge University Press.

Slater, Dan. 2010. *Ordering Power: Contentious Politics and Authoritarian Leviathans in Southeast Asia*. Cambridge: Cambridge University Press.

Smith, Tony. 1975. *The End of the European Empire: Decolonization after World War II*. Lexington: D.C. Heath and Company.

Springhall, John. 2001. *Decolonization since 1945: The Collapse of European Overseas Empires*. Basingstoke: Palgrave.

Spruyt, Hendrik. 2005. *Ending Empire: Contested Sovereignty and Territorial Partition*. Ithaca: Cornell University Press.

Stewart, C.F. 1964. *The Economy of Morocco 1912–1962*. Cambridge, MA: Harvard University Press.

Stora, Benjamin. 2001. *Algeria 1830–2000: A Short History*. Ithaca: Cornell University Press.

2003. "Algeria/Morocco: The Passions of the Past. Representations of the Nation that Unite and Divide." In *Nation, Society and Culture in North Africa*, ed. James McDougall, 14–34. London: Frank Cass.

Strang, David. 1990. "From Dependency to Sovereignty: An Event History Analysis of Decolonization, 1870–1987." *American Sociological Review* 55 (6): 846–860.

1992. "The Inner Incompatibility of Empire and Nation: Popular Sovereignty and Decolonization." *Sociological Perspectives* 35 (2): 367–384.

Le Sueur, J.D. 2003. *The Decolonization Reader*. New York: Routledge.

Suny, Ronald Grigor. 1993. *The Revenge of the Past: Nationalism, Revolution, and the Collapse of the Soviet Union*. Stanford: Stanford University Press.

2001a. "The Empire Strikes Out: Imperial Russia, 'National' Identity, and Theories of Empire." In *A State of Nations: Empire and Nation-Making in the Age of Lenin and Stalin*, eds. Ronald Grigor Suny and Terry Martin, 23–66. New York: Oxford University Press.

2001b. "Constructing Primordialism: Old Histories for New Nations." *Journal of Modern History* 73 (4): 862–896.

Tarrow, Sidney. 1994. *Power in Movement: Social Movements, Collective Action and Politics*. Cambridge: Cambridge University Press.

Tessler, Mark A., John P. Entelis, and Gregory W. White. 1995. "Kingdom of Morocco." In *The Government and Politics of the Middle East and North Africa*, eds. D.E. Long and B. Reich, 369–393. Boulder: Westview Press.

Tetlock, Philip E., and Aaron Belkin. 1996. *Counterfactual Thought Experiments in World Politics*. Princeton: Princeton University Press.

Tetlock, Philip E., and Richard Ned Lebow. 2001. "Poking Counterfactual Holes in Covering Laws: Cognitive Styles and Historical Reasoning." *American Political Science Review* 95 (4): 829–843.

Thomas, Martin. 1998. *The French Empire at War, 1940–45*. Manchester: Manchester University Press.

2005. *The French Empire Between the Wars. Imperialism, Politics and Society*. Manchester: Manchester University Press.

Thompson, Elizabeth. 2000a. "The Climax and Crisis of the Colonial Welfare State in Syria and Lebanon During WWII." In *War Institutions and Social Change in the Middle East*, ed. Steven Heydemann, 59–99. Berkeley: University of California Press.

2000b. *Colonial Citizens: Republican Rights, Paternal Privilege and Gender in French Syria and Lebanon*. New York: Columbia University Press.

Tilly, Charles. 1978. *From Mobilization to Revolution*. New York: McGraw-Hill.

———. 1995. "States and Nationalism in Europe, 1492–1992." In *Perspectives on Nationalism and War*, ed. John L. Comaroff, 187–204. Amsterdam: Gordan and Breach Science Publishers.

Tilly, Charles, and Sidney G. Tarrow. 2007. *Contentious Politics*. Boulder: Paradigm Publishers.

Tlili, B. 1984. *Nationalismes, Socialisme et Syndicalisme dans le Maghreb des Années 1919–1934*. Tunis: Publications de l'Université.

Trépied, Benoît. 2007. "Politique et Relations Coloniales en Nouvelle-Calédonie." Thèse de doctorat en anthropologie sociale et ethnologie, Paris: École des hautes études en sciences sociales.

Tronchon, Jacques. 1974. *L'Insurrection Malgache de 1947*. Paris: Librairie François Maspero.

Tucker, Spencer C. 1999. *Vietnam*. London: UCL Press.

Tunisia, Government of. 1969. *Le Neo-Destour et le Front Populaire en France: La Rupture, 1936–38*. Tunis: Centre de Documentation Nationale.

———. 1989. *La Tunisie de 1939 à 1945*. Tunis: Presse de l'Imprimerie Officielle de la République Tunisienne.

Varshney, Ashutosh. 2003. "Nationalism, Ethnic Conflict, and Rationality." *Perspectives on Politics* 1 (1): 85–99.

von Albertini, R. 1975. "The Impact of the Two World Wars on the Decline of Colonialism." In *The End of the European Empires: Decolonization After World War II*, ed. Tony Smith, 3–19. Lexington: D.C. Heath and Company.

Wallerstein, Immanuel Maurice. 1961. *Africa, the Politics of Independence; an Interpretation of Modern African History*. New York: Vintage Books.

Waterbury, John. 1970. *Commander of the Faithful: The Moroccan Political Elite – A Study in Segmented Politics*. London: Weidenfeld and Nicolson.

Weber, Eugen. 1976. *Peasants into Frenchmen: The Modernization of Rural France, 1870–1914*. Stanford: Stanford University Press.

Wedeen, Lisa. 2003. "Seeing Like a Citizen, Acting Like a State: Exemplary Events in Unified Yemen." *Comparative Studies in Society and History* 45 (4): 680–713.

———. 2008. *Peripheral Visions: Publics, Power, and Performance in Yemen*. Chicago: University of Chicago Press.

———. 2009. "Ethnography as Interpretive Enterprise." In *Political Ethnography: What Immersion Contributes to the Study of Power*, ed. Edward Schatz, 75–93. Chicago: University of Chicago Press.

Weyland, Kurt. 2010. "The Diffusion of Regime Contention in European Democratization, 1830–1940." *Comparative Political Studies* 43 (8–9): 1148 –1176.

Wilder, Gary. 2005. *The French Imperial Nation-State: Negritude and Colonial Humanism between the Two World Wars.* Chicago: University of Chicago Press.

Wilkinson, Steven I. 2004a. *Votes and Violence: Electoral Competition and Ethnic Riots in India.* Cambridge: Cambridge University Press.

2004b. "Colonial Institutions, Governance and Conflict: An Introduction to a New Dataset." Unpublished paper presented at *LiCEP 10,* Columbia University.

Wilson, William J. 1976. *Power, Racism and Privilege.* New York: Free Press.

Wimmer, Andreas. 2002. *Nationalist Exclusion and Ethnic Conflict.* Cambridge: Cambridge University Press.

2008. "Elementary Strategies of Ethnic Boundary Making." *Ethnic and Racial Studies* 31 (6): 1025–1055.

Wintrobe, Ronald. 1998. *The Political Economy of Dictatorship.* Cambridge: Cambridge University Press.

2002. "Slobodan Milosevic and the Fire of Nationalism." *World Economics* 3 (3): 1–26.

Wolf, J. 1994. *Les Secrets du Maroc Espagnol: l'Épopée d'Abd-el-Khaleq Torrès 1910–1970.* Paris: Coédition Balland-Eddif.

Wood, Elisabeth Jean. 2003. *Insurgent Collective Action and Civil War in El Salvador.* Cambridge: Cambridge University Press.

Woolman, David S. 1968. *Rebels in the Rif: Abd El Krim and the Rif Rebellion.* Stanford: Stanford University Press.

Yacono, Xavier. 1971. *Les Étapes de la Décolonisation Française.* Paris: Presses Universitaires de France.

Yashar, Deborah J. 2005. *Contesting Citizenship in Latin America: The Rise of Indigenous Movements and the Postliberal Challenge.* Cambridge: Cambridge University Press.

Young, M. Crawford. 1994. *The African Colonial State in Comparative Perspective.* New Haven: Yale University Press.

2004. "Revisiting Nationalism and Ethnicity in Africa." *James S. Coleman Memorial Lecture Series,* University of California, Los Angeles.

Zade, Mohammed. 2001. *Résistance et Armée de Libération au Maroc (1947–1956): de l'Action Politique à la Lutte Armée: Rupture ou Continuité.* Doctoral thesis: Université Nice-Antipolis.

Zartman, I. William. 1964. *Morocco: Problems of New Power.* New York: Atherton Press.

Zisenwine, Daniel. 2010. *The Emergence of Nationalist Politics in Morocco: The Rise of the Independence Party and the Struggle against Colonialism after World War II.* London: Tauris Academic Studies.

Zniber, M. 1984. "Mohammed V: Un Symbole en Ascension." In *Le Memorial Du Maroc*, ed. Larbi Essakali, 6: 29–41. Rabat: Nord Organisation.

Index

NOTE: page numbers with italicized *f, n,* or *t* indicate figures, notes, or tables respectively.